Édouard
Glissant

ALSO AVAILABLE FROM BLOOMSBURY

Alienation and Freedom, Frantz Fanon
Gilles Deleuze, Postcolonial Theory, and the Philosophy of Limit, Réda Bensmaïa

Édouard Glissant: A Poetics of Resistance

SAM COOMBES

BLOOMSBURY ACADEMIC
LONDON • NEW YORK • OXFORD • NEW DELHI • SYDNEY

BLOOMSBURY ACADEMIC
Bloomsbury Publishing Plc
50 Bedford Square, London, WC1B 3DP, UK

BLOOMSBURY, BLOOMSBURY ACADEMIC and the Diana logo are trademarks
of Bloomsbury Publishing Plc

First published in Great Britain 2018

Copyright © Sam Coombes, 2018

Sam Coombes has asserted his right under the Copyright, Designs and Patents
Act, 1988, to be identified as Author of this work.

Cover design by Irene Martinez Costa
Cover image © Édouard Glissant (2009) Alain DENANTES, Getty Images

All rights reserved. No part of this publication may be reproduced or
transmitted in any form or by any means, electronic or mechanical,
including photocopying, recording, or any information storage or
retrieval system, without prior permission in writing from the publishers.

Bloomsbury Publishing Plc does not have any control over, or responsibility for,
any third-party websites referred to or in this book. All internet addresses given
in this book were correct at the time of going to press. The author and publisher
regret any inconvenience caused if addresses have changed or sites have ceased
to exist, but can accept no responsibility for any such changes.

A catalogue record for this book is available from the British Library.

A catalog record for this book is available from the Library of Congress.

ISBN: HB: 978-1-3500-3683-3
PB: 978-1-3500-3684-0
ePDF: 978-1-3500-3682-6
eBook: 978-1-3500-3685-7

Typeset by Newgen KnowledgeWorks Pvt. Ltd., Chennai, India

CONTENTS

A Note on Translation vii
List of Abbreviations viii
Introduction ix

PART ONE Later Glissantian thought as alternative perspective on globalization 1

1   *Poetics of Relation* (1990): a manifesto for the twenty-first century? 3
2   From Relation to the 'common-place': the later Glissantian conceptual schema 21

PART TWO Creolization, anti-universalism and twenty-first-century radical thought 45

3   Creolization and creoleness: proximity and divergence 47
4   The paradoxes of universalism and the ambivalence of the postcolonial condition 67
5   Glissant: postmodernist apologist for neoliberal-led globalization? 87
6   Glissant's latter-day political commitments 105

PART THREE Envisioning the twenty-first century otherwise: utopianism, anarchism and the critique of neoliberalism 123

7 Globalization and its critics: neoliberalism, alter-globalization and contemporary anarchism 125
8 A poetics of resistance and change: Glissant, a maître à penser for twenty-first-century dissident thought? 163

Bibliography 191
Index 197

A NOTE ON TRANSLATION

Quite a number of Glissant's theoretical works of the last twenty or so years have not yet been translated into English. In cases where published translations are available, I have used those. Otherwise, the translations of citations from Glissant's works included in this book are my own. In both cases, the translated version has been included in the text and the original French included in a footnote, it being important in the case of an author such as Glissant who, moreover, is such a distinctive prose stylist, that the actual wording he himself uses be visible at all times to the reader.

ABBREVIATIONS

The following abbreviations are used throughout this book for primary source texts by Glissant:

CL	*La Cohée du Lamentin* (Gallimard, 2005)
DA	*Le Discours antillais* (Gallimard, 1997 [1981])
EBR	*Les Entretiens de Baton Rouge* (Gallimard, 2008)
IBM	*L'Intraitable Beauté du monde: adresse à Barack Obama* (Galaade, 2009)
IL	*L'Imaginaire des langues* (Gallimard, 2010)
IP	*L'Intention poétique* (Gallimard, 1997 [1969])
IPD	*Introduction à une politique du divers* (Gallimard, 1996)
ME	*Mémoires des esclavages* (Gallimard, 2007)
MPHN	*Manifeste pour les "produits" de haute nécessité* (Galaade, 2009)
NRM	*Une Nouvelle région du monde* (Gallimard, 2006)
PR	*Poétique de la Relation* (Gallimard, 1990)
QMT	*Quand les murs tombent. L'Identité hors la loi?* (Galaade, 2007)
SC	*Le Soleil de la conscience* (Seuil, 1956)
TTM	*Traité du tout-monde* (Gallimard, 1997)

INTRODUCTION

It will be by now almost a truism that centuries do not always begin and end when their chronological dates indicate. The twentieth century is often thought to have properly begun in political and social terms only at the outbreak of the First World War which, by implication, suggests a rather longer nineteenth century than chronology would have it. It may still be too early to cast judgment on the starting point of the twenty-first century and, in any case, it is unlikely that there will ever be a consensus opinion on the matter as there are a number of significant watershed moments which would seem to be equally worthy contenders. In particular, one might ponder whether it was the demise of the Soviet bloc in the period following the fall of the Berlin wall in 1989 and the subsequent end of the Cold War which signalled the end of a short but extremely violent century. Or conversely whether it was the event which came to be known simply as '9/11' in the United States, with the myriad of consequences for global politics which that event has had, that is a more fitting moment to designate as marking the start of the new century.

Either way, it is by now common knowledge that the twenty-first century is going to be fraught with far-reaching problems which humanity will have to at least attempt to mitigate even if it cannot solve them. What's new, one might retort? Human history was ever thus. This objection to a pessimistic prognosis which is shared by ever-growing numbers of people around the world today would be convincing were it not for a number of factors which are specific to the current conjuncture and which render that conjuncture more problematic when viewed in a long-term perspective than previous bleak moments in human history. To some extent one can set aside contemporary trends which, although nevertheless of major importance, are however perhaps not as decisive for the future of humanity as a whole: the chronic systemic problems which lie at the heart of our Western-led global finance system and which were finally laid bare when the financial crisis came to a head in 2007–8; the slow but sure decline of the United States as world economic leader and the increasing pre-eminence of China; the considerable demographic increase that has been taking place since at least 1950, which is set only to intensify in the twenty-first century; and perhaps even the problem of an ever-widening chasm between the ultra-rich and the poor and poverty-stricken around the planet.[1] One might add moreover that at least three out of four of the above trends are all systemically linked to the workings of the now globalized capitalist system, the failings of which are, if not necessarily self-evident, well documented in scholarly literature.[2] Of ultimately much greater significance in a long-term historical perspective is the chronic problem of global warming which is set to have profound consequences for human life in the twenty-first century.[3] In conjunction with the ongoing problem of inequality, the consequences of environmental change run the risk of being the source of a wide range of difficulties which ultimately, if not addressed in the short and medium terms, have the potential to give rise to conflicts and wars over land and resources later in the century. As peoples and communities feel impelled to migrate *en masse* to escape natural disasters and shortages in food and supplies, conflicts will be a likelihood, and the chasm between the privileged few who are in a position to fence themselves into luxurious gated communities and the disenfranchised masses will only grow. The expected migration problem is perhaps going to have much further-reaching structural consequences than the present one growing out of the civil war situation in Syria. This latter situation alone has

---

[1] At the 2014 annual World Economic Forum conference held in Davos, inequality of incomes was singled out as a major cause of economic stagnation and instability. It is significant that the political class currently steering the globalized economy has been coming around to the view that inequality is reaching levels which are detrimental to the growth of even the wealthier as well as the emerging economies.

[2] Moreover, it is of particular note that in the aftermath of the financial crisis of 2007–8, there was renewed interest in the work of Karl Marx even in the mainstream press, a number of weeklies such as *Le Point* and *Der Spiegel* making Marx their front cover feature in 2008.

[3] Naomi Klein, in *This Changes Everything: Capitalism vs. the Climate* (New York: Simon and Schuster, 2014), argues that global warming is the big game changer in our era.

given rise to nationalist anti-globalism reaction in a certain number of Western nations.

Where does the thought of Édouard Glissant stand in relation to this conjuncture that I have described? I will approach this question by briefly addressing another matter of a general nature: where do minoritarian communities and cultures such as post-colonial communities like those of the francophone Caribbean or those that immigrated into host nations larger than their own stand in relation to such a situation? In this question lie preoccupations which go to the heart of Glissant's intellectual project. Indeed the matter of how the situation of post-colonial communities is to be understood is intimately linked in Glissant's work to that of immigrant communities for reasons which I will set out. As his oeuvre developed from the late 1980s onwards, the latter question became ostensibly subsumed in the former to some extent, but in reality the matter of the situation of minoritarian cultures in relation to larger and indeed hegemonic cultures remained at the very core of his entire theoretical world view. While up until the 1980s Glissant's central preoccupation in this regard was the matter of where a culture like that of Martinique and the other French Caribbean islands stood in relation to their neocolonial master, from *Poetics of Relation* (1990) onwards it was the standing of all specific cultures in relation to what was the hegemonic economic and hence linguistic preeminence of the United States and the anglophone mindset. The colonialism of former colonial nations like France and Britain had been replaced by another type of imperialism, that which Glissant variously calls 'standardisation'[4] (*IPD*) or, at a linguistic level specifically, 'the Anglo-American pidgin' *(PR,* 93).[5] In this globalized context, France itself and the French language and culture joined the ranks of those cultures threatened by the influence of a more powerful nation. Of course, there was a difference between being from mainland French and being from, say, Nouvelle Calédonie or Cap Verde, and there are not many indications in Glissant's writing that he felt a great deal of sympathy for the French in their moments of anxiety about the encroachments of anglophone culture on their own. Nevertheless, although France was overshadowed by a larger neo-imperial power just as it had enjoyed influence over others, in

---

[4] 'la standardisation' (*IPD*, 97).
[5] 'le sabir américain' (*PR*, 107).

this new context its concerns were legitimate and, on a point of principle, Glissant would defend the right of all national cultures to their own specificity.

This study aims both to explore Glissant's response to the politico-economic arrangement to which the label 'globalization' has commonly been applied over the last twenty-five to thirty or so years, and in some sense to sum up the theoretical contribution that his works of that period constituted. Glissant is considered by many in the field of post-colonial studies to be one of, if not the most significant, thinkers in the francophone context. He died in 2011 after a more than fifty-year career as a publishing author, and it is hence now possible not only to include in our assessment analysis of works published in the later years of his life, which many earlier studies devoted to Glissant could not do, but also to form conclusions about the import of his later oeuvre. I should indicate at the outset that it is the later period of Glissant's theoretical writings which form the focus of this study. Although consideration of his poetry and novelistic writings could certainly have been a worthwhile addition to my analyses, Glissant's theoretical writings of the last twenty-five or so years constitute a sizeable body of work in its own right and can in my view be discussed independently of the literary works as a stand-alone contribution to theory.

Hence this book aims to serve as an introduction to the later Glissantian theoretical oeuvre for those not familiar with it. It also presents an original view of the central positions set out in that later oeuvre. A defence of Glissant is offered against the criticisms of his later positions, which were made by a certain number of mainly anglophone critical commentators in the early 2000s. The view of the later Glissant which I advocate is grounded in political convictions as is that of these commentators but it involves adopting a stance that is diametrically opposed to theirs. While they have berated Glissant for supposedly abandoning radical politics, I argue on the contrary that radical critique of contemporary globalization is not only accepted by the later Glissant but is also positively encouraged. Far from being an expression of apathy in the face of the growing systemic problems of global capitalism, the later Glissant's oeuvre offers vital strategies for countering them and proposes valuable alternatives.

Part One offers an overview and appraisal of the key concepts which Glissant either introduced or, in the case of ideas which he had formulated previously, adapted, thereby formulating a distinctive theoretical vision or world view. This is followed in Part Two by more in-depth consideration of a number of issues which are vital to understanding Glissant both in his own context and within the framework of the intellectual debates of that context, namely the French West Indies. Chapter 3 examines the ways in which Glissant's ideas cohere with, but also diverge from, the Creolist movement which has been advocated by such recognized Caribbean writers as Patrick Chamoiseau and Raphaël Confiant. In Chapter 4, the central issue of universalist versus particularlist thinking is examined and appraised. This is followed by a defence of Glissant in the face of criticisms made by radical commentators in Chapter 5. Chapter 6 covers the overtly political theoretical works which Glissant published in the years 2007–9, which are a powerful reminder that politically radical views lay at the very core of his world view. Part Three offers a distinctive account of later Glissantian politics which involves the central claim that areas of clear reciprocity and overlap can be identified with the Alter-Globalization Movement (AGM). I conclude this study by arguing notably in Chapter 9 that the AGM would have much to gain from incorporating later Glissantian concepts into its thinking. Every political movement, however unhierarchically structured, can gain immensely from the sense of direction which an intellectual and/or spiritual guide can offer them. I argue that Glissant could very usefully act as one maître à penser among others for the AGM movement today and in years to come.

PART ONE

Later Glissantian thought as alternative perspective on globalization

CHAPTER ONE

Poetics of Relation (1990): a manifesto for the twenty-first century?

Throughout his career, an unwavering support for minoritarian, oppressed and repressed communities and cultures is a mainstay of Glissant's work. Hence from *Poetics of Relation* (*Poétique de la Relation*) onwards a questioning of globalization in its present-day form is added to and a logical extension of the anti-colonialism of earlier works. Why do I suggest that *Poetics of Relation* might be a manifesto for the twenty-first century? Because it on the one hand describes in key ways so presciently some of the key cultural consequences of the phenomenon known as globalization that came to full maturity a few years later. It describes what globalization and the information revolution mean for questions of identity, for the future of individual languages, for the possibilities afforded to multinational big business and international communication networks. But on the other hand, it also offers the beginnings of a blueprint for a profound questioning of globalization thus conceived and hence an outline for an alternative kind of globalization, one which places people and their distinctive cultures at the centre of the equation, not profit-oriented strategies. But a questioning of a very different sort from that we have seen since 2016 where fears concerning the arrival of migrants notably from the Middle East were used to fuel a right-tending nationalist agenda.

What is also significant about *Poetics of Relation* is that it marks an important turning point in Glissant's oeuvre. Although there are many lines of continuity between the various concepts which Glissant sets out in this work and earlier theoretical works like *Poetics Intention* (*L'Intention Poetique*) and *Caribbean Discourse* (*Le Discours Antillais*), nevertheless *Poetics of Relation* marks a paradigm shift in Glissant's thinking in a number of respects. I will set out in broad terms the distinctive theoretical vision which forms *Poetics of Relation*'s principal substantive content in this chapter prior to examining the specific Glissantian concepts making up that theoretical vision in Chapter 2. It is important to bear in mind with respect to the new paradigm contained in *Poetics of Relation* that it was to remain *the* operative paradigm in Glissant's work until the end of his life. All of Glissant's theoretical endeavours after this seminal work remain broadly faithful to, repeat and reiterate in new ways, as well as build on in modest ways, the arguments contained in this work of 1990. Hence its centrality and my having chosen it to be the starting point for this study.

One final introductory remark I would like to make is that although the theoretical vision which is set out in *Poetics of Relation* presents the reader with a subtle but determined counter-narrative of the economics-driven globalization which became the leading paradigm in the West following the adoption of neoliberal agendas in the 1980s, in the exegesis of Glissant's ideas which follows, I have sought to present Glissant's vision in a politically neutral manner. Where there are clear and undeniable political implications to Glissant's concepts I mention those as part of my account, but I have left the more contentious debates, notably concerning the political usefulness of Glissant's world view, until Chapter 5 and beyond. In these later chapters I discuss the objections which certain radical critics have made to Glissant's thought and explain why I am in disagreement with them. I will set out why I believe that not only those objections are misguided but also why, contrary to what these critics suggest, Glissant's thought should be welcomed by radical[1] thinkers and political activists today. I do not believe

---

[1] I employ the term 'radical' to encompass quite a wide range of people and groups today who are critical of the neoliberal agenda that has been pursued by Western, and notably Anglo-American, governments for well over thirty years now. These people and groups include the traditional political left which was affiliated to socialist and

that Glissant's vision by any means offers a comprehensive blueprint for much-needed progressive political thought and activism today, but I am of the view that it should nevertheless be welcomed as a vital contribution to reflection on how meaningful opposition to the reactionary tendencies of today's world should be countered.

Poetics of Relation: a new vision for a globalized age

Approaching later Glissantian theory for the first time can be a somewhat disorienting experience. The reader finds him or herself presented with an array of neologistic concepts, all of which are interlinking and yet set out by the author in a non-systematic way. Indeed, the very notion of a 'non-system of thought' is part of the Glissantian world view. There is also the fact that Glissant believed that it was up to the reader to make sense of the ideas contained in his writings, a characteristic which gives his work an abstruse quality. As early as his first theoretical work *Le Soleil de la Conscience* (1956) he had written the following in this regard: 'one must leave it up to others to unearth in one's work the "deep resonances," and give only the appearance of ease.'[2] However, there is an overarching coherence to the concepts which Glissant proposes such that it is not only tempting but also helpful to understand this putative 'non-system' as if it were a philosophical system of sorts. For the remainder of this chapter I will provide a brief overview of this non-systematic body of ideas.

There is no one best order in which to set out Glissant's conceptual apparatus. To assume that there was would already be to run counter to the orientation of Glissant's intellectual project as his thought involves a fundamental critique of intellectual, as indeed socio-historical hierarchies. Hence, his various concepts are all interlinking but could and in theory should – if one were keen to avoid the trap of performative contradiction – be set out in any

---

Marxist thinking but also an increasingly wide spectrum of left-tending disaffected individuals and groups which would like to see the West rethink and restructure the ways in which it approaches globalization.

[2] '[i]l faut laisser à d'autres le soin de découvrir en votre travail "les résonances profondes…", et n'offrir d'apparence que celle de l'aisance' (*SC*: 17).

order as indeed they tend to be in his own writings. With this being in part an introductory work though, I will nevertheless attempt to present them in a way which I think offers the easiest way in for the non-acquainted reader.

As good a place to begin as any is Glissant's conception of identity. Drawing on the work of Gilles Deleuze and Félix Guattari, Glissant rejects the idea that identity should be conceived of as being derived from a unitary root. This established and familiar idea involves the notion that an effect has a single or principal point of origin just as this latter similarly emanated from one unified source, and so on. The history of such an idea has strongly essentialist connotations, which is to say that it links up closely with the assumption that individuals have a predefined essence, that is that they have a determinate, even largely fixed, identity and that they tend to behave in accordance with that identity. Like many thinkers notably since the post-Second World War period, Glissant finds such a conception of identity limiting, be it applied to individuals or cultures. However, as I shall explain, he also believes it to be factually inapplicable to the context which he considers home, namely the francophone Caribbean, with its history of forced mass immigration of individuals via slavery, colonial domination and, as he sees it, neocolonial subordinacy. Hence, Glissant adopts Deleuze and Guattari's concept of 'rhizomatic' identity. The metaphor of the rhizome is used by Deleuze and Guattari to suggest a transversal (i.e. horizontal) set of interconnecting phenomena as opposed to the more vertical, because chronologically sequential and one-dimensional, relationship between cause and effect which the traditional idea of the unitary root implies. Individuals and cultures which are conceived of as existing 'rhizomatically' exist by definition *relationally*, which is to say that their identities are subject to redefinition when they come into contact with each other. This manner of conceiving of identity tends to imply strongly an emphasis on the *difference* or *diversity* of the given social phenomena in relation to each other and it also links closely with the idea that individual identities exist and can be acted upon by horizontal networks comprising other identities which can be affected similarly. Glissant claims that what he calls *Relation identity* (PR, 144):[3]

---

[3]*'identité-relation'* (PR, 158).

- is linked not to a creation of the world but to the conscious and contradictory experience of contacts among cultures;
- is produced in the chaotic network of Relation and not in the hidden violence of filiation;
- does not devise any legitimacy as its guarantee of entitlement, but circulates, newly extended;
- [...]
- Relation identity exults the thought of errantry and of totality. (*PR*, 144)[4]

The idea of relationality which is central to the rhizomatic conception of identity serves as the basis for the concept around which so many of Glissant's concepts revolve, namely what Glissant terms 'Relation'. This concept, it is worth noting at the outset, is so expansive and seemingly all-inclusive in Glissant's world view as to be difficult to grasp when one first encounters it. Although included in the very title of the work of 1990 which constitutes our present focus, *Poetics of Relation*, Relation was not a new concept in Glissant's work at this time as it had made important appearances in earlier theoretical works such as *Poetic Intention* (although in this work written with a small 'r') and *Caribbean Discourse*. However, in *Poetics of Relation* it takes on a new dimension as a central operative concept, along with 'creolization', in an account of a globalized world (here I am using the term 'globalized' specifically in line with the sense that we have come to take to be the commonly understood meaning of the term 'globalization' since the early 1990s). It is hence absolutely vital to the image of late twentieth-century and early twenty-first-century society which Glissant so presciently envisions *avant la lettre*.

---

[4]– est liée, non pas à la création du monde, mais au vécu conscient et contradictoire des contacts des cultures;
- est donnée dans la trame chaotique de la Relation et non pas dans la violence cachée de la filiation;
- ne conçoit aucune légitimité comme garante de son droit, mais circule dans une étendue nouvelle;
[. . .]
L'identité-relation exulte la pensée de l'errance et de la totalité' (*PR*, 158).

Relation comes about as a process of interaction between phenomena which, though distinct, can be seen as integrally linked to each other through those interactions themselves. It preserves the particularities of the entities in question because it is inimical to simplifying generalization. It is a totality[5] and yet Relation is an 'open totality' (*PR*, 171),[6] by which Glissant means that it is in constant movement and is constantly subject to change and modification. Otherwise put, it is entirely made up of differential relations which can and do constantly affect the whole. 'Relation is a product that in turn produces.' (*PR*, 160)[7] It is 'an open totality evolving upon itself' (*PR*, 192).[8] In *Poetics of Relation*, Glissant makes an analogy with Einstein's theory of relativity. 'What part of this theory do we retain [...]? That there is no thought of the absolute' (*PR*, 134).[9] This is an assertion which, although not needing to imply a thoroughgoing relativism (as this would itself be to uphold only another type of absolutism), nevertheless marks a paradigmatic shift in the way physics is approached. Departing from Newtonian physics, Einstein's theory presented a view of the universe in which all its component entities exist in a space-time relation which made them constantly subject to potential mutation. The Glissantian concept of Relation involves positing a similar relativity of phenomena in the world owing to the presence of other phenomena. To introduce another of Glissant's concepts, the diverse phenomena of the world we inhabit are part of what Glissant terms the 'chaos-world'. That is to say that they make up a world of phenomena which are apparently disparate but whose underlying coherence can be sought. 'Relation [...] is the *chaos-monde* relating (to itself).' (*PR*, 94)[10] Once this process of relating has been successfully undertaken, multiple, diverse and yet harmonious 'échos-monde' supplant the 'chaos-monde'. 'Echos-monde' are phenomena which, although ostensibly contrasting, exhibit similarities to the degree that they in some sense reflect or are reminiscent of each other. In short, where

---

[5] This point has led to comparisons with the work of Hegel.
[6] 'totalité ouverte' (*PR*, 185).
[7] 'La Relation est un produit, qui produit à son tour' (*PR*, 174).
[8] 'totalité ouverte en mouvement sur elle-même' (*PR*, 206).
[9] 'Que retenons-nous de cette Théorie [...]? Qu'il n'y a pas de pensée de l'absolu' (*PR*, 148).
[10] 'La Relation [...] est le chaos-monde qui (se) relate' (*PR*, 109).

discordance is the initial situation ('chaos-monde'), an overarching harmoniousness can be aspired to and achieved ('échos-monde'). What both states of affairs have in common is the dialectical idea of interactions between phenomena which are advancing a totality.

It is worth noting that Glissant's comparison with Einsteinian relativity is not just an analogy because Glissant's notion that all phenomena exist in interlinking relations involves the very same idea of the *relativity* of each of those phenomena through their relations with each other as in Einstein's theory. In short, where an analogy involves comparison of two distinct phenomena, Glissant would in fact appear to be talking about the exact same thing as Einstein. However, this is nevertheless not entirely the case and it is for this reason that it remains fair to speak of an analogy that is being made in Glissant's writing here. It is not entirely the case for the following important reason: although the discipline of theoretical physics has often been said to be highly hypothetical and not first and foremost postivistic, as there has been a tendency in the humanities to assume mistakenly, nevertheless it is grounded in phenomena which can in theory be proven. To give an example, one area of current physics research involves researching into the implications thrown up by the existence of the Higgs Boson. The Higgs Boson for many years remained nothing but a hypothesis but today advancing research techniques, such as those provided by the CERN in Switzerland, have allowed physicists to prove that it actually exists.

Conversely, Glissant's Relation, however persuasive the concept might seem, can only ever remain a hypothesis, that is to say a speculative theory, because it is not grounded in states of affairs the reality of which could ever be proven. Glissant is well aware of this fact and accepts it entirely. He does not in other words see it as a shortcoming in his thought. 'Relation cannot be "proved," he comments, 'because its totality is not approachable. But it can be imagined' (PR, 174).[11] Otherwise put, Glissant realizes that one could never posit the existence of Relation with absolute certainty. Indeed, to attempt to do so is in a sense missing the point. Relation is best understood as a theoretical schema derived from observation of the multiple interactions of phenomena in the world, as well as from a certain reading of history (more on this later when

---

[11]'La Relation ne peut pas etre "prouvée", parce que sa totalité n'est pas approchable—mais imaginée' (PR, 188).

we will discuss 'creolization'), which helps us to understand the nature of those interactions and the different ways in which the diverse phenomena of our world are thoroughly interconnected with each other at a wide range of levels. Nevertheless, it is this hypothetical character of Glissant's world view which has led some commentators to query the relevance of his thought to political and social thought today. Even as sympathetic a commentator as francophone critic Alain Ménil has rightly categorized Glissant's thought as an atheist mysticism, a categorization which would not appear to render it compatible with politics, whether mainstream or progressive. Others whose arguments I will discuss in Chapter 5 have been much more severe in their judgments than Ménil, arguing that Glissant's thought is not only irreconcilable with progressive politics but is even politically reactionary and a betrayal of the politically committed orientation of his earlier writings. I will explain subsequently why I disagree profoundly with both of these assessments of the work of the later Glissant, and notably the latter reading.

Ménil's assessment however is accurate. In so far as Glissant has made the centrepiece of his thought a theory which could never be proven, there is undeniably a mystical dimension to his world view. At this stage I will limit my response to this admission to the following two observations. First, it is important never to lose sight of the intellectual heritage and context in which most of Glissant's oeuvre was produced. Towards the end of his life Glissant divided his time for the most part between his home country Martinique and the United States. Whatever his anglophone connections in his later years might have been, the fact is that Glissant lived, was educated and worked in the francophone context for much of his life. Certainly his oeuvre from the early works through until his very last publications bear the hallmarks of the European 'continental' speculative tradition of philosophical writing, any influence from the anglophone 'analytic' and pragmatic philosophical heritage being very largely absent. In the European tradition hypothetical theoretical writing has always been accorded a much greater validity than in the anglophone world. Moreover – but this is far too complex a topic for me to address with the rigorousness it merits in the context of a chapter of this length – the relationship between the cultural and political spheres has long been understood differently notably in the French and francophone contexts of intellectual debate from the way it appears to the anglophone mindset. To speak in general and inevitably simplifying terms, in the French and francophone contexts in the twentieth century, there has commonly been an assumption that theoretical oeuvres which were not explicitly politically progressive nevertheless were of a fundamentally left-wing political persuasion unless demonstrably otherwise. Intellectual, like political, liberalism never took hold in France in the way it did in Britain and the United States, and the majority of the writers and intellectuals in the twentieth century in France and the francophone world whose works have constituted what we think of today as the canon were of a broadly even if not explicitly left-wing political orientation.

Second, as I indicated in the Introduction and as will be discussed in detail in later chapters of this study, Glissant's concept of Relation is closely associated in his work with a utopian vision. In so far as it links up with concepts such as the 'Whole-World' ('Tout-monde'), 'worldiness' ('mondialite') and the 'écho-monde', Relation speaks of an ideal world in which all languages and cultures, and hence the peoples they represent, irrespective of how influential they currently are, would be accorded equal respect. Glissant is aware that this aspiration is unrealizable but he nevertheless continues to make it the centrepiece of his thought. Otherwise put, and this is a point which has been overlooked by Glissant's anglophone critics in particular, utopianism is defended by Glissant not as concrete political project but as a *regulative ideal*. This aspect of his later work became apparent notably in the work he wrote with Patrick Chamoiseau in 2009 which was addressed to Barack Obama, entitled *L'Intraitable Beauté du monde*. In this work, Glissant combines very concrete observations about the implications of the election of Obama to the US presidency with his customary association of progressive politics with utopian aspirations. Glissant and Chamoiseau direct at the newly elected US president the remark that his presence 'gives this wonderful utopia a chance. Power only lies in Relation, and this power is that of, and belongs to, all'.[12] It is not that Glissant really believed of course that even Barack Obama, on whose shoulders immense hopes rested in 2009, could make

---

[12]'offre une chance à cette [...] belle utopie. Il n'y a de puissance que dans la Relation, et cette puissance est celle de tous' (*IBM*, 55).

utopia become a reality. Rather, he was of the view that that the real politics of the present could only hope to achieve progressive political results if utopian outcomes remain our guide. Glissant's utopianism, then, is neither synonymous with an abandonment of practical political commitments nor with political naivety. It *coexists* in relational interaction with those commitments. These two drives in his work, the theoretical and the political, are far from being mutually exclusive or, as even Ménil appears to almost end up conceding, paradoxical.[13] They are contrasting, but mutually supporting, aspects of a vision which is at once philosophical, political, aesthetic and ethical.[14] I shall argue in Part III of this book that this utopian vision coheres in a myriad of ways with that which animates and inspires numerous currents associated with the alter-globalization movement. This movement coalesced around the Global Justice Movement (GJM) in the late 1990s and 2000s and has, from that time until the present day, been incarnated in the annual meeting of the World Social Forum (WSF), a politically progressive counterpart to the World Economic Forum which takes place annually in Davos. More significantly, the alter-globalization movement has manifested itself in an increasingly wide range of movements of contestation and trends such as Occupy Wall Street, Occupy, the Indignados in Spain and an ever-more pervasive mistrust of financial institutions and the political authorities which have backed them up by bailing them out of debts, allowing them to carry on rewarding bankers and traders, and turning a blind eye to many years of blatant tax evasion strategies aided and abetted by the big accountancy firms.

---

[13]Alain Ménil, *Les Voies de la créolisation Essai sur Édouard Glissant* (De L'Incidence Editeur, 2011), 567 suggests that in the publications of the later part of Glissant's career there might be a tension between the theoretical vision and more concrete political concerns. However, he is quick to defend Glissant from a specifically political standpoint in the following terms: 'This appraisal only concerns the objective content of the published theoretical writings, and gives us no indications about Glissant's personal convictions [...]. The positions he took publically reveal him to have remained faithful to his earliest commitments.' ('Cette appréciation ne porte que sur le contenu objectif des essais publiés, et ne préjuge en rien des convictions personnelles de Glissant [...]. Ses prises de position publiques l'ont montré fidèle à ces plus anciens engagements'.)
[14]Ibid., chapter 5.

Glissant's concept of Relation is closely linked to a concept which he coined to describe both a historical reality in the Caribbean and a process which he believes is increasingly widespread in our ever-globalizing world, namely 'creolization'. Indeed, there is a limited, or localized sense of 'creolization' which corresponds to an anthropological and historical understanding of how Caribbean cultures developed in the context of colonialism and the mass importation of slaves. The creolizing of the constituent cultural elements, Glissant points out, took place in spite of, and not because of, the coloniser. Secondly, there is a more expansive sense in which Glissant uses the term 'creolization' that involves extrapolating out from the Caribbean context to identify similar processes of cultural mixing and intermingling in today's globalized world. In this sense, the Caribbean becomes for Glissant a paradigm and harbinger for a world of constant interactions between different languages and cultures. As he was to put it succinctly in *Introduction à une poétique du divers* (1996), '*the world is creolising*' (italics Glissant's).[15]

Creolization takes place when two or more linguistic and cultural spheres are brought into contact with one another and an unpredictable result occurs. It is this unpredictability which sets creolization apart from the otherwise closely related phenomenon of cultural mixing ('métissage'). In the latter case it is possible to ascertain what will result from the crossing of two or more cultural components, but not in the case of creolization. Creolization is in no sense some sort of cultural hotchpotch though, Glissant insists, and nor is it to be assimilated to the American 'melting pot' model of multiculturalism. Moreover, creolization is always to be understood as a process, that is to say as an on-going negotiation, rather than as a static state of affairs. It does not lend itself to being a statement of cultural identity as such in the way that affirmations of 'creoleness' were in the francophone Caribbean from the late 1980s onwards.[16] It hence cannot be used for nationalist ends, even though it does

---

[15]'*le monde se créolise*' (*IPD*, 15, italics Glissant's).
[16]Bernabé, Chamoiseau, Confiant, *Eloge de la créolité*. '[Creoleness], unlike creolization, is "*an attempt to get at Being. But that would consitute a step backward in comparison with how creolizations can function*"' (*PR*, 89) ('[Créolité] serait une visée à l'être. Mais c'est là un recul par rapport à la fonctionnalité des créolisations' [*PR*, 103, italics Bernabé, Chamoiseau, Confiant's]).

not imply a rejection of the idea of the nation itself either.[17] Where nationalist agendas tend to rest on essentializing conceptions of cultural identity, creolization is by definition open-ended and always subject to change. It is this dimension of the concept which allows Glissant to extrapolate so easily, in works from *Poetics of Relation* on, from the Caribbean to the transnational and globalized contexts of today's world.

Processes of creolization are closely associated with Relation, both concepts involving interactions between disparate phenomena. Relation though is wider-reaching in its scope and has the potential to be much more all-encompassing. Central to both concepts is the idea of 'the Diverse' (*PR*, 62) ('le Divers', *PR*, 75) which is vital to modes of thought which resist assimilation to absolutes and reductive generalizations: "Diversity, the quantifiable totality of every possible difference, is the motor driving universal energy, and it must be safeguarded from assimilations, from fashions passively accepted as the norm, and from standardized customs.' (*PR*, 30)[18] Difference, then, not only characterizes reality for Glissant but is a positive value. Its affirmation is an act of resistance in the face of all forms of assimilationist thinking which would prefer to impose would-be universal values in the interests of reasserting the dominance of one culture in relation to others. Glissant has the neocolonial influence of mainland France over the francophone Caribbean uppermost in his mind, but notably from *Poetics of Relation* onwards it is the pre-eminence of the United States in economic and cultural terms which he also has in his sights. A form

---

[17]In *Philosophie de la Relation* (2009) Glissant refutes the accusation that his vision involves a repudiation of the idea of the nation: 'Nobody is claiming [...] that the notion of the nation has been become obsolete. The way it discreetly brings things together is necessary to human groups in order that they can frequent the places they live and the landscapes they create on a daily basis, and in order that connections be established between these and other places and landscapes.' ('Nul n'entend [...] que la dimension de la nation est hors jeu: sa secrète corrélation [...] est nécessaire aux collectivités humaines pour fréquenter les lieux qu'elles habitent et les paysages qu'elles suscitent jour après jour, et pour les relier aux autres lieux et aux autres paysages' [*Philosophie de la Relation*, 41]).

[18]'Le Divers, la totalité quantifiable de toutes les différences possibles, est le moteur de l'énergie universelle, qu'il faut préserver des assimilations, des modes passivement généralisées, des habitudes standardisées' (*PR*, 42).

of English is becoming increasingly common today internationally, he argues, which is neither that spoken by the British nor that of the Americans strictly speaking, but is a technico-commercial esperanto born of economic dominance. The dangers of what Glissant calls 'the leveling effect' (*PR*, 112)[19] or 'standardisation' (*PR*, 138 [153]) are great today, that is to say of 'some reduced universal monolingualism' (*PR*, 112).[20] Running counter to these old and new types of negative universalism, the full acknowledgment of differences is a profoundly egalitarian and anti-hierarchical gesture. Economic and cultural hierarchies, but also hierarchies of thought, can thereby be undermined in the name of a manner of approaching the cultural other which is respectful of his or her particularities. These particularities can be approached transversally rather than hierarchically, that is to say from the standpoint of equal to equal rather than dominant in relation to subordinate. Glissant highlights the specificity of individual languages as a key instance. The type of world he would like to see is one in which every language is accorded its full and rightful place irrespective of whether the culture it is associated with is majoritarian or minoritarian. The world should in other words remain fully multilingual and the only way forward in this respect, Glissant believes, is for the practice of translation to be increasingly encouraged and promoted in the twenty-first century.

Thinking of cultures rhizomatically rather than in terms of having a unitary root emphasizes and facilitates this horizontal and egalitarian mode of thinking, and is one of the key bridge areas with the idea of networks which has become so familiar in our globalized age. Such networks should be thought of as open-ended and always subject to potential change, according to Glissant's world view, and are of a piece with another important concept in his thought, namely that of errantry. The errant, by very nature of his 'nomadism' (a concept which Glissant derives from Deleuze), 'challenges and discards the universal—this generalizing edict that summarized the world as something obvious and transparent, claiming for it one presupposed sense and destiny. He plunges into the opacities of that part of the

---

[19] 'l'égalisation' (*PR*, 126).
[20] 'la réduction à un monolinguisme universel, neutre et standardisé' (*PR*, 126).

world to which he has access.' (*PR*, 20)[21] By putting himself in cultural contexts he is not familiar with the errant undermines any pretention that he might have to thinking monolithically or hegemonically. He accepts the impossibility for any mode of thinking to become universalized and embraces this lack wholeheartedly: 'in the poetics of Relation, one who is errant (who is no longer traveller, discoverer, or conqueror) strives to know the totality of the world yet already knows he will never accomplish this—and knows that this is precisely where the threatened beauty of the world resides'. (*PR*, 20)[22] Errantry hence implicitly involves a respect for and modesty in relation to the other, the 'opacity' of whose culture is a positive value, not something to be effaced or erased.

The concept of opacity is one of the most central in Glissant's thought, if not the most central, in terms of offering clear evidence that his vision was in no sense complicit with the economics-derived cultural homogenization wrought by globalization in the 1990s and 2000s but was staunchly opposed to it. Opacity 'protects the Diverse' (*PR*, 62).[23] It stands opposed to 'the preconceived transparency of universal models' (*PR*, 193)[24] – and here Glissant has French universalist republicanism in mind in particular – without being in any sense synonymous with obscurity. It is not 'enclosure within an impenetrable autarchy but subsistence within an irreducible singularity' (*PR*, 190).[25] Put otherwise, the right to opacity which Glissant thinks should be accorded to all cultures, and in particular the minoritarian ones which really need it, safeguards cultural specificity from assimilation to the imperialist designs of majoritarian cultures and communities, or the proto-imperialist cultural consequences which can result from their pre-eminence. The particularities of French culture in a globalized age, for example, have just as much right to remain 'opaque' to

---

[21]'récuse l'édit universel, généralisant, qui résumait le monde en une évidence transparente, lui prétendant un sens et une finalité présupposés. Il plonge aux opacités de la part du monde à quoi il accède' (*PR*, 33).

[22]'dans la poétique de la Relation, l'errant, qui n'est plus le voyageur ni le découvreur ni le conquérant, cherche à connaître la totalité du monde et sait déjà qu'il ne l'accomplira jamais – et qu'en cela réside la beauté menacée du monde' (*PR*, 33).

[23]'protège le Divers' (*PR*, 75).

[24]'la transparence préconçue de modèles universels' (*PR*, 207).

[25]'l'enfermement dans une autarcie impénétrable, mais la subsistance dans une singularité non réductible'(*PR*, 204).

Anglo-American linguistic, cultural, and institutional practices today as did and do francophone Caribbean cultures in relation to what Glissant has always seen as mainland French neo-imperialism.

We have discussed the central Glissantian concepts of Relation and creolization but what of the 'poetics' which are also mentioned in the title *Poetics of Relation*? It is worth noting moreover that it was in 1997 when Glissant's oeuvres to date were republished by Gallimard that series subheadings were given to his theoretical works, some of which were placed in the 'Poétique' category. Hence *Le Soleil de la conscience* (1956), *Poetic Intention* (1969), *Poetics of Relation* (1990), *Treatise on the Whole-World* (*Traité du Tout-monde* (1997)), and *La Cohée du Lamentin* (2005) make up the 'Poétique' series running from numbers I through to V. Equally if not more importantly still is the fact that Glissant was himself a poet and novelist as well as a theorist. Hence the aesthetic dimension of his thought cannot be lost from view even though, for reasons mentioned in the Introduction, I have chosen not to discuss his literary works in the present study.

There are at least two senses of 'poetics' which one needs to be mindful of when approaching Glissant's oeuvre, a familiar sense which is purely aesthetic in the traditional vein, and a broader meaning which can in no way be reduced to the aesthetic sphere. I think it is important to set out this vital distinction at an early stage in this study, and in order to do so it will be useful to refer to some of the works Glissant wrote subsequent to *Poétique de la relation* but whose arguments nevertheless apply to that work. Turning to the first sense of 'poetics', it is not simply that Glissant was in part a poet but that he elevates poetry to primary status in relation to novelistic writing and arguably philosophical writing too. In an interview with Lise Gauvin of 2009, Glissant remarked that '[p]oetry has always been at the crux of literature, because poetry is the only literary artform which states without stating whilst nevertheless making statements'.[26] Poetry, Glissant wrote in a work published the same year, 'is the only narrative giving expression to the world'.[27] When one considers that theoretical writing is itself subordinated by Glissant to the aesthetic sphere,

---

[26]'[l]a poésie a toujours été le nœud de la littérature. Parce que la poésie est le seul art littéraire qui dit sans dire tout en disant.'(*IL*, 116).
[27]'est le seul récit du monde' (*NRM*, 99).

the importance of poetic thinking and discourse in his work becomes fully apparent: 'Philosophy is an artform, and it is difficult to define it, for the reason that noone initially acknowledges this characteristic. Philosophy does not invoke the truth, but arranges the truths of the world in order to single out beauty.'[28]

However, there is a second sense of 'poetics' employed by Glissant which is broader in its reach encompassing not only aesthetics but also politics and ethics, and which could be described as a way of apprehending the world as a totality not just as it presently is but as it could be. It is most commonly this sense of the term 'poetics' which Glissant uses in his theoretical works but the conflation of the two senses can lead to misreading Glissant's politics as debilitatingly abstract.[29] In this second sense of the term, 'the poetics of the Whole-World emanate from the imaginary representations of our most determined and wide-reaching policy-making, here and everywhere, struggles that have been ignored, badly heard demands, fragile associations and objectives that are impossible to meet; *poetics never stop fighting*. Specific poetics that have come into the world are policies that could be put into action everywhere'.[30] 'Poetics' are not expressed in the form of idle musings ('rêvasseries'), Glissant points out. Rather, they can motivate the will to resist when it is necessary to do so: 'The initial desire to resist the effects of those catastrophes that are so deeply connected to the machinations of the tryannical is a poetics before it is a politics.'[31] Poetics, then, are a necessary prerequisite for

---

[28]'La philosophie est un art, et il est difficile de la définir, pour la raison que nul n'avoue d'abord cette qualité. La philosophie n'appelle pas la vérité, elle agence les vérités du monde pour désigner la beauté' (*NRM*, 123).
[29]C. Bongie, in *Friends and Enemies: The Scribal Politics of Post/Colonial Literature* (Liverpool: Liverpool University Press, 2008), 329–330, takes a critical stance with respect to the political dimension of the later Glissant's writings, arguing that Glissant's work becomes very largely disconnected from real-world political concerns.
[30]'[l]es poétiques du Tout-monde', argues Glissant, 'sont issues des imaginaires de nos politiques les plus disséminées, les plus obstinées, ici et partout, combats ignorés et cris malentendus et rassemblements fragiles et visées tellement impossibles à tenir' (*NRM*, 152); '[l]es poétiques ne cessent de combattre. Les poétiques particulières survenues au monde sont des politiques réalisables partout' (*Philosophie de la relation*, 85).
[31]'La première volonté de résistance aux effets des catastrophes, tellement profondément liés aux manœuvres des tyrannies, est une poétique avant d'être une politique' (*NRM*, 162).

progressive politics, not some sort of distraction or diversion from them. As François Paré puts it, 'in Glissant's latter-day publications [...] a close connection is established between a genuine poetics and a politics worthy of the name.'[32] It is in this light that the later Glissant's pessimism with respect to the possibilities of 'substantive' politics *stricto sensu* is best understood. Actual politics today are increasingly limited in terms of the scope of their progressive possibilities, the later Glissant believes, and it is only by way of a 'poetics', that is to say an imagined view of future potential agendas for change regulated by a utopian ideal, that meaning and value can be reinfused into politics. Hence Glissant's insistence in the text he and Chamoiseau addressed to Barack Obama that the newly elected US president was in need of a poetics.

It has to be conceded that there is some ambivalence in Glissant's writing in places which may go some way towards explaining why misunderstandings have arisen with respect to his political commitment. Glissant states in *Philosophie de la relation*, for example, that Relation has no intrinsic moral content but that we can inscribe moral content into it (*PR*, 73), a point which is belied by statements elsewhere and indeed the whole orientation of his thought, all of which suggest strongly that Relation is by its very nature not just a concept with ethical implications but also that it is only conceivable as part of a progressive political project. It is also undeniable that Glissant does not make clear that he is often using terms like 'poetics' and 'aesthetics' in a non-standard way. When he writes, for example, that 'aesthetics [...] allows us to forsee an ethics, exhorting us to define moral conduct and behaviours',[33] the reader could certainly be forgiven for feeling somewhat perplexed. How can Glissant substantiate the idea that laudable ethical conduct should derive from aesthetics, that is to say from something relating to art, one might justifiably ask? It is only when one remembers that in such instances Glissant is using the

---

[32]'dans les derniers écrits de Glissant [...] s'établit un lien étroit entre une véritable poétique et une politique digne de ce nom' (F. Paré, 'Sur quelques pages d'Édouard Glissant. L'Immensité du lieu', in C. W. Francis and R. Viau, (eds) *Trajectoires et dérives de la litterature-monde. Poétiques de la relation et du divers dans les espaces francophones* [Amsterdam, New York: Rodopi, 2013], 452).

[33]'[l]'esthétique [...] augure d'une éthique, pousse à définir les conduites morales' (*Philosophie de la Relation*, 74).

term aesthetics, as he does 'poetics', to mean an apprehension of the world as we would hypothetically and ideally like it to be that such statements are plausible. The 'Whole-World' ('Tout-monde'), in so far as it, like Relation, has to be conceived in thought as opposed to being perceived because already in existence, has an instrinsically hypothetical character and is by its very nature *prospective*, that is to say that it is oriented towards a desired future which cannot be actually known in the present. It is this aspirational dimension, linking up as it does with desired but not-yet-actual realities, which is the conceptual bridge area between the two senses of 'aesthetics' employed by Glissant. It ties in with the traditional sense of 'aesthetics', that is, the science of the beautiful, as well as also being roughly synonymous with the 'Whole-World'.

CHAPTER TWO

From Relation to the 'common-place': the later Glissantian conceptual schema

I have argued in Chapter 1 that the philosophico-poetic vision which Glissant sets out in *Poetics of Relation* both announces a new paradigm in his thought and shows remarkable prescience in terms of anticipating some of the leading tendencies which came to be viewed notably in the 1990s and 2000s as characteristic of contemporary globalization. Otherwise put, *Poetics of Relation* can be seen as emblematic of the manifold and diverse ways in which the later Glissantian theoretical corpus gives expression to way we experience today's world. In this chapter, we will examine some of the key concepts we discussed in Chapter 1 in more detail and will also cover other concepts which form part of Glissant's world view. There will inevitably be some repetition of themes already discussed because Glissant's works of the last twenty or so years revisit and explore in new ways the concepts set out in *Poetics of Relation*. However, they also build on and in certain important ways extend those concepts so there will certainly be new material to discuss too. In fact, one of the specific challenges facing any reader of Glissant – and this is particularly true in Glissant's case even though it can also be said of many thinkers and writers who produced sizeable oeuvres – is being able on the one hand to chart areas of development in his thought while at the same time as identifying continuities. Moreover, there is not just continuity in the expositions Glissant offers of his ideas from work to work and period to period, but even repetitiveness. This is a feature of his writing which he acknowledged openly and even presented as a positive quality of his work. We will examine this dimension of his writing later in this chapter. Suffice it to say for the time being that readers of Glissant have on the one hand to take into account the fact that his ideas are deliberately set out in a non-systematic manner (Glissant being very critical of all hierarchically structured systems and their Cartesian overtones), and on the other hand the fact that his ideas frequently recur in similar but not quite identical ways. Allowing a degree of repetition into our critical exposition of Glissant's ideas is hence a quintessentially Glissantian gesture and will allow us to go some way towards atoning for presenting his ideas in a systematic manner as we will inevitably do to some extent. By way of a final introductory remark, I should stress also that although I and other commentators view *Poetics of Relation* as marking a new paradigm in Glissant's thinking, there are all sorts of thematic and conceptual connections between that work and earlier theoretical works like *Poetic Intention, Caribbean Discourse* and even Glissant's very first theoretical treatise *Le Soleil de la conscience* (1956). Getting to the heart of Glissant's account of the contemporary world is to some extent a journey back to points of origin where one discovers, sometimes to one's own surprise, that he was always-already thinking in the terms of his mature vision many years earlier. We discover that globalization is not as recent a phenomenon as is commonly thought today, or at least that it certainly is not for individuals and communities whose history is that of the Caribbean.[1]

The ways of the chaos-world

Relation has a utopian dimension to it, but can only emanate from an initial acknowledgement of the disparateness of worldly phenomena. What Glissant calls '"the poetics of chaos"'[2] (speech

---

[1] In this regard see Eva Sansavior and Richard Scholar. (eds) *Caribbean Globalizations, 1492 to the Present Day* (Liverpool: Liverpool University Press, 2014).
[2] 'les poétiques du chaos' (*IPD*, 81, speechmarks Glissant's).

marks Glissant's) constitute a moment of recognition of this fundamental disparateness; they amount to doing what he describes as 'para-philosophising about chaos theory.'[3] 'I call *Chaos-monde*', he writes in *Treatise on the Whole-World*, 'the colliding of so many cultures today that are spreading like wildfire, repelling each other, disappearing, and yet which subsist [...]: those outbursts of which we as yet have only a limited understanding'.[4] Indeed, it is at the point that we start to gain an understanding of it that Relation can be conjured up: 'I call *Poetics of Relation* that potential of the imaginary which allows us to conceive of the intangible whole of such a Chaos-world'.[5] Chaos-world involves cultural mixing but not after the fashion of the American melting pot model of cosmopolitanism (*IPD*, 82). As with the parallel he establishes with the Einsteinian theory of relativity which I explained in Chapter 1, Glissant draws inspiration from the sciences to elucidate his thought:

> Chaos theory states that there are dynamic, pre-determined systems which become erratic. In theory, a deterministic system has a fixedness, a "mechanicalness" and a regularity in its functioning; [...] there is an infinity of dynamic, pre-determined systems which become erratic[6]

The phenomena of the world, then, are not naturally ordered but are in flux and unpredictable. Order and harmoniousness have to be sought and involve an imaginary leap.

Relation, Whole-World and Worldliness

It is worth noting that Glissant's thought contains quite a number of conceptual parallels and comparisons which could be described

---

[3] 'paraphilosopher autour de la science du chaos' (*IPD*, 82).
[4] 'le choc actuel de tant de cultures qui s'embrasent, se repoussent, disparaissent, subsistent pourtant [...]: ces éclats dont nous n'avons pas commencé de saisir le principe' (*TTM*, 22).
[5] 'j'appelle *Poétique de la Relation* ce possible de l'imaginaire qui nous porte à concevoir la globalité insasisisable d'un tel Chaos-monde' (*TTM*, 22).
[6] 'La science du chaos dit qu'il y a des systèmes dynamiques déterminés qui deviennent erratiques. En principe, un système déterministe a une fixité, une "mécanicité" et une régularité de fonctionnement; la découverte des sciences du chaos et qu'il y a une infinité de systèmes dynamiques déterminés qui deviennent erratiques' (*IPD*, 84).

as 'rough conceptual equivalences'. That is to say, his thought is made up concepts quite a number of which resemble, or at least cohere with each other very closely, indeed to the degree that they could be said to be by and large equivalent. I have already indicated the conceptual reciprocity of Relation and the Whole-World in Chapter 1 for example, but one might also point to the coherence of 'errantry' with Glissant's scepticism of hierarchies of thought and preference for 'transversality',[7] or to the 'erraticness' of the disparate phenomena of the Chaos-world and his defence of the Diverse and of multiplicities. One might think that such conceptual equivalences essentially amount to little more than the overarching coherence which one would expect from any theory which presents itself as a more or less unified body of ideas or world view. However, this tendency to present roughly equivalent terms does seem to be particularly marked in Glissant's case and is indeed entirely appropriate to a philosophical vision at the centre of which lies the idea of relationality. Indeed, it is apt that a philosophy which emphasizes the horizontal interactions between phenomena would stress the possibility of their ultimate harmonization within an overarching totality. The disparate phenomena of the world are not conceived of as mutually exclusive or contradictory, in Glissant's 'non-system of thought'. Rather, they are different from each other and that difference is viewed as a positive value. Phenomena have the potential to be harmonized with each other despite not being the same or inherently similar.

This idea of the centrality of difference to the concept of Relation was articulated many years before the publication of *Poetics of Relation* in Glissant's second significant theoretical work *Poetic Intention* (1969). 'Poetics of relation presupposes that each and every one of us be brought face to face with the density (opacity) of the other.'[8] The particularity of each phenomenon, then, is not simply to be accommodated by and included in a relational conception of reality but is even necessary to such a conception. The irreducible specificity and inassimilability of each phenomenon in relation to others – others with which it is nevertheless connected via the dialectics of relationality – is affirmed by Glissant. 'It is certainly not

---

[7] 'errance'; 'transversalité'.
[8] '[L]a poétique de la relation', writes Glissant in this work, 'suppose qu'à chacun soit proposée la densité (l'opacité) de l'autre' (*IP*, 24).

the Same and the Other, nor the fact of their being in agreement, which weaves the fabric of Relation', Glissant would write twenty-seven years later in *A New Region of the World* (*Une Nouvelle Région du monde* (2006)), 'it is that which is different which gives an impetus to the jumps and repercussions of the Whole-World and allows the Same and the Other to exist'.[9]

The concept of Relation occupies a significant place in Glissant's magisterial work *Caribbean Discourse* (1981) and is from this point on in his oeuvre written with a capital 'R'. This work which was originally written as a 'thèse d'état', a now obsolete doctoral diploma in France which involved submitting a much more lengthy and substantial thesis than the standard doctoral thesis. *Caribbean Discourse* is a lengthy and imposing analysis of francophone Caribbean history and culture which encompasses thought, customs, and music among other topics and analyses them in a historical and postcolonial perspective. Standing at over 800 pages, *Caribbean Discourse* is divided up into four 'Books', the second of which is entitled 'POETICS OF RELATION', and chapter 45 within the same book carries the same title, although is written in lower case letters. Early on in this work, when addressing the issue of slavery, Glissant argues that through forced migration and resettlement slave populations had no choice but to change; they had to transform into something they had never been before. 'It is in this metamorphosis that we must try to detect one of the best kept secrets of creolization', observes Glissant. 'Through it we can see that the mingling of experiences is at work, there for us to know and producing the process of being. We abandon the idea of fixed being.' (*CD*, 14)[10] The distinction between 'l'étant' (being) and 'l'être' (fixed being) is complicated by the difficulty of translating the two terms into English. Both translate as 'being' but whereas in the case of 'l'être' being is a noun, in that of 'l'étant' in verbal form hence designates a process as opposed to an ontological state of

---

[9]'Ce n'est certes pas le même et l'autre, ni leur accord, qui tissent la Relation, c'est le différent, qui anime les sauts et les rebonds du Tout-monde et permet que soient le même et l'autre' (*NRM*, 103).

[10]'C'est en ce changement qu'il faut essayer de surprendre un des secrets les mieux gardés de la Relation', observes Glissant. 'Par lui nous comprenons que des histoires entrecroiséées sont à l'oeuvre, proposée à notre connaissance et qui produisent de l'étant. Nous renonçons à l'Etre' (*DA*, 40).

fact. To return to the quotation, changing identities such as those of the slaves reinforce the idea of mobile selves and communities who are constantly subject to processes of change and evolution.

It will by now be apparent that there is a powerful anti-essentialist strain to Glissant's thought. The challenge for communities which were forcibly removed from their home cultural environment and have had to adapt in far-reaching ways to a new setting is precisely resisting the impulse to identify with their former and now lost cultural identity. The impulse to identify in this way reifies this latter identity and falsely essentializes their own sense of selfhood. 'The first impulse of a transplanted population [...] is that of reversion. Reversion is the obsession with a single origin [...] To revert is to consecrate permanence, to negate contact.' (CD, 16)[11] We will set aside discussion of Glissant's views on 'the One' until Chapter 4. For the time being, we will limit ourselves to observing that the desire to reconnect with a past cultural identity amounts to a desire for fixity and stasis; this latter is a reaction against the difficulty of facing up to the contingencies and uncertainties of the present situation. Although never mentioned by Glissant, the ontology of Jean-Paul Sartre would appear to be a precursor here: indeed, the impulse to return to a past state of affairs or being which Glissant warns against bears all the hallmarks, at the level of the subjective consciousness which is orienting itself in this direction, of Sartre's well-known concept of *mauvaise foi*.[12] As regards the specificity of Glissant's concept of Relation, where there is fixity there can be no Relation, Glissant argues, as Relation is entirely predicated on the idea of the ongoing interaction between diverse phenomena. 'Relation is the knowledge in motion of beings' (PR, 187),[13] notes Glissant. Hence Relation is a sort of ongoing synthesis of 'being' which, as a verb in this case, refers to phenomena that are

---

[11] 'La première pulsion d'une population transplantée [...] est le Retour. Le Retour est l'obsession de l'Un [...]. Revenir, c'est consacrer la permanence, la non-relation' (DA, 44).
[12] A wealth of criticism has discussed or been devoted to this concept of Sartre's. My own discussions of it have focused on establishing a long-overlooked connection between *mauvaise foi* and ideology. See my *Early Sartre and Marxism* (Lang, 2008), chapter 3, and my article 'Sartre's Concept of Bad Faith in Relation to the Marxist Notion of False Consciousness: Inauthenticity and Ideology Re-Examined' (*Cultural Logic*, Vol. 4, No. 2, Spring 2001, 1–7. http://clogic.eserver.org/4-2/coombes.html).
[13] 'La Relation est connaissance en mouvement de l'étant' (PR, 201).

constantly subject to processes of change and evolution. Relation requires an active 'prise de conscience' of those phenomena but is itself not static.

The type of non-fixed conception of identity which Glissant favours is what he terms an 'identité *relation*' (*IPD*, 24), or 'Relation identity'.[14] As with the concept of creolization which we will examine in Chapter 3, such a conception of identity is in Glissant's work *both* that which has characterized the realities of cultural identity-construction for the peoples of the Caribbean *and* that which he believes is increasingly representative of identities in today's globalized world. Moreover, it is only through poetics that such processes today can be properly understood: 'It is only a poetics of Relation, that is to say a set imaginary representations, which will allow us to "comprehend" those phases and those implications of the situations of peoples in today's world, and which will permit us, if the opportunity presents itself, to try to escape the solipsistic existence we are confined to.'[15] The 'confinement' ('enfermement') he refers to comes in many forms: displaced Caribbean and also north American communities, for example, that mistakenly try to hark back to a putatively lost collective past; postcolonial societies which are tempted by communitarian-type affirmations of collective identity, as was the case at the time of the Martinican 'creoleness' ('créolité') movement from the late 1980s onwards;[16] or even societies, such as former colonial power France, that are becoming increasingly threatened by groups and governmental policies which assert a fixed conception of national identity out of fear of others, be those others immigrants or supranational institutions such as the European Union.[17]

---

[14]'identité-relation' (*PR*, 158).
[15]'c'est seulement une poétique de la Relation, c'est à dire un imaginaire, qui nous permettra de "comprendre" ces phases et ces implications des situations des peuples dans le monde d'aujourd'hui, qui nous autorisera s'il se trouve à essayer de sortir de l'enfermement auquels nous sommes réduits' (*IPD*, 24).
[16]This issue will be discussed in detail in Chapter 3.
[17]In *Quand les murs tombent. L'Identité nationale hors la loi?* (Editions Galaade, 2007) Glissant and Chamoiseau criticise the creation of a Ministry of Immigration, Integration, National Identity and Codevelopment in 2007, a governmental measure which they interpret as all about reasserting some putatively determinate 'Frenchness' against others. More marked still is the nationalism of the French National Front which involves the assertion of a semi-fantasized notion of a determinate and unitary French identity down through the ages.

Glissant's ideal is summed up in a term that makes an appearance in *Poetics of Relation* as 'totality-world'[18] but will subsequently be referred to as the 'Whole-World'.[19] 'I call Whole-World our world all in its changeability and in the durability of its exchanges', writes Glissant, 'and at the same time, the "vision" that we form of it. The totality-world in all its physical diversity and in the representations which it conjures up in our minds: that we would no longer sing, speak nor work localized in the place where we are situated, without steeping ourselves in imaginary representations of that totality.'[20] Like Relation, the 'Whole-World' is best understood as a manner of apprehending the world in all its diversity as a totality; this involves the work of the imaginary in the sense that it is inevitably an imaginary construction. The 'Whole-World' is irreconcilable with contemporary globalization understood in terms of its negative, culturally homogenizing effects: 'standardisation cannot be a mode of the Whole-World.'[21] This, in conjunction with its inextricable connection with Relation, is central to it being an ethical concept, as François Paré rightly points out.[22] As a concept the Whole-World is broadly speaking coterminous with Relation, describing the same phenomenon from a different angle. In the case of Relation the interactions and interrelating of diverse phenomena are foregrounded whereas in the case of the Whole-World it is the idea of all those phenomena making up the world constituting a totality which is emphasized, but there can be no doubt that they are sister concepts. The Whole-World is not, as one might perhaps think at first brush, a geographical concept but rather, as Dominique Chancé puts it, 'first of all the "world that you have mulled over in thought,"

---

[18] 'totalité-monde'.
[19] 'Tout-monde' (*EBR*, 120; *IPD*, 91, 97). The concept of the 'tout-monde' (with a small 't') was first introduced however in Glissant's novel *Mahogony* (1987).
[20] 'J'appelle Tout-monde', Glissant writes, 'notre univers tel qu'il change et perdure en échangeant, et en même temps, la "vision" que nous en avons. La totalité-monde dans sa diversité physique et dans les représentations qu'elle nous inspire: que nous ne saurions plus chanter, dire ni travailler à souffrance à partir de notre seul lieu, sans plonger à l'imaginaire de cette totalité' (*TTM*, 176).
[21] 'la standardisation ne peut pas être un mode du Tout-monde' (*IPD*, 97).
[22] F. Paré, 'Sur quelques pages d'Édouard Glissant. L'Immensité du lieu', in C. W. Francis and R. Viau (eds) *Trajectoires et dérives de la litterature-monde. Poétiques de la relation et du divers dans les espaces francophones* (Amsterdam, New York: Rodopi, 2013), 451.

that is to say a subjective, known, problematised world.'[23] It is 'both inside and outside, both problematic exteriority that we are trying to account for, and interiority which absorbs that exteriority entirely.'[24] 'Moreover, one can live the "Whole-World" without so much as moving at all'.[25] Moreover, as in the case of Relation, there is a utopian dimension to the 'Whole-World'. The term designates a conception of the world *to which we should aspire* as opposed to being a mere description of an existing state of affairs. As such it is similarly of a piece with the concept of creolization which Glissant presents as in part an act of resistance: 'We have lived creolisation in two respects: the negative dimension of slavery and of enslavement and today another dimension which is assimilation to French culture. [...] *Within creolisation many ways of escaping from negativity have manifested themselves.* [...] On the positive side: a way of living creolisation, but a real way which prefigures future solidarities.'[26]

In *La Cohée du Lamentin* (2005) Glissant introduces the concept of 'worldliness' ('mondialite') to designate a mentality corresponding to the phenomenon of transnational interconnectedness which is increasingly the common experience of globalized citizens. 'Worldliness' is politically progressive by its very nature. It is a way of conceiving of the world as being of a fundamentally interconnected nature but in order to push back rather than accept, let alone exacerbate, the alienations wrought by transnational capitalism. Glissant refers to 'an elevated world philosophy, which I would not call globalization (it is even its opposite) but worldliness'.[27]

---

[23]'d'abord le "monde que vous avez tourné dans votre pensée," c'est-à-dire un monde subjectif, reconnu, problématisé.' (Dominique. Chancé, *Édouard Glissant. Un "traité du deparler" Essai sur l'oeuvre Romanesque d'Édouard Glissant* (Paris: Karthala, 2002), 220).
[24]'à la fois dedans et dehors, à la fois extériorité problématique dont le penseur tente de rendre compte, et l'intériorité qui l'absorbe tout entier.'(Ibid., 221).
[25]"On peut d'ailleurs vivre le "tout-monde" sans bouger' (Ibid., 222).
[26]'Nous avons vécu la créolisation sous deux aspects: l'aspect négatif de l'esclavage et de l'asservissement et aujourd'hui un autre aspect qui est l'assimilation à la culture française. [...] *A l'intérieur de la créolisation il s'est présenté bien des moyens d'échapper à la négativité.* [...] C'est le positif: une manière douloureuse de vivre la créolisation, mais une manière réelle, qui préfigure les solidarités futures' (*IPD*, 31, Emphasis added).
[27]'une haute pensée du monde, que j'appelerais non pas la mondialisation (c'en est même le contraire) mais la mondialite' (*CL*, 22–23).

This concept lends itself to parallels with the vision for global understanding which the Paul Gilroy of the early 2000s articulated by way of the concept of a 'planetary mentality'. In fact, Gilroy's work generally is a valuable point of reference and comparison in relation to later Glissantian theory. Gilroy's context and references have always been anglophone but it is perhaps for that reason that consideration of his claims in relation to those of Glissant is of particular interest. The respective focuses of each author in terms of linguistic and specific postcolonial (French or British) contexts are contrasting and yet they have often been trying to get to grips with similar fundamental questions including: the nature of the postcolonial condition; that condition as experienced by black communities in or originating from the Caribbean; and the ways in which that condition can be seen as a harbinger of sorts for Western cosmopolitan societies and also for globalization. One major divergence in terms of focus is that Glissant's interest in the Caribbean experience has always been centred on the communities of the Caribbean islands themselves whereas Gilroy initially interested himself in the Caribbean population living in the UK[28] and subsequently the African diaspora conceived more broadly, and notably the African-American community, its culture and intellectual legacy.[29] However, there are enough areas of significant commonality of interest to merit these two authors being studied together in a comparative perspective.[30]

As will become apparent in Chapter 8, I am more in sympathy with the militant-edged vision set out in *The Black Atlantic* (1993) than I am with the Gilroy of today, despite the great interest which his more recent work still holds. Gilroy's concept of the 'black Atlantic' in my view remains of abiding interest as a paradigm seeking to account for a commonality of experience among diasporized black communities of African descent. What I will call middle-period Gilroy, that is to say the Gilroy of works like *Between Camps*

---

[28]Paul Gilroy, *There Ain't No Black in the Union Jack* (1988).
[29]Paul Gilroy, *The Black Atlantic* (1993). After this work Gilroy increasingly turned his attentions to questions pertaining to cosmopolitanism and postcoloniality conceived more broadly in Western societies.
[30]See my article 'Black Postcolonial Communities in a Globalised World as Articulated in the Work of Paul Gilroy and Édouard Glissant: A Comparative Analysis', in *Commonwealth Essays and Studies*, Vol. 36, No. 2, May 2014, 11–18.

(2000) and *After Empire* (2004), also remains valuable in terms of bridging the divide between questions pertaining to postcoloniality and the attempt to conceptualize the experience of living in the cosmopolitan and ever-globalizing societies of today's developed and emerging nations. In *Between Camps* (2000) Gilroy advocates a 'planetary mentality'[31] which shares with 'worldliness' the fact that it is an attitude of mind, a way of relating to the situation of being in a world made up of transnational interconnectedness. The planetary mentality is defined by a similar desire for inclusiveness and reciprocity and these qualities are contrasted with the violence with which transnational capitalism imposes its agendas on communities around the world. Gilroy hopes for a new type of multiculturalism which could be considered a present-day extension of the 'counterculture of modernity' that cultures in what he had termed the 'black Atlantic' had developed.

La Pensée de la Trace

As I indicated earlier, there is a pronounced tendency towards anti-essentialism in Glissant's conception of reality. However, from at least the *Introduction à une poétique du divers* (1996) onwards[32] the recurrence of the concept of the 'trace' might at first view be perceived as posing a challenge of sorts to this general orientation. In this mature form of the concept, the term 'trace' is principally used metaphorically and, though difficult to define with absolute precision, designates some sort of cultural inheritance or conditioning. For the Africans who were deported and transplanted to slave colonies in the so-called New World, for example, the 'trace' was one of the only things which sustained them at a cultural level (*TTM*, 18–19), Glissant argues, because they carried with them 'the trace of their gods, their customs, and their languages'.[33] This claim

---

[31]Paul Gilroy, *Between Camps: Race, Identity and Nationalism at the End of the Colour Line* (London: Allen Lane, 2000), 356.

[32]In fact, the concept had made a notable earlier appearance in chapter 32 of *Le Discours antillais* (1981) which was entitled 'Traces' (the official translation *Caribbean Discourse* does not contain this chapter). In this chapter the term is used in the literal sense of the footprints or beaten path followed by a fugitive.

[33]'la trace de leurs dieux, de leurs coutumes, de leurs langages' (*TTM*, 19).

could be interpreted as suggesting a conception of identity that is in fact closer to the traditional idea of the unitary root as point of origin than it is to relationality; the idea also of some determinate identity which has been preordained by one's cultural moorings. I believe however that Glissant's thought is not contradictory in this respect, and perhaps not even paradoxical, as might be thought.

First of all, Glissant consistently opposes the 'pensée de la trace' to all types of stasis-inducing modes of thinking which would suggest a foreclosing on change and mutability in the present. It is the 'trace' which 'puts us in Relation, irrespective of where we come from.'[34] It implies conditioning, insofar as a cultural inheritance often involves such conditioning, but without the determinism of the unitary root model of identity. The inheritance it bequeaths to individuals and communities is of great importance to their sense of identity but is not limiting. Their sense of identity can remain open-ended and subject to constant change and evolution.

By its very nature, the 'thought of the trace' ('pensée de la trace') is, 'like errantry which shows the way',[35] intrinsically opposed to every form of system of thought. In his *Introduction à une poétique du divers* (1996) Glissant explains this opposition in the following metaphorical terms using poetic imagery:

> It is an opaque way of learning about how the wind bends branches, of being oneself whilst deriving from the other, sand scattered in a truly utopian disorderly fashion, the unfathomable, the river's concealed undercurrents unleashed. Antillean rural settings link up with others further away, and each tale secretes its singular trace into it, from streams to rivers establishing points of contact.[36]

There can be little doubt, as I argued in Chapter 1, that there is a mystical dimension to Glissant's thought. Indeed, a certain mysticism is inscribed in the very notion of the 'trace' as it is

---

[34]'nous met, nous tous, d'où que venus, en Relation' (*TTM*, 18).
[35]'comme une errance qui oriente' (*TTM*, 18).
[36]'C'est une manière opaque d'apprendre la branche et le vent, d'être soi dérivé à l'autre, le sable en vrai désordre de l'utopie, l'insondé, l'obscur du courant dans la rivière dételée. Les paysages antillais enjoignent les autres au loin, et chaque conte y insinue sa trace singulière, de rivières en fleuves, établissant corrélation (*IPD*, 70).

described here. But the above description also illustrates a tendency towards a syncretic synthesizing of natural and cultural phenomena which, given the long history of syncretic thinking in what Paul Gilroy has termed 'black Atlantic' cultures, cannot simply be put down to mysticism. To do so would arguably be only to reconfirm a decidedly Western separation of rational from irrational thinking, thereby judging Glissant according to criteria which his thought intrinsically challenges in fundamental ways. The right to difference and 'opacity' which Glissant so fervently defends throughout his oeuvre is also a demand not to be judged only according to the criteria by which Western commentators would usually apply when reading the works of Western writers and theorists.[37]

The thought of the trace does not imply lapsing into indeterminate, vague thought processes, as the Western reader might infer. Rather it reconfirms conceptual thinking but 'as forward movement'; it 'turns it into a recitative, makes it a basis for relation, reminds us of its relative character.'[38] Systems of thought paradoxically undermine conceptual thinking, Glissant argues, by propagating a 'false universality',[39] that is to say a mode of thinking with universalist ambitions which, with its

---

[37] That said, it has to be conceded that this is a very complex matter and one which runs right to the heart of a range of central debates foregrounded by postcolonial discourses. For to suggest that the thought of a writer like Glissant, who was educated in Paris and who published throughout his career in French with French publishing houses, cannot be judged *at all* according to Western criteria would also be an error and would involve falling into the opposite trap, namely a sort of positive discrimination whereby the cultural other is presented as being intrinsically beyond reproach. It would be to suggest that what we cannot understand in Glissant is simply beyond criticism on the grounds that it is different, and this would amount to ceding too much ground to cultural relativism and dispensing altogether with criteria of judgment which, at some level at least, would normally be considered universally applicable. As we will see in Chapter 4, Glissant is a staunch opponent of universalist thinking. However much validity we wish to accord to affirmations of difference, though, in reality universals, be they considered an imposition or in certain respects valuable, cannot be dispensed with entirely, or at least not without great cost. The cost is that of lapsing into complete cultural relativism which, if pushed to its furthest extreme, itself becomes a form of universalism that is even more tyrannical in intellectual and perhaps even political terms than a more modest universalism which can in my view be defended.
[38] 'comme élan'; it 'en fait le récitatif, le pose en relation, lui chante relativité' (*TTM*, 83).
[39] 'fausse universalité' (*IPD*, 17).

neocolonial rejection of otherness, undermines the very bases of genuine thought. The attempt to iron out differences amounts to nothing less than a denial of the real nature of thought which involves the transmission of values, knowledge and a cultural inheritance from one period to another. Otherwise put, the affirmation of values claimed to be timelessly valid for all is a negation of a fundamental truth, namely the historical origin and the geographical situatedness of modes of thinking. Universalist systems of thought are consequently nothing less than a type of intellectual *imposture*, in Glissant's view. They deny minoritarian cultures the right to difference, but they also involve a refusal to acknowledge their own conditions of possibility and hence the historical developments – both intellectual, social and cultural – by which they themselves came into existence.

Glissant mentions jazz music as an example of a form of present-day cultural expression which illustrates the phenomenon he calls the 'trace'. 'Jazz music', writes Glissant, 'is a reconstituted trace'.[40] In an interview of 2009 which is quite short but nonetheless highly revealing and in many respects representative of his thought more broadly conceived, Glissant stresses that from its inception jazz was the result of both creolizing processes and of 'traces' of a past cultural identity: 'The African Americans landed naked, without any instrument. It's for this reason that they had to reconstruct their identities, digging deep into the traces lying in their memories, and it's from that trace alone [...] that they were to invent jazz.'[41] Blacks in the New World, continues Glissant, did not express something that had existed beforehand because their African musics had been taken away from them. All that remained was the trace of that music:

> It's the case with jazz, but also with reggae, calypso, beguine, salsa ... This trace expressed itself also in the drumming of Guadeloupe, Dominica, Jamaica and Cuba ... No two are the

---

[40] 'La musique de jazz', writes Glissant, 'est une trace recomposée' (*TTM*, 19).
[41] 'Les Africains-Américains sont arrivés nus, sans aucun instrument. C'est pour cela qu'ils ont dû se reconstruire, en fouillant les traces de leur mémoire, et c'est à partir de cette simple trace [...] qu'ils vont inventer le jazz.' Interview with Glissant, 'Édouard Glissant: le jazz est une négritude dépassée' in *Jazzman*, no.159, July/August 2009, 46–48, 47.

same, each style grows out of this idea of the trace, seeks it and enters into relation.[42]

The importance of the trace in its genesis does not mean that jazz should be allowed to be canonised or systematized today though. It should not become a backward-looking or traditionalist celebration of past musical achievements. If jazz is a form of 'negritude which acknowledges itself as such' it is also a 'transcended negritude'.[43] This means that without denying its origins jazz is a music which must nevertheless move forwards and express its time. It has a capacity to 'take hold of the world' ('saisir le monde') of today while also containing within it the elements which allowed it to come into existence.[44] It 'goes beyond questions of identity.'[45]

Trembling ('*Le Tremblement*')

There is another sense in which Glissant's statements on jazz offer an illuminating illustration of the trace and that is in the connection between the latter and a concept which Glissant first started to formulate in the 2000s, namely the concept of 'trembling'. 'Jazz music is a type of trembling', he writes in *La Cohée du Lamentin*. 'It first made its mark in the United States, in archipelic music, before becoming continentalised.'[46] We will return shortly to the question of what is meant by the 'archipelic thought' ('pensée archipélique') which is alluded to in this quotation and the opposition Glissant sets up between it and 'continental thinking' ('pensée continentale'). For the time being we will focus on 'trembling' which, claims Glissant, 'presupposes improvisation but also control.'[47] In the case

---

[42]'C'est le cas du jazz, mais aussi du reggae, du calypso, de la biguine, de la salsa … Cette trace s'exprime aussi dans les tambours guadéloupéens, dominicains, jamaïcains, cubains … Aucun n'est le même, tous repartent de cette idée de trace, la cherchent et se mettent en relation' (Ibid., 47).
[43]'négritude assumée'; 'négritude […] dépassée.'(Ibid., 47).
[44]Ibid., 47.
[45]'dépasse les questions identitaires' (Ibid., 48).
[46]'La musique de jazz est un tremblement', 'elle a d'abord rayonné dans le sud des Etats-Unis, en musique archipélique, avant de se continentaliser' (CL, 77).
[47]'suppose à la fois l'improvisation mais aussi la maîtrise' (Ibid., 48).

of jazz, it manifests itself in the balance between improvisation and the reiteration of traditional elements conveyed via the 'trace'.

It should be stressed that 'trembling' ('tremblement') is first and foremost a non-musical concept in Glissant's thought. While the adjective 'trembling' ('tremblant') had made appearances in earlier works, it is notably in *La Cohée du Lamentin* (2005) that it becomes a noun thereby taking on the status of a philosophical concept. To return briefly to the 'trace', it is vital to 'trembling' coming about: 'The trace [...] is that by which, on which, in which trembling moves forward.'[48] But the 'trace' is itself 'trembling': 'The trembling, fragile and pressing character of the Trace explains why the unexpected happens in our societies.'[49] And if the 'trace' is hence central to processes of creolization, which are defined by their unexpected outcomes, it is also vital to the relational, rhizomatic conception of identity (*CL*, 84).

What, then, is designated exactly by term 'trembling'? 'The image of trembling', writes Chris Bongie, 'functions throughout *La Cohée du Lamentin* as a poetic metaphor for understanding the contingent nature of life in the Tout-Monde'.[50] It 'picks up on passing mentions of the 'trembling value' of cultural *metissages* and cultures of *metissage* in the *Traité du Tout-Monde* and can even be traced as far back as *L'Intention poetique*.'[51] 'Trembling thought wells up from everywhere' and 'protects us from system-thinking and systematic thinking';[52] because it 'deliberately aims to give up all systematic, long-range perspectives ... and linear thinking'; 'trembling plunges us into an intimate understanding of depths'.[53] It stands opposed to the smooth surface exterior of systematic thinking and reveals the necessity of delving much deeper in order to understand the cultural other. Systems of thought ('Pensées de système') have historically

---

[48]'La trace [...] est ce par quoi, sur quoi, en quoi le tremblement avance' (*NRM*, 188).
[49]'Le caractère tremblant, fragile et impérieux de la Trace, explique comment l'inattendu survient dans nos sociétés' (*CL*, 84).
[50]Chris Bongie, *Friends and Enemies: The Scribal Politics of Post/Colonial Literature* (Liverpool University Press, 2008), 333.
[51]Ibid., 334.
[52]'La pensée du Tremblement surgit de partout' and 'nous préserve des pensées de système et des systèmes de pensée' (*CL*, 12).
[53]'la vocation deliberée de renoncer aux longues vues systématiques, [...] au principe lineaire'; '[l]e tremblement nous plonge dans l'intuition des profondeurs' (*NRM*, 188).

gone hand in hand both with Western colonial aspirations and a concomitant insistence on transparency: the alleged transparency of the colonial power's language, thinking and institutional arrangements; but also an exhortation to the cultural other to align himself to that way of thinking in order supposedly that his thinking gain from the 'universally applicable' values, procedures and criteria of the coloniser's practices. In reality, the aim of such a strategy was to subjugate the cultural other ideologically to ensure political obedience. The 'pensée du tremblement' involves an acceptance that such an aspiration to transparency cannot succeed in this sense of transparency, that is, as complete clarity. It is hence entirely of a piece with Glissant's insistence on the right of all cultures to opacity. At the same time, it is an expression of a fundamental uncertainty which is that of the existential present and the effects which contingent circumstances can always have on the substantive content and/or identities of given phenomena. The improvisatory character of jazz makes it a prime example of the 'tremblement'. As jazz is created in real time, even if the performers employ elements which they have assimilated beforehand, the direction which the music takes can always be subject to fluctuation and change. The end result is consequently always dependent on contingent factors and may not be quite what any of the participants or the audience anticipated.

'Errantry' ('*L'errance*')

The concept of errantry makes an appearance in *Poetic Intention* (1969) to describe the questing spirit of Western colonialists and their illegitimate appropriation of the lands of others. 'The poetics of errantry', notes Glissant in this regard, 'is in the very fabric of mindless violence. Violence serving a cause can become a politics of rootedness.'[54] In this instance, then, errantry is self-justifying; it gained its justification solely from the fact that it was an expression of the will of the Western coloniser. The violence of colonial appropriation needed neither provocation nor legitimation. Once the violent act of appropriation had taken place, it then took

---

[54]'La poétique de l'errance est tissée dans la violence sans cause. La violence qui s'oriente devient politique de l'enracinement' (*IP*, 183).

root and became normalized by the coloniser. Moreover, Glissant adds, the intellectuals of the day more often than not gave their support to such colonialist practices. In a manner reminiscent of Karl Marx's view of ideological incorporation in *The German Ideology* (1845) and Sartre's account of the nineteenth-century intellectual in *What Is Literature?* (1947), Glissant condemns the intelligentsia of the day flatly: 'sold-out or cowardly, allegedly free or mistakenly loud-mouthed, they always served those working in the sugar cane business. (Their educated class was created for this purpose.)'[55]

In other works Glissant endeavours to explain the Western impulse to wander in search of other lands and peoples to appropriate. There was a 'Western errantry' ('errance occidentale'), he remarks in *Introduction à une poétique du divers* (1996), which was directed towards conquering other peoples. For a long period it was this type of questing nomadism which set the pace. Western errantry, Glissant adds, was not only a colonial project though. For some, such as the poet Rimbaud, it manifested itself in 'very personalized adventures' (*PR*, 14–15).[56] '[F]or Rimbaud errantry is a vocation only told via detour. The call of Relation is heard, but it is not yet a fully present experience.' (*PR*, 15)[57] Figures such as Rimbaud, then, by contrast with their colonialist counterparts, in fact prefigured the type of errantry which Glissant advocates as a mode of thinking today. Their attitude anticipated the celebration of diversity which Glissant believes is central to Relation.

It is important to note that Glissant as often as not refers not simply to errantry but to errant thinking ('la pensée de l'errance'). In other words, errantry is, like the Whole-World, above all a mode of thinking or an attitude of mind. In *Introduction à une poétique du divers* errantry is associated directly with 'drifting' ('la dérive'), both of which are 'an availability of being' and what Glissant terms an 'appetite for the world'.[58] This latter involves a willingness to

---

[55] 'vendus ou pusillanimes, prétendument libres ou faussement aboyeurs, ils servent toujours ceux qui exploitent la canne. (Leur classe de lettrés fut créée à cette fin.)' (*IP*, 183).
[56] 'des aventures très personnelles' (*PR*, 27).
[57] '[A]vec Rimbaud, l'errance est vocation, qui ne se dit qu'en detours. C'est l'appel, et non pas encore la plénitude, de la Relation' (*PR*, 27).
[58] 'une disponibilité de l'étant' and what Glissant terms an 'appétit du monde' (*IPD*, 130).

come into contact with cultural contexts other than one's own either literally (as with Rimbaud's self-exile, or Fanon's years in Algeria) or, as is more often the case, in thought alone. The errant, through coming into contact with the infinite diversity of the world, incorporates that diversity into his or her thinking. This is a vital step on the road to conceptualizing Relation and the Whole-World.

'Errant thinking is a poetics, which always infers that at some moment it is told. The tale of errantry is the tale of Relation.' (*PR*, 18)[59] It is clear from this statement that errantry and Relation are mutually supportive and interconnecting concepts for Glissant. The same can be said for errantry in relation to the 'tremblement': 'Trembling thought is in tune with the errantry of the world and what it cannot express.'[60] The receptiveness and openness of mind of the errant is of a piece, then, with the concept of a contingent reality that is always subject to potential fluctuation and change. Among other things, a process of creolization could potentially result in those cases where errantry involves actual as well as mental movement as given individuals thereby come into direct contact with other cultures. Creolization will be the subject of the next chapter.

Archipelic thought

As with the trace and errantry, there is a literal sense of the 'archipelago' which becomes both metaphor and concept when linked with 'thought' or 'thinking' (as in 'la pensée de l'errance'). As we will discover when discussing creolization, there is a tendency for Glissant to take the particular characteristics of the Caribbean as both model and template for other contexts in the world today. In Glissant's view, the islands that make up the archipelago that is the Caribbean have long had the particularity of being distinct by dint of their status as individual islands on the one hand while enjoying a sense of shared identity which transcends the boundaries between them on the other. 'And if, with a sense of dignity, each of

---

[59]'La pensée de l'errance est une poétique, ce qui sous-tend qu'à un moment elle se dit. Le dit de l'errance est celui de la Relation' (*PR*, 31).
[60]'La pensée du tremblement s'accorde à l'errance du monde et à son inexprimable' (*CL*, 25).

us in these islands, each person in his or her own country, looks out towards the horizon', comments Glissant, 'what we see is not only another country but the whole of the Caribbean, and this alters the way we see things and teaches us not to underestimate anything in this world.'[61] This reality in the Caribbean provides the model for what Glissant terms 'archipelic thought' ('la pensée archipélique') and he is of the view that this phenomenon is becoming more and more widespread in the globalized age:

> What I see today is that the continents of the world are becoming like archipelagos [...] The Americas are becoming archipelagos. Linguistic regions and cultural regions beyond the frontiers between nations are islands, but islands that are outward-looking and this is the principal basis for their survival.[62]

Archipelic thought is a non-systematic, inductive mode of thinking which accepts the idea of the unexpected, Glissant argues. It maintains coherence but not at the expense of ironing out differences or becoming a closed system. As such it contrasts with 'pensée continentale' which aspires to reasserting the One ('l'Un'), that is the idea of one entirely unified, non-differential entity, and codifies its universalist ambitions in systematic thinking. The archipelago is tantamount to a supranational agglomeration of contrasting elements; it is greater in extent than the individual islands, or nations, which compose it and yet is devoid of the neocolonial tendencies of continental thinking ('la pensée continentale'). It goes hand in hand with creolization where the bringing together of distinct phenomena produces unexpected results while leaving the specificity of those phenomena intact. It 'recognises the scope of the imaginary representations of the Trace, which it confirms',[63]

---

[61]'Et si, debout, chacun dans une de ces îles, chacun dans son pays, nous regardons sur l'horizon', comments Glissant, 'nous voyons non pas un autre pays seulement, mais la Caraïbe entière, qui change notre regard et lui enseigne à ne rien mésestimer de ce monde' (*CL*, 85–6).

[62]'Ce que je vois aujourd'hui, c'est que les continents "s'archipélisent" [...] Les Amériques s'archipélisent, elles se constituent en régions par-dessus les frontières nationales [...] L'Europe s'archipélise. Les régions linguistiques, les régions culturelles, par-delà des barrières des nations, sont des îles, mais des îles ouvertes, c'est leur principale condition de survie' (*IPD*, 44).

[63]'reconnaît la portée des imaginaires de la Trace, qu'elle ratifie' (*TTM*, 31).

the preservation of the 'trace' being dependent on the persistence of distinctive, often age-old, characteristics in present-day cultural or identitarian phenomena. Moreover, 'archipelic thought is a philosophy of trembling [...] it explodes onto all horizons, *in all directions*'.[64] While it preserves valuable inheritances from the past, it is open to the contingencies of the present and the future. 'The World is trembling, is creolizing [...] Archipelic thinking itself trembles as a result of this trembling'.[65]

The detour

Archipelic thinking is of a piece with what Glissant terms 'le détour' (*TTM*, 31), a concept which links up with that of errantry. The detour, Glissant specifies, is neither 'escapism nor renunciation',[66] contrary to what one might imagine. Whereas the primary obsession of displaced communities is a desired Return, Glissant explains in *Caribbean Discourse*, the detour involves going elsewhere in order to understand the nature of the domination of one's own land and culture by a colonial power. The need to go elsewhere is owing to the fact that 'the system of domination (which is not only exploitation, which is not only misery, which is not only underdevelopment, but actually the complete eradication of an economic entity) is not directly tangible' (*CD*, 20).[67] The detour, in very simple terms, is a need to go elsewhere in order to understand the situation of one's own country and culture. The concept would appear to be somewhat reminiscent of the cultural relativism of the eighteenth-century French 'philosophes', as exemplified notably in Diderot's *Lettres persanes*, were it not for the fact that Glissant's focus is those communities and nations which the colonial power perceives and portrays as a cultural *other* trying to make sense of the ways

---

[64]'la pensée archipélique est une pensée du tremblement [...] elle éclate sur tous les horizons, *dans tous les sens*' (*CL*, 75).
[65]'Le Monde tremble, se créolise [...] La pensée archipélique tremble de ce tremblement' (*CL*, 75–6).
[66]'fuite ni renoncement' (*TTM*, 31).
[67]'la matérialité de la domination (qui n'est pas l'exploitation seulement, qui n'est pas la misère seulement, qui n'est pas le sous-développement seulement, mais bien l'éradication globale de l'entité économique) n'est pas directement visible' (*Le DA*, 48).

in which they have been oppressed by the French. In short, it is Diderotian cultural relativism *inverted*, as the following passage illustrates:

> We can find quite logically one of the most dramatic manifestations of the need for the strategy of diversion in a threatened community in the migration of French Caribbean people to France (which has often been described as an officially sanctioned slave trade in reverse) and in the psychic trauma that it has unleashed. It is very often only in France that migrant French Caribbean people discover they are *different*, become aware of their Caribbeanness. (CD, 22–23)[68]

Frantz Fanon is the most significant example of the practice of the detour, Glissant continues. In his wholehearted embracing of the Algerian cause in the 1950s, Fanon is the only leading Martinican intellectual to have severed ties with his home country. Although his views on the 'Martinican problem' specifically remained entirely ambiguous following his emigration to Algeria, nevertheless his writings have contributed hugely to reflection about that colonial and subsequently neocolonial problem back in his homeland: 'the political act of Fanon, led us *somewhere*, authorizing by diversion the necessary return to the point where our problems lay in wait for us' (CD, 25).[69]

The 'common-place' ('lieu-commun')

It will be apparent from the above quotation that the importance of geographical location is not a dimension of cultural identity or political history that is overlooked by Glissant. Indeed, without an

---

[68]'L'une des manifestations les plus spéctaculaires de cette nécessité du Détour pour une communauté ainsi menacée, nous la trouvons en toute logique dans le mouvement d'émigration des populations antillaises vers la France (dont on a assez dit qu'il constituait, encouragé par les pouvoirs publics, une traite à rebours) et dans les retentissements psychiques qu'il déclenche. C'est en France le plus souvent que les Antillais émigrés se découvrent *différents*, prennent conscience de leur antillanité' (Ibid., 52).

[69]'l'acte politique de Fanon nous ont mené *quelque part*, autorisant par détour que nous revenions au seul lieu où nos problèmes nous guettent' (Ibid., 56).

awareness of the interconnectedness of these parameters and the places in which they are articulated, the detour would be all but meaningless. It would not be possible to rethink the predicament of the people of one's own island or nation from *elsewhere* were that predicament not closely associated with that community's own shared geographical location or physical space.

François Paré has highlighted effectively the importance of place in Glissant's thought, stressing the centrality of the place from which statements are made to the import of those enunciations.[70] 'The "totality-world,"' writes Paré, 'would only be acceptable ultimately if it continued discreetly to shelter and nourish the troublesome matter which constitutes "Place," perhaps as a repressed and unacknowledged premise.'[71] One might add that just as creolization involves bringing together distinct elements which nevertheless remain intact, and just as Relation in no sense involves subsuming the 'opaque' particularities of specific cultures in a sea of relativism, so the particular history and cultural heritage of any given *lieu* remains intact within the much broader and synthetic totality that is the 'totality-world' (or 'Whole-World' as Glissant was later to label this concept).

Glissant employs the concept of the 'common-place' to specify such shared spaces. The common-place is not a platitude or *idée reçue* but 'literally places where worldly thinking meets other types of worldly thinking'[72] or, in other words, actual physical places or locations where different sets of cultural values meet. In the relatively late work *Une Nouvelle region du monde* (2006) Glissant introduces a distinction between the 'lieu-commun', with a hyphen between the two terms, and the 'lieu commun' without a hyphen. The latter 'is just as necessary for us, in order to summarize the (hi)stories of the world'.[73] In short, it is a form of linguistic practice, not all that dissimilar from the everyday sense of the expression,

---

[70]Paré, 'Sur quelques pages d'Édouard Glissant. L'Immensité du lieu', in Francis and Viau (eds), 378–389, 381.
[71]'[L]a "totalité-monde" ne serait recevable au bout du compte', writes Paré, 'que si elle continuait d'abriter et de nourir clandestinement, peut-être sous forme d'interdit et de refoulé, la matière gênante du "Lieu"' (Ibid., 388).
[72]'littéralement des lieux où une pensée du monde rencontre une pensée du monde' (*IPD*, 33).
[73]'nous est aussi nécessaire, pour récapituler les histoires du monde' (*NRM*, 111).

involving giving expression once again to tales and stories which, via their familiarity within specific contexts, serve to consolidate and galvanize communities by reaffirming their heritage or 'trace'. Unlike the everyday sense of commonplace ('lieu commun'), however, in Glissant's usage the term is conceived entirely positively.

PART TWO

Creolization, anti-universalism and twenty-first-century radical thought

CHAPTER THREE

Creolization and creoleness: proximity and divergence

The concept of creolization is central to Glissant's world view, both in terms of his reading of Caribbean history and identity, and with respect to his vision for the future of our globalized world today. Moreover, as I indicated in Chapter 2, there is a tendency for Glissant to project outwards from reflections on the Caribbean to discussing the kind of globalized world he would ideally like to see, namely one divested of primarily market-led neo-imperialist tendencies. The Caribbean context, then, is from a philosophical as well as literary point of view both a home base for Glissant and a starting point for reflecting on the future of global society in the late twentieth and twenty-first centuries. And it is fair to say that there is no one concept in Glissant's 'non-system of thought' which is more representative of his vision as a whole, or more decisive in terms of colouring its overall orientation, than that of creolization. In this chapter we will make this concept our focus, firstly with the intention of explaining the role Glissant allots to it in terms of accounting for Caribbean cultural identity, and secondly in order to shed further light on his mature vision for an alternative conception of globalization today. We will also discuss an important development in Caribbean thinking in this regard which came to prominence from the 1980s onwards, namely the 'Créolité' movement. The idea of 'Créolité', or 'Creoleness' was promoted as a cultural agenda notably by intellectuals and writers in Martinique, the central postulates of the theory being elaborated notably in the *Eloge de la créolité* (*In Praise of Creoleness*, 1993 [1988]), authored by Jean Bernabé, Patrick Chamoiseau and Raphaël Confiant. It will be of value to our analysis of Glissantian thought to discuss this cultural manifesto with political overtones not only because of the significant impact which it had on cultural politics in the Caribbean but also because its advocates claimed to have derived their ideas from the oeuvre of Glissant who they, and in particular Chamoiseau, considered to be their 'maître à penser'.

'Creolization': a new theoretical paradigm with a dual application in Glissantian theory

We established in Chapter 1 that creolization is the result of two or more linguistic and cultural spheres coming into contact with each other and giving rise to an unpredictable outcome. In the case of cultural mixing ('métissage'), conversely, the results can be predicted, Glissant argues. Creolization, then, is a fundamentally much more open-ended phenomenon than that of cultural mixing, the concept being antithetical to fatalism in all its forms. Moreover, the open-ended nature of creolization is also what makes it so well suited to the diverse contexts and situations to which Glissant applies it. In Glissant's mature theory, as we have seen, creolization is an operative concept applied to phenomena so diverse that it becomes the central paradigm employed to account for today's globalized world itself as well as for the alter-globalist vision which Glissant would ideally like to see supplant globalization in its present-day form.

If creolization comes to take pride of place in Glissant's account of today's world, even a cursory examination of the concept confirms that it derives from an understanding of the cultural history and make-up of the Caribbean. In his *Mémoires des esclavages* (2007) Glissant presents creolization as a positive consequence of the human tragedy that was the forced transplanting of Africans to the New World to labour as slaves. Glissant speaks of 'the creolization of this large section of the world, a creolisation which is just as wonderful as its democratisation'.¹ The cultural identity of the Caribbean is owing to the forced meeting of culturally diverse groups, namely the descendants of the African slaves and the French colonizers. In *Caribbean Discourse*, Glissant argues for a specific Antillean identity which he coins the neologism 'antillanité' (Caribbeanness) to describe. As J. Michael Dash comments a propos of *Caribbean Discourse*, '[t]he panoramic picture of the Caribbean is almost one in which a shared part and a common landscape remain a submarine and unconscious reality, and the 'field of islands' represents zones of consciousness where *Antillanité* is manifested in given linguistic, national and political configuration. As Glissant writes, *antillanité* is lived 'de manière souterraine' ('in a subterranean manner') by the people of the Caribbean.'² 'Antillanité' is of course a paradigmatic instance of 'archipelic' thinking but will be progressively supplanted by the concept of creolization in Glissant's writings. Although 'antillanité' is not an essentialist conception of local identity,³ its successor will place an even more marked emphasis on processes thereby evacuating any remaining vestiges of some determinate essence.

'The world is creolizing. It is not becoming creole but is becoming this unpredictable entangled continuum that every process of creolization bears within it'.⁴ This statement will be familiar to readers of the mature Glissantian theoretical corpus as variations on it appear in a number of works from the mid-1990s onwards. It sums up in relatively few words Glissant's view of the direction today's world is taking. How exactly then does Glissant define this

---

¹"the creolisation of this large section of the world, a creolisation which is just as wonderful as its democratisation' ('la créolisation de ce grand pan du monde, créolisation aussi belle que sa démocratisation' (*ME*, 137)).
²J. Michael Dash, *Édouard Glissant* (Cambridge University Press, 1995), 147.
³Alain Ménil, *Les voies de la créolisation Essai sur Édouard Glissant* (De L'Incidence Editeur, 2011), 163. There is some critical uncertainty on this point, Chris Bongie (1998, 67) for instance mistakenly ascribing to Dash the view that 'Antillanité' is open to the charge of essentialism. Dash refers to 'Antillanité' as a 'definition of the Caribbean in terms of openness, of *errance*' (147), which would seem to sit uncomfortably with ascribing essentialism to Glissant in this regard. As I shall indicate later, Bongie's misreading would appear to derive from his own critical stance with respect to the later Glissantian world view.
⁴"Le monde se créolise, il ne devient pas créole, il devient cet inextricable et cet imprédictible que tout processus de créolisation porte en lui' (*CL*, 229).

central concept of creolization beyond the relatively brief summary I have already provided? Creolization does not lead to any kind of loss of identity or sacrificing of the self to outside influences, Glissant points out in *Treatise on the Whole-World* (*Traité du tout-monde* (1997)), but it does suggest a distancing from the fixity of Being (*TTM*, 25). In fact it is 'non-Being finally enacted',[5] even though 'non-Being is not non being'.[6] Creolization is hence not a denial of Being as such but involves casting aside any essentialist emphasis or insistence on Being in favour of highlighting ongoing processes of change. A close connection is established here with the figure of the archipelago which is also defined as 'the dispersal of non-Being, which brings together the being of the world'.[7] 'Being', then, as a verb rather than a noun.

Creolization is 'the meeting point, interference, impact, harmoniousness and disharmony between cultures'.[8] Beyond the unpredictability of outcomes, the speed of interactions is noteworthy, as is 'the process of mutual valourization which results from it and makes it necessary that each person re-evaluate for himself the component elements that have been put into contact with each other'.[9] Creolization is ongoing and has no determinate end point: there will be processes of creolization for the full duration of human history. These processes are also devoid of any intrinsic moral content (*ME*, 91). There is hence nothing intrinsically ethically laudable or reprehensible about creolization. It is simply a fact, and only its results that can be judged in terms of their moral implications.

If creolization clearly has nothing whatsoever to do with the French assimilationist policy towards the cultural other in the name of supposedly universally applicable values, Glissant is also keen to dissociate it from the American 'melting pot' model of social integration and associated American multiculturalist agendas. 'Land of multiculturalism, the United States is not a country of

---

[5] 'le non-Etre enfin en acte' (*TTM*, 238).
[6] '[l]e non-Etre n'est pas non être' (*TTM*, 237).
[7] '[l]a dispersion du non-Etre, qui rassemble l'étant du monde' (*TTM*, 237).
[8] 'la rencontre, l'interférence, le choc, les harmonies et les disharmonies entre les cultures' (*TTM*, 194).
[9] 'l'intervalorisation qui en provient et qui rend nécessaire que chacun réevalue pour soi les composantes mises en contact' (*TTM*, 194).

creolization, not yet at least',[10] remarks Glissant. However, the election of Barack Obama to the US Presidency marked a watershed moment for Glissant in terms of thinking about creolization in a future perspective. In their *Intraitable beauté du monde. Adresse à Barack Obama* (2009), Glissant and Chamoiseau marvel at the fact that an individual who in their estimation incarnates in his very person the results of creolization processes should have been elected to such an influential post (*IBM*, 4). They express the ardent hope, shared by many at the time, that Obama's election would lead to the pursuing of a more progressive political agenda worldwide; in Glissant's terms, that the political line pursued by Obama would work to further the poetics of Relation (*IBM*, 55–57).

The creolist turn in Antillean thought

In the interests of presenting a broader and better contextualized account of this central Glissantian concept of creolization I now propose to take a step back to the late 1980s and 1990s to discuss the Antillean 'Creoleness' ('Créolité') movement. This movement was born when a new generation of mainly Martiniquan intellectuals and writers, under the influence of Glissant, advocated a form of creole cultural expression, named 'Créolité', which they believed to be the most representative of Antillean identity. The *Eloge* (1993 [1988]), the movement's manifesto text, written by Jean Bernabé, Patrick Chamoiseau and Raphael Confiant situated its recommendations and demands very clearly under the aegis of positions which Glissant had set out in his magisterial *Caribbean Discourse* (1981). The movement's cultural and political basis lay in the desire to reaffirm Martiniquan creole identity in opposition to metropolitan French structures in a new way following the eventual decline of 'Négritude'-inspired thinking in the 1970s and 1980s.[11] In the years which have elapsed since the *Eloge* Chamoiseau has

---

[10]'Pays du multiculturalisme, les Etats-Unis ne sont pas un pays de créolisation, pas encore' (*TTM*, 39).

[11]Negritude was a cultural movement with pronounced anti-colonial overtones which came to prominence from the late 1940s onwards. In its earlier years it was associated notably with Martinican poet and politician Aimé Césaire and Senegalesian poet and future President (1960–80) Léopold Senghor.

remained the most faithful to the example of Glissant among the creolists, explicitly citing Glissant's works in many of his publications and ultimately joint-authoring two books with him in recent years.[12]

In his largely autobiographical memoir *Ecrire en pays dominé* [*Writing in a Dominated Land*] (Gallimard, 1997), Chamoiseau explains that it was reading Glissant, and in particular the latter's *Malemort* (Paris: Seuil, 1975), which proved to be the decisive turning point in his development as a young writer.[13] Chamoiseau states that by the latter part of the 1970s he had come to see the limitations of the Négritude-inspired poetry he had been writing, following a trend among Martiniquan authors which lasted through until the 1980s. After some inauspicious initial experiments with prose writing on his part it was the example of Glissant which he felt best indicated a way out of the impasse, pointing the way, Chamoiseau suggests, to a more profound engagement with Martiniquan culture (*EPD*: 79–82, 84). In the *Eloge* Bernabé, Chamoiseau and Confiant actually devote no less than a third of the book to articulating positions which they explicitly state derive from the recommendations which Glissant makes for Antillean writing in *Caribbean Discourse*. A significant number of broader Glissantian positions are adhered to in the *Eloge* including, to list the most important: the idea of a specifically Antillean as opposed to neo-African culture; a rejection of universalist, and in particular French universalist, attitudes towards cultural identity in the name of stressing difference; a belief in the centrality of articulating the collective memory of Martiniquan society; a belief in the need to give the oral culture of Martinique a voice in literature; and the idea that 'créolité' as a condition can be identified in the wider world beyond the Antilles. The authors extrapolate from and expand considerably on what are relatively briefly sketched out points notably concerning literary writing in Glissant's study in order to present the case for creole literature and identity in a more polemical, militant way than Glissant had done. It is as if they were attempting to articulate more fully what they believe Glissant had

---

[12]Glissant and Chamoiseau, *Quand les murs tombent. L'identité nationale hors-la-loi ?* (Paris: Galaade, 2007), and *L'intraitable beauté du monde. Adresse à Barack Obama* (Paris: Galaade, 2009).
[13]Chamoiseau, *Ecrire en pays dominé*, 69–95 (Hereafter *EPD*).

been tentatively pointing towards. On closer inspection, however, it is apparent, first, that the vision of 'Créolité' which they present is not founded on an accurate reading of the ideas of their 'maître à penser', and second, that they do not build on his ideas in a manner which is really consistent with his thinking either. Glissant for example had highlighted the value of the long repressed oral culture of the Antilles and had voiced his support for those literary works in which there is an 'oralization of the written' (*CD*, 244).¹⁴ He had nevertheless indicated that he had reservations about whether such writing could lead to literary production of consistently high quality:

> But could Creole writing reconcile the rules of writing and the teeming, irrepressible element in 'oraliture'? It is much too early to reply, and the countless publications I have read have not for the most part abandoned the facile effects of a folkloric naivete. (*CD*: 245)¹⁵

Little hesitation of this sort is perceptible in the *Eloge* by contrast, the creolists singing the praises of oral expression in the following unequivocally eulogious terms:

> A real galaxy with the Creole language as its core, Creoleness has, still today, its privileged mode: orality. Provider of tales and proverbs [...] orality is our intelligence; it is our reading of this world. (*EC* : 104)¹⁶

The promotion of oral culture is presented in the *Eloge* not simply as a literary approach worth exploring and developing but as absolutely indispensable to literary production, indeed almost

---

¹⁴Glissant, *Le Discours antillais* 'oralisation de l'écrit', 778 (Hereafter *DA*).
¹⁵'Mais si l'écriture créole conciliait ce qu'il y a de régi dans la littérature et ce qu'il y a de foisonnant et d'irrépressible dans l'"oraliture" Il est bien trop tôt pour répondre, et les nombreuses publications que j'ai pu lire n'ont pas pour la plupart quitté les facilités du folklorisme naïf' (*DA*, 778).
¹⁶'Véritable galaxie en formation autour de la langue créole comme noyau, la Créolité connaît aujourd'hui encore un mode privilégié : l'oralité. Pourvoyeuse de contes, proverbes [...] l'oralité est notre intelligence, elle est notre lecture de ce monde' (*EC*, 33).

above criticism, because 'oralité' (orality) is viewed by the creolists as a central pillar of creole identity.

Elsewhere in the *Eloge*, Bernabé, Chamoiseau and Confiant can be seen to elaborate on and add to the positions set out by Glissant in *Caribbean Discourse*. One area of discrepancy with Glissant which has received a certain amount of attention is a marked tendency towards an essentializing view of Martiniquan 'créolité' which would seem to be divergent with Glissant's preference for a rhizomatic over a roots-based conception of identity.[17] The creolists' thinking seems more reminiscent of the Négritude movement's essentialist insistence on a unitary root than of Glissant's Deleuzian-influenced theory, favouring as the latter does the multiplicity of the rhizome. A possible counterargument to this reading might run that the creole condition is *by its very nature* intrinsically rhizomatic rather than unitary and that the insistence on 'Créolité' is hence not susceptible to the charge of essentialism. A defence of this sort, though of interest, is ultimately not convincing. There is something about the authors' of the *Eloge*'s insistence on recreating and indeed personally identifying with a putatively lost collective past[18] while seeking to stipulate so forcefully what that social history was which essentializes both that history itself and the historian-come-writer in pursuit of it. In *Caribbean Discourse* Glissant had expressed the hope that 'the countries of the Caribbean will develop an original Afro-Caribbean culture whose cultural reality is already in evidence.' (*CD*, 235),[19] he had suggested that the contemporary Antillean artist needed to be also 'his own ethnologist, historian, linguist, painter of frescoes' (*CD*, 236),[20] and had argued for a type of literature which would ultimately 'reconcile the values of the culture of writing and the long-repressed traditions of orality.' (*CD*, 249)[21] None of these ambitions for Antillean literature however

---

[17] Richard Burton (1993, 23) and Mary Gallagher (2002, 44) are just two of a number of academic commentators who have picked up on the difficulties surrounding the essentialist tendencies of creolist thinking.

[18] Mary Gallagher (2002, 32–33) remarks on the 'strikingly retrospective' vision of the creolist aesthetic outlined in the *Eloge*.

[19] 'les pays des Antilles développeront une culture originale de type afro-caraïbe dont la réalité s'affirme dès maintenant' (*DA*, 757).

[20] 'un ethnologue, un historien, un linguistique, un peintre de fresques' (*DA*, 759).

[21] 'concilier enfin les valeurs des civilisations de l'écrit et les traditions longtemps infériorisées des peuples de l'oralité' (*DA*, 793–4).

necessarily entailed the sort of wilfully traditionalist, not to say parochial, focus which Chamoiseau and Confiant appeared to favour in their own literary publications.

Another area of discrepancy is to be found in the attitude to the creole language articulated in the *Eloge*. Glissant had lamented the fact that creole oral culture had been repressed but he had nevertheless expressed reservations about the possibility of considering creole as fully representative of a putatively authentic Martiniquan cultural identity in opposition to French because, he pointed out, the 'békés', that is the white ruling class in the Antilles, had understood and spoken creole too. Creole had not been the exclusive cultural property of Martiniquans of Afro-Caribbean descent. The *Eloge* seems to gloss over this sort of reservation suggesting as it does that there is some intrinsic and insoluble link between the creole identity which the authors believe is central to being authentically Martiniquan and the creole language of 'oralité': 'Creole [...] is the initial means of communication of our deep self' (*EC*: 104),[22] the authors argue. 'It remains the river of our alluvial Creoleness' (*EC:* 104)[23] Acknowledging that creole writers are bilingual, they refer to such writers' use of the French language, perhaps for understandable political reasons, with a certain disdain. '*We did conquer it, this French language* [...] Creoleness left its indelible mark on the French language' (*EC*: 106–107),[24] they proclaim somewhat immodestly, by way of an adjunct to their insistence on creole. It is worth noting however- *ironie du sort*- that almost all the literature which has been published by the creolists themselves since the *Eloge* appeared has been principally in French.

There are hence significant areas of divergence between the manifesto-style *Eloge de la Créolité* [*In Praise of Creoleness*] and the work which served as its principal theoretical source of inspiration, *Caribbean Discourse*. By the time of the *Eloge*, Creolité as a mindset and movement of thought had become a statement of identity, of a right to difference. It had, in other words, become a political statement and a demand for a greater acknowledgement

---

[22]'Le créole [...] est le véhicule originel de notre moi profond, notre inconscient collectif'.
[23]'[C]ette langue demeure la rivière de notre créolité alluviale' (*EC*, 43).
[24]'*Nous l'avons conquise, cette langue française* [...] Nous nous sommes approprié cette dernière' (*EC*, 46).

of the cultural specificity of the Antilles. In the process of evolving in this direction the intellectual subtlety of the positions set out by Glissant in *Caribbean Discourse* was significantly compromised. To essentialize creoleness is to run counter to the phenomenon of creole identity as presented in Glissant's account. Moreover, in his *Introduction à une poétique du divers* (1996), Glissant himself observed that the *Eloge* had been founded on a misunderstanding of his thought. Whereas, for him, 'créolization' meant 'a perpetual movement of cultural and linguistic impenetrability which means that no definition of being can be arrived at',²⁵ the creolists attributed a determinate being, or essence to creoleness, he argued. Moreover, prior to this in *Poetics of Relation* (1990), published only two years after the *Eloge*, Glissant had evidently felt strongly enough about the misappropriation of his ideas by his creolist compatriots to issue a discreet but nevertheless forceful disavowal of their theory. '*Creolization [...] is only exemplified by its processes and certainly not by the "contents" on which these operate. This is where we depart from the concept of creoleness*' (PR, 89, italics Glissant's).²⁶

Caribbean critical responses to 'Créolité'

The 'Créolité' movement and in particular its formulation in the *Eloge* have come in for some harsh criticism not just from academic commentators²⁷ but also from other Caribbean writers and intellectuals. The reaction of the latter group is of particular significance because they have clearly felt the most affected by the publicity surrounding the promotion of 'Créolité' and in some cases evidently saw a need to take sides for or against a movement which they realized was likely to influence perceptions of their own work

---

²⁵'un mouvement perpétuel d'interpénétrabilité culturelle et linguistique qui fait qu'on ne débouche pas sur une définition de l'être' (Glissant, *Introduction à une poétique du divers*, 125).
²⁶'*La créolisation [...] n'a d'exemplaire que ses processus et certainement pas les "contenus" à partir desquels ils fonctionneraient. C'est ce qui fait notre départ d'avec le concept de "créolité."*' (PR, 103, italics Glissant's).
²⁷Bongie (1998), Burton (1995), Gallagher (2002), Le Brun (1994), McCusker (2003) and Suk (2001) amongst others have all voiced significant reservations about the tenability of the case which is made for a pro-creolist approach and agenda in the *Eloge*.

whether they liked it or not. The Saint Lucian poet Derek Walcott, in a text entitled 'A Letter to Chamoiseau'[28] of 1997, applauds *Texaco* (1992) on the grounds of literary merit, but sees in the declarations and exhortations of the *Eloge* something of an own goal. He queries the decision to write the text in French rather than Creole, seeing in this a performative contradiction: 'Why was it not written in Creole if it is that passionate about authenticity?'[29] He objects to this criticism, which could be fairly made about much creolist literature since the 1980s, Walcott adds observations about the quintessentially French tone of the manifesto style of the *Eloge*. Although its polemicism 'is not one of which Creole is incapable, [...] it is nevertheless academic, even classical thereby taking it some way from Creole's *oralité* [...] Nothing is more French than the confident rhetoric of this manifesto.'[30]

Martiniquan intellectual and well-known activist René Ménil, in his *Antilles déjà jadis* (Jean Michel Place, 1999), homes in on the creolists' cultivation of a folkloristic naturalism which undermines in his view the aesthetic quality of their literary writing. Whereas, for Ménil, 'the aim of any artistic approach is to reveal, via its own particular means of expression, aspects and truths as yet unknown to us and to the period we are living in',[31] the creolists' approach is founded on the erroneous assumption that all Antillean literature has to do is 'reflect, describe and photograph the various types of folklore in order to accomplish its task'.[32]

Creolist writers believe that rooting their prose in this type of naturalism gives it more credibility but in reality their descriptions of folkloristic customs and practices amount to little more than a regionalist exoticism best suited to tourists. Ménil emphasizes the artificial and contrived dimension of 'Créolité' pointing out that with the exception of a brief flourish in the 1930s, folklorism has

---

[28]DerekWalcott, included in *What the Twilight Says* (New York: Farrar, Straus and Giroux, 1998), 213–232.
[29]Ibid., 224.
[30]Ibid., 224.
[31]'la vocation de toute démarche artistique est de révéler, grâce aux moyens qui lui sont propres, des aspects et des vérités encore inconnus de nous-mêmes et de l'époque que nous vivons' (René Ménil, *Antilles déjà jadis* (Paris: Jean Michel Place, 1999), 276).
[32]'refléter, décrire, photographier les formes du folklore pour accomplir sa tâche' (Ibid., 276).

not been a feature of the Martiniquan cultural landscape in the course of the twentieth century. It is, to some extent at least then, a construction or superimposition, a 'forgery', as Maeve McCusker puts it.[33] Folkloristic naturalism, though, also demonstrates a naivety about literary writing in that it is proof that insufficient attention has been paid to aesthetic form. 'The error in aesthetic terms consists in relating the folkloristic in a folkloristic way',[34] argues Ménil. Successful literary writing does not simply involve transposing features of real life, such as folk customs, to novelistic prose. In those cases where such naturalism is employed to good effect 'the folkloristic object like all unfiltered cultural forms is already shot through with a set of imaginary and ideological representations.'[35] It is integrated into some sort of world view, which is to say, to borrow Sartre's expression, some sort of 'novelist's metaphysical perspective'.[36] If it is important for Antillean writers to include images drawn from folk culture in their literary work, then their ultimate aim, Ménil argues, should be to convey 'folklore without folklorism.'[37]

It is worth noting in this regard that the problem of folklorism is one which had been anticipated by the creolists. I mentioned earlier that Glissant had warned against the dangers of writers falling into 'the facile effects of folkloric naiveté' (*EC*, 245)[38] when reintegrating the oral tradition into literary prose. Taking Glissant's lead, the authors of the *Eloge* are also critical of the tendency towards folklorism. There have been, they suggest, works written by mediocre authors who succumbed to the malady of folklorism in the context of the commercial promotion of Antillean culture:

There were some insignificant reproducters of misunderstood gestures, some modest collectors of useless memories ; there

---

[33]Maeve McCusker, 'The Contradictions of 'créolité', in *Francophone Postcolonial Studies: A Critical Introduction* (London: Arnold, 2003), 114, by C. Forsdick and D. Murphy (eds), 112–121.
[34]'Raconter le folklorique de façon folklorique, voilà l'erreur esthétique' (Ibid., 279).
[35]'l'objet folklorique comme toute forme culturelle immédiate est déjà pénétré d'idéologie imaginaire' (Ibid., 278).
[36]'métaphysique du romancier' (Sartre, J. -P., *Situations I* (Gallimard, 1947), 71).
[37]'le folklore sans folklorisme.' Ménil, *Antilles déjà jadis*, 279.
[38]'les facilités du folklorisme naïf' (*DA*, 778).

were some obscure directors of commercialized culture for tourists more curious about us than we were ; there were some dull epigones of a hackneyed speech [...] They rarely escaped the assertion – shouted or whispered – of doudouism and folklorism. (*EC* : 97)[39]

Such authors played an important role in keeping Creole culture alive but the creolists declare their intention to learn from their errors:

taking over the oral tradition should not be considered in a backward mode of nostalgic stagnation, through backward leaps. To return to it, yes, first in order to restore this cultural continuity (that we associate with restored historical continuity) without which it is difficult for collective identity to take shape. To return to it, yes, in order to enrich our enunciation, to integrate it, and go beyond it. (*EC*: 97)[40]

Creolist literature, then, should not be nostalgic but rather a means of sustaining the collective memory of Antillean societies. Although this statement of intention must be given due consideration, offering as it does ample proof of the creolists' lucidity about the pitfalls of promoting local culture by means of a reinstated oral tradition, it is far from certain that in their literary practice the creolists escape the charges levelled at them by Ménil. Chamoiseau, the most celebrated of the creolists, and arguably Confiant even more so, have clearly tended in the direction of a nostalgic recreation of past periods of Martiniquan creole culture in a number of their literary and autobiographical works, not just

---

[39] Il y eut [...] d'insignifiants reproducteurs de gestes incompris, de modestes cultivateurs de souvenirs inutiles, il y eut d'obscurs metteurs en scène d'une culture commercialisée pour touristes plus curieux que nous de nous-mêmes, il y eut de plats épigones d'une parole ressassée [...] Rarement ils échappèrent à l'assertion – proclamée ou sussurrée – de doudouisme et de folklorisme (*EC*, 35–36).

[40] [...] prendre le relais de la tradition orale ne doit pas s'envisager sur un mode passéiste de nostalgique stagnation, de virées en arrière. Y retourner, oui, pour d'abord rétablir cette continuité culturelle (associée à une continuité historique restaurée) sans laquelle l'identité collective a du mal à s'affirmer. Y retourner, oui, pour en enrichir notre énonciation, l'intégrer pour la dépasser (*EC*, 36).

the reaffirmation of historical continuities.[41] In his *Une Enfance créole. Antan d'enfance* (1990) Chamoiseau's nostalgia for his own lost past hangs over the narrative throughout, and is anticipated by his account, in a preface devoted to the incident, of how he learnt of the fire which burnt down the house he had grown up in. For Chamoiseau, the obliteration of his childhood home had the effect of fixing his thoughts in time, an attitude which is particularly revealing in the light of the pronounced retrospective outlook throughout his oeuvre as a whole to date. 'I can't say any more on this subject without it being an expression of nostalgia and profound regret . . .'[42]

His first novel *Chronique de sept misères* (*Chronicle of the Seven Sorrows*, 2000 [1986]), focused on the lives of the *djobeurs*[43] working on the local market, not only conveys a sense of nostalgic admiration for a lost dimension of Martiniquan culture but also in numerous places undeniably validates Ménil's criticism that the creolists succumb to folklorism. Indeed, the narrative tends towards being a populist and rather romanticized celebration of the lives of the labouring classes. Although the artistry of the writing should not be underestimated, Chamoiseau's prose in this work being far from naïve, unworked naturalism, the obstinate focus on the lower classes, as in a number of Chamoiseau's works, combined with the narrator's somewhat rose-tinted perspective on their lives creates a one-sided, distorted image of Martinique's creole past (were there no educated creoles, one wonders, reading Chamoiseau?).

There is hence often as much nostalgia as there is reactivation of collective memory in Chamoiseau's prose as indeed in much other creolist writing, a tendency which ties in with a certain conservatism, even parochialism, of outlook. Guadeloupian author Maryse Condé has voiced her opposition to these characteristics of 'Créolité', objecting to what she sees as the heavily prescriptive tone of the *Eloge*. The creolists, proceeding from a proclamation of the

---

[41]Richard Burton (1995, 29) has argued that the creolists retrospective vision is excessive in that it renders their work irrelevant to contemporary Martiniquan life. Martinique today, he claims, is a 'post-Creole' society.

[42]'Je ne pourrai plus y ajouter une ligne', he states in the closing sentence of the preface, 'qui ne soit de nostalgie et de regret profond' (Patrick Chamoiseau, *Une Enfance créole I. Antan d'enfance* [Paris: Hatier, 1990]).

[43]The term *djobeurs* designates odd-jobbers working on the markets.

obvious fact that they are creoles, suggest that the only 'authentic' Antillean literature is that imbued with the idioms of the creole language and that which treats a certain range of literary themes such as the *djobeurs*, the *dorlis*, and other such topics associated with creole culture specifically, she argues.[44] What is absent from the urgings of the *Eloge* is any acknowledgement that literary writing is above all about authors finding their own voice and identity and expressing them via whatever linguistic strategies and narrative techniques they feel most appropriate.[45] The objection made by Confiant about Aimé Césaire that the latter had never published in the creole language, is hence misplaced, she argues: 'Does he not know that all the writer seeks to do is find his own language beyond languages, be they mother tongue or otherwise? Cesaire created the Cesairian language.'[46]

Condé's readiness to give priority to aesthetic and personal considerations over the political implications of linguistic and literary expression in the Caribbean is reinforced by her explicit preference for Robbe-Grillet's dissociation of literature from commitment over any sort of (neo-Sartrean) view of writing as inextricable from politics. 'Créolité', she argues, offers nothing new and is a hackneyed rehashing of the well-worn insistence on literary commitment.[47] This objection could be interpreted as somewhat reductive of the specific political import of the creolists' demands in the postcolonial context which is theirs. There is a certain aestheticist naivety in the idea that Césaire's consistent attachment to the French language, for example, was either of no political significance or that the political implications of that attachment were of little importance. However, Condé's position on this issue is part of a wider argument about Antillean cultures today being best understood as characterized by a porous intermingling of cultural

---

[44]Condé in *Caribbean Creolization* (University Press of Florida, 1998), Balutansky and Sourieau (eds), 106–7.
[45]Ibid., 107.
[46]'Ne sait-il pas qu'il suffit pour l'écrivain de trouver son langage au-delà des langues, maternelles ou non? Césaire a forgé la parole césairienne.' (Condé 'Chercher nos verites' in *Penser la créolité* (Karthala, 1995), Condé and Cottenet-Hage (eds), 309.) It is worth noting in this regard that Confiant's criticisms of Césaire also provoked the ire of some in the critical community. Annie Le Brun (1994) in particular jumped to Césaire's defense, dismissing the creolists as intellectually mediocre.
[47]Condé in *Caribbean Creolization*, Balutansky and Sourieau (eds), 108.

influences and, as such, being in chime with the broader conjuncture in the era of globalization. In today's Guadeloupe, she points out, one finds gwoka being fused with rap and other such 'new cultural mixtures which challenge those cultural mixes that have already become established over time and already have socially stratified connotations.'[48] These 'new cultural mixtures' should be embraced, she believes, not frowned upon in the name of preserving an image of the Antilles which is out of step both with where the Caribbean and the wider world stand today. 'Créolité', she argues, allows Caribbeans to exorcise their fear of the future and in fact reaffirms the binary opposition between French and creole which 'is nothing but an inheritance from the obsessive colonial mindset of both victor and victim.'[49]

The matter of what a culturally, socially and politically progressive outlook should consist of in the postcolonial Antillean context is extremely complex. I will offer only the following observation on the question in the context of the present discussion: it is not insignificant that the example Condé gives of new 'métissages' involves the fusing of gwoka, a traditional Gwadeloupian musical form, with rap. The latter musical style has in recent years become a feature of global pop culture but originated in the United States. While Condé is surely right to dismiss the creolists' inward looking attempts to recreate a lost creole past as parochial and out of date, can one really assert that an embracing of globalized American pop cultural forms is preferable even if it is more in step with the times? If one were to limit one's judgment to the creolist agenda on the one hand and popular culture on the other, one would have to conclude that modern-day Caribbeans are caught between the Scylla and Charybdis of a somewhat parochial heritage culture on the one hand and the uniformness, to borrow François Jullien's concept,[50] of (often market-fuelled) globalized culture on the other; between continuing the ideological struggle against the French ex-colonial

---

[48]'nouveaux métissages culturels qui remettent en question les métissages traditionnels déjà stratifiés par l'usage' (Condé in 'Chercher nos vérités' in *Penser la créolité* [Karthala, 1995]), Condé and Cottenet-Hage (eds), 309).
[49]'n'est qu'un héritage de l'obsession coloniale entre vainqueur et victime' (Ibid., 309).
[50]See Jullien's *De l'universel, de l'uniforme, du commun et du dialogue entre les cultures* (Fayard, 2008), 31–8.

master and the dissolution of that struggle in the sea of globalized cultural forms.

Condé's open-ended view of Antillean identity and culture is clearly perceptible in her skilful intratextual response to Chamoiseau's *Solibo Magnifique* (*Solibo Magnificent*, 1999 [1988]). Her *Traversée de la Mangrove* (*Crossing the Mangrove*, 1995 [1989]) inverts all the principal underlying intellectual positions articulated in Chamoiseau's work of the preceding year.[51] That Condé's novel is a very deliberate rewrite of *Solibo* is evident from a similarity of narrative construction which is too readily apparent, even to the point of being semi-parodic, to be the result of pure coincidence. *Crossing* opens, like *Solibo*, with the discovery of the death of the male protagonist and the remainder of both novels is taken up with the enquiries of other characters both into the cause of the deaths and memories of them when they were alive. This formal mirroring of the Chamoiseau text is where the similarities stop however as the two protagonists are radically different types of individuals. Solibo, the local creole storyteller, is presented as being rooted in popular creole culture. This rootedness is confirmed by his dead body being found lying entangled in the roots of a tamarind tree and as being associated in various ways throughout the narrative with the tree. Solibo clearly is the voice of oral literary culture, and a pronounced opposition is in evidence throughout *Solibo Magnificent* between the oral and the written, the latter being associated with French language and thought. Chamoiseau presents his own association with Solibo as a coming to awareness involving a profound questioning of his own intellectual background and training. Solibo's manner of storytelling is presented as the most suitable vehicle for conveying Antillean cultural values: 'Solibo used the four facets of our disglossia : the Creole basilect and acrolect, the French basilect and acrolect, quivering, vibrating, rooted in an intellectual space that I thought to be our most exact socio-linguistic reality.'[52]

---

[51] Quite remarkably, there has been a tendency amongst critics to consider *Traversée* to be a text celebratory of 'créolité' when, as Suk (2001) points out, in reality it does the opposite: in *Traversée* the very notion of there being any real continuity to shared or collective memory is undermined.

[52] 'Solibo Magnifique utilisait les quatre facettes de notre diglossie: le basilecte et l'acrolecte créole, le basilecte et l'acrolecte français, vibrionnant enracinement dans un espace interlectal que je pensais être notre plus exacte réalité socio-linguistique'. Chamoiseau, *Solibo Magnifique*, 45.

By contrast with such rich linguistic expression representative of creole social reality, the lance sergeant's request for 'français mathématique'[53] and the police inspector's 'scientific efforts and cold logic',[54] which 'often skidded'[55] even 'despite his long stay in the land of Descartes',[56] seem hopelessly and ridiculously otiose. In short, Solibo is presented throughout as the personification of local authenticity in opposition to educated sophistication, Frenchness and any sort of aspiration to universality.

Francis Sancher, Condé's protagonist, despite having distant Guadeloupian ancestors, was born in Columbia and has travelled the world before settling in the Caribbean. He is educated and cuts a marginal figure among the local community in Guadeloupe who are wary of him as they do not know where he has come from and cannot identify with him. We learn from one of his lovers that he belonged to no one, as if his real nature was beyond the grasp of any of the local people: 'The creature he belonged to was hiding in the shadows amid the sounds of the night'[57] (*CM*: 159). Describing himself as 'shipwrecked',[58] Sancher insists that '[y]ou've got to live with your times' (*CM*: 61) '[i]l faut vivre avec son temps' rather than continuing to carry the tragedies of the past around with you.[59] Sancher, then, is a worldly character who is psychologically beyond limiting himself to specifically local concerns. Yet, towards the end of *Crossing the Mangrove* numerous remarks in the accounts offered by the Guadeloupian characters who had known Sancher accord him a sort of posthumous moral victory. One such notable comment is that made by Lucien Evariste, the polemical sting of which is readily apparent: 'There's more humanity and riches in that man than in all our lecturers in Creole' (*CM*, 187).[60] In spite of his radical otherness, Sancher's example and outlook is hence posthumously accepted. Whereas Chamoiseau's narrative had been

---

[53]Ibid., 105.
[54]'efforts scientifiques et de logique glaciale'.
[55]'dérapaient bien souvent'.
[56]'malgré son long séjour au pays de Descartes' (Ibid., 118).
[57]'L'être à qui il appartenait se cachait dans l'ombre et les bruits de la nuit.' Condé *La Traversée de la Mangrove*, 192.
[58]'naufragé' (Ibid., 127).
[59]'[i]l faut vivre avec son temps' (Ibid., 82).
[60]'Il y a plus d'humanite et de richesse dans cet homme-là que dans tous nos faiseurs de discours en créole' (Ibid., 226).

inward-looking, seeking to reassert the value of a lost cultural past through the figure of the oral storyteller, Condé's *Crossing* constitutes a clear rejection of the attachment to roots taken as any sort of stamp of authenticity.

Creolization: from local past to international future

It will be already apparent from what has preceded that the difficulties thrown up both by the essentialist and fundamentally backward-looking 'Créolité' ('Creoleness') on the one hand and the embracing of market-fuelled globalized cultural forms on the other – the former dissolving the globalizing present in a re-created local past, the latter amnesiac about and dismissive of local history – are absent from Glissant's thought. Creolization fully acknowledges the crucial role played by past and local cultural inheritances in making present-day phenomena of all sorts what they are. When phenomena come into contact with each other and their meeting produces unexpected results, they nevertheless remain intact and uncompromised in and of themselves. This means that the 'traces' of the cultures they emanated from are still carried within them and remain vital to making them what they are. They also, as cultural phenomena growing out of specific local contexts, preserve an opacity for others which protects them from dissolution in today's increasingly internationalized forms of cultural expression. On the other hand, as we saw at the start of this chapter, creolization as Glissant presents it, unlike 'Créolité', is always open-ended and receptive to changes and contingencies in the present; it can take place just as easily in international as national or local contexts. Creolization is hence an effective concept in the context of today's globalized world, especially if one is in favour of a reorienting of globalization in its present form in the direction of an alternative, more egalitarian type of globalization which is respectful of the cultural specificities of minoritarian cultures. Creolization is hence a concept which offers an effective marriage of local concerns and specific local national histories on the one hand and a necessary openness to international exchanges and cultural intermingling on the other.

It is ironic that a critical examination of the creolist paradigm only serves to reconfirm the comparative philosophical superiority of Glissant's concept of creolization, especially given that the advent of creolism owed so much to Glissant's work in the first place. It is not that Glissantian theory supercedes or offers some sort of antidote to 'Créolité' because it predated the creolists' publications by many years. It is rather that Glissant's ideas were misread by his creolist followers, and that these followers (and Chamoiseau in particular) became so well known in the 1990s that certain confusions and conflations took place in the minds of many readers.

CHAPTER FOUR

The paradoxes of universalism and the ambivalence of the postcolonial condition

We will now turn our attention to a dimension of Glissant's thought which we have touched on in numerous ways in the preceding chapters without addressing it directly, namely his views on universalism, that is, the doctrine that it is possible to advocate a system of ideas, values and procedures which are applicable to all. The topic merits singling out for special attention both because the orientation of so many of Glissant's concepts links up with his views in this regard and because debates about the possibility and validity of universals is a perennial subject in the history of philosophy. However, when considering this issue the quintessentially anglophone tendency to think of philosophy as having little to do with society and politics should immediately be resisted. The continental philosophical tradition has tended not to compartmentalize to anything like the same degree and has consequently devoted much more energy to consideration of ethical, political, aesthetic and social issues within the discipline of philosophy itself, one consequence of which being that the discipline is much more widely studied in European countries than in the anglophone world. To this the caveat should be added that Glissant, although educated and steeped in the continental intellectual tradition, is not a European thinker and insists on his right to be judged in accordance with other criteria, some of which non-Western. It would be a tragic irony if a thinker as staunchly anti-universalist as Glissant were to be judged exclusively according to criteria habitually employed to assess European thinkers. However, in so far as Glissant's preoccupation with universalism was for many years linked with his views on the French republican colonial and neocolonial imposition of values and institutional arrangements on the francophone Caribbean islands to a significant degree, the role of universalist thinking in French culture specifically must be a central concern of our analysis.

The role accorded to universalist thinking in French culture is a far too broad and far-reaching topic to be given adequate consideration in a chapter of this length. For our purposes, it suffices to note that there has been a pronounced tendency in French political history to favour and encourage a universalist mindset and universalist institutional models. In comparative terms, and even if we limit our appraisal to the period from the Revolution of 1789 onwards, the French have proved themselves to be vigorous defenders of the doctrine that it is possible and desirable to insist on sets of values and related practices which are valid for all. Indeed, the extent to which this ideology remains deeply rooted in the French mindset was forcefully reconfirmed as recently as early 2015 by the so-called esprit du 11 janvier ('spirit of January 11th'), which was defined as a gathering of all genuine French republicans in response to the terrorist attacks in Paris four days earlier. Political groups and citizens of all persuasions (with the exception of the National Front who were excluded from the ceremonies) were requested to set aside their differences of opinion supposedly in the interests of defending the French Republic itself. The assassination of journalists was perceived to be an attack on the principle of free speech itself, not just on the journalists at Charlie Hebdo, and as this is a principle which French Republicanism holds to be a fundamental inalienable right, the terrorist attacks were presented by the government and the media as an attack on the French Republic as a whole. Those who identified with the 'esprit du 11 janvier' hence subscribed to the view that the principle of free speech, in the version of this principle that the French uphold, is universally valid and that all French citizens who think of themselves as bonafide republicans should assent to it.

It goes without saying that my intention is not in any sense to cast doubt on the validity of a forceful response to the horrific terrorist acts of 7 January 2015. My focus in these remarks is the *way* in which the French establishment, media, and certain sections of the French population[1] responded to the events, and what the nature of that response reveals as far as French cultural values are concerned.

Glissant's aversion for universalism

Acknowledging that universalist thinking has long been central to the French political and cultural landscape goes some way towards explaining why a francophone postcolonial Caribbean thinker and writer like Glissant has shown himself to be so consistently opposed to universalism in all its forms. The colonial and, as Glissant and creolist compatriots such as Chamoiseau and Confiant see it, neocolonial relationship which France has maintained with Martinique has meant that French ideas, cultural practices and institutional arrangements have long been promoted in the francophone Caribbean at the expense of local language and culture. The according to Martinique of French 'département' status in 1946 led to a situation, so these writers claim, in which the island, like Guadeloupe and La Guyane, became subordinated to the former colonial master in a neocolonial relationship. It is important to note though that it was colonialism itself, and not just French colonialism, which was the purveyor *par excellence*

---

[1] Historian Emmanuel Todd, in an interview in the *Nouvel Observateur* of the 29 April 2015 entitled 'Le 11 janvier a été une imposture' ['The 11th January was a total sham'], was the first to break the silence in media and political circles, offering the first genuinely critical response to the official line. Among other criticisms, Todd challenged the idea that the 'esprit du 11 janvier' was universally assented to France. He argued that ironically it was in areas of France that have traditionally always been the most Catholic and the least pro-Republican that the greatest level of identification with the 'esprit du 11 janvier' was perceptible. He also warned against the dangers of growing and unwarranted Islamophobia in France. Todd's intervention was so striking that it gave rise to a direct response from the then Prime Minister Manuel Valls which was published on 7 May 2015 in *Le Monde* and entitled 'Non, la France du 11 janvier n'est pas une imposture' ['No, the France of the 11th January is not a total sham'] in which Valls sought to refute Todd's claims.

of universalist doctrines and practices. The so-called 'civilizing mission' of colonialism in the nineteenth century was advocated as vigorously by British colonialists as it was by their French counterparts. This doctrine was presented as a justification for the perpetuation of colonialism on the grounds that non-Western cultural others were being 'civilized', that is, culturally conditioned by European languages, ideas and values which they would otherwise be without. European thinking was hence presented as being of universal validity and applicability.

The ills of colonialism in general notwithstanding, the neocolonial implications which Glissant et al. perceive as inevitable in the 'departmentalized' status of Martinique could be viewed as a peculiarly French arrangement. The British Commonwealth did not seek to maintain the same level of influence over its former colonies as the French. Accusations of paternalism and intrusiveness in internal affairs have long been made with particular force against the French,[2] a key reason for this being the French's preference for 'assimilationist' policies with respect to cultural others. Both in relation to colonized peoples abroad and with respect to immigrant communities living in mainland France, the French long argued, and indeed still do argue as far as immigrants are concerned, that the cultural other should adopt French modes of thought and practices. As far as the francophone Caribbean is concerned, acknowledging this fact is not to assert or assume in an uncritical way however that French involvement in the region by way of 'départementalisation' has only had negative consequences for the inhabitants of islands like Martinique and Guadéloupe. For reasons which I will explain, the reality of the situation has always been much more ambivalent than this. Nevertheless, it does go some way towards explaining the particularly forceful opposition of an intellectual like Glissant to universalist thinking. One question we will ponder later in this chapter is whether Glissant's aversion for the mode of thinking which the French employed to subjugate the peoples of the francophone Caribbean islands is in fact excessive. Might it be that in rejecting universalism in all its forms, rather than just the abstract type of universalism which the French tend to advocate, Glissant's world view is deprived of certain dimensions of

---

[2]See Bancel, Blanchard and Vergès, *La République coloniale* [*Colonial Republic France*] (Albin Michel, 2003).

universalist thinking which are not only worth salvaging but even actively worth promoting?

How, then, is the opposition to universalism expressed in Glissant's works? It is worth noting that this aversion is one of a number of constants in Glissant's thought and is perceptible from his earliest theoretical works onwards. Even as early as *Le Soleil de la Conscience* (1956) his weariness with the dominant European paradigm is clearly perceptible, as in the following statement: 'Has Europe not lived out until saturation point that almighty splendour which sent it off towards other horizons? Has it not, in its thirst for power, perceived far from its own shores the exploding of its own eternal life?'[3] Here 'eternity', or timelessly applicable values, can be taken as synonymous with universalism and is presented as outmoded. In *Poetic Intention* Glissant refers to the '*faux-semblant* of the universal' (*PI*, 147),[4] and distinguishes the totality from the levelling out of difference: 'unity is not uniformity' (*PI*, 53), 'the Totality is not the Same' (*PI*, 53).[5] This will prove to be an important distinction as Glissant defends the idea of phenomena constituting a totality but considers the overall coherence which it implies as different from a universally applicable set of ideas or values.

Relation, like totalities, has little to do with universal modes of thought; it can and should be aspired to without universalism being implied (*IL*, 117). Moreover, the traditional conception of identity as derived from a unitary root leads unfailingly to the promoting of universalist thinking, Glissant argues (*PR*, 142), just as the aspiration to 'transparency' goes hand in hand with Western 'cultures of the One' (*PR*, 191).[6] From a socio-historical standpoint, the later Glissant is concerned both about the ways in which American dominance, both in cultural and economic terms, has largely superceded that of former empires like that of France or Britain in terms of becoming the principal new purveyor of supposedly universal ideas, values and practices. He also enquires into the extent to which the 'West' itself taken as some sort of

---

[3]'L'Europe n'a-t-elle pas vécu jusqu'à satiété cette splendeur souveraine qui la déporta vers d'autres cieux? N'a-t-elle pas, l'assoiffée, appris bien loin l'éclatement de son éternite?', *Le Soleil de la Conscience*, 32.
[4]'faux-semblant de l'universel' (*IP*, 153).
[5]'l'unité n'est pas l'uniformité', 'le Total n'est pas le Même' (*IP*, 59).
[6]'cultures de l'Un' (*PR*, 205).

entity is coextensive with the aspiration to universally applicable value-systems.

From *Poetics of Relation* in particular onwards Glissant's concern that Anglo-American culture is imposing itself on the world as a new pseudo-universal paradigm becomes self-evident: 'the levelling effect of Anglo-American is a persistent threat for everyone and that this language, in turn, risks being transformed into a technical salesman's Esperanto' (*PR*, 112).[7] The 'levelling effect', or as Glissant elsewhere calls it 'standardization', is a form of uniformization which is entirely of a piece with universalist thinking. The new 'esperanto' Glissant speaks of is a version of English that is shorn of the full range of idioms actually employed in British or American English, and is 'a negative *écho-monde,* whose concrete force weaves the folds of Relation and neutralizes its subsistence' (*PR*, 93).[8] It works to homogenize the cultures of the world rather than genuinely respecting their differences. In the later work *La Cohée du Lamentin* (2005) Glissant devotes no less than fifteen pages to speculating on what the consequences of world domination by the United States or any other nation would be. In fact, arguably by 2005 the idea of American world domination was already starting to look somewhat dated, not just because of the failure of the US's neocon-led imperialist agenda in the Middle East, starting with Iraq, but also because of the prodigious and sustained economic growth of China on the one hand and convincing evidence on the other that the long-term economic trend of the United States was a downward one.[9] The American empire, contrary to appearances and last-ditch attempts to reverse the trend, was already caught in a downward spiral.

Glissant's concern with Anglo-American dominance tends to be expressed with reference to its cultural effects and notably the pre-eminence of the aforementioned debased, technico-commercial version of English. He suggests, however, that this negative universalizing tendency is closely associated with the West itself.

---

[7] 'se maintient pour tous la menace de l'égalisation par l'anglo-américain, lequel risque à son tour de se transformer en un espéranto du technico-commercial' (*PR*, 126).
[8] 'un écho-monde négatif, dont la puissance concrète trame les plis de la Relation et en neutralise la subsistance' (*PR*, 107).
[9] See Emmanuel Todd, *After the Empire: The Breakdown of the American Order* (London: Constable and Robinson, 2004 [2002]).

In fact, it is the very ideal of universal values which is the main export of the Western world to its subordinates (*EBR*, 29). And Western dominance continues to this day in this way: 'It is still the case that western countries collectively dictate the Universal and what constitutes the dignity of the individual, in spite of all the abuses, oppressive policies and profiteering which their societies have inflicted on the world.'[10]

Interestingly, it is not just minoritarian communities but also poets who put up resistance to the universal aspirations of the dominant. The poet creates a language within the language in which he writes and his work is of a piece with the process of establishing Relation (*TTM*, 122). As such it can have nothing to do with universalism which is the antithesis of Relation (*TTM*, 123). 'The poet strives to 'enrhizome' his place entirely, to spread the totality throughout his place: permanence in the moment and conversely, elsewhere in the here and now and vice versa.'[11]

It will by now be apparent that there is a series of oppositions in Glissant's work all relating to universalism and what Glissant considers to be its opposites: The One vs. The Diverse ('L'Un' versus 'Le Divers'); the universal vs. difference; colonialism, neocolonialism and uniformization vs. defending minoritarian cultures' right to autonomy and opacity. To these oppositions can be added monolingualism vs. promoting multilingualism and the practice of translation, a topic which we will discuss in Chapter 5. However, despite the coherence of Glissant's opposition to universalism, he is careful not to dismiss the idea of universals altogether. In *Une Nouvelle région du monde* (2006) the concept makes a return in a manner best summed up by the following statement: 'The sizeable expanse of contrasts, that is to say the large energy field of differences, is the only conceivable universal within diversity'.[12] The universal is hence conceived as 'the *total sum* of all the differences

---

[10]'Aujourd'hui encore, les cultures occidentales tiennent ensemble la généralité de l'Universel et la dignité de la personne humaine, malgré tant d'exactions, d'oppressions et de profitations dont leurs sociétés ont accablé le monde' (*TTM*, 98).
[11]'Le poète tâche à enrhizomer son lieu dans la totalité, à diffuser la totalité dans son lieu : la permanence dans l'instant et inversement, l'ailleurs dans l'ici et réciproquement' (*TTM*, 122).
[12]'L'étendue des différents, c'est-à-dire le grand champ d'énergie des différences, est le seul universel concevable, dans la diversité' (*NRM*, 134).

and that alone',[13] as Glissant resumed in an interview of the same year. While it is not difficult to see there are good reasons for wanting to avoid the pitfall of denying universalism so vehemently that relativism itself becomes a new universal, it is not clear what distinguishes this new, very limited brand of universalism which Glissant concedes from the ideas of totality, 'totality-world' and 'Whole-World' which are central to his world view. A universalism which is constituted of nothing but differences, the objection might run, is surely no genuine universalism at all. I hence would argue that this acceptance of universals does little to mitigate the consistently oppositional stance which Glissant adopts in relation to universalism elsewhere in his theoretical output.

The ambivalent situation of overseas Caribbean French citizens

To this day, Glissant's home island Martinique remains a French Overseas Department (a 'Département d'Outre-Mer', or D.O.M.). It took on 'départment' status in 1946 and was governed under the watchful eye of the vehemently anti-colonialist poet, politician and thinker Aimé Césaire for no less than forty-eight years.[14] It is this departmental status which, as mentioned in Chapter 3, has led the island's long-standing independentists, of which Glissant, Chamoiseau and Confiant are just some of the more high-profile, to argue that France's stance is neocolonial. Martinique, like Guadeloupe whose protesters erupted into urban violence in 2009, is French and yet many of its citizens do not feel they are treated equitably by the government in Paris.

Following a protracted 'mouvement social', or social protest movement, which became a general strike in Guadeloupe and Martinque between January and March 2009, a referendum was held in January 2010 on the political future of the French D.O.M. Martinique, Guadeloupe and Guyane. The outcome of the two

---

[13]'la quantité *réalisée* de toutes les différences et elle seule' (*IL*, 91).
[14]The stark contrasts in Césaire's stance, as not just poet and politician, but also advocate of 'Négritude' while being fully incorporated into the workings of the French political system are discussed at length in Raphaël Confiant's *Aimé Césaire. Une traversée paradoxale du siècle* (Paris: Ecriture, 2006) [Editions Stock, 1993].

rounds of this referendum is very revealing of the ambivalent position of the francophone Caribbean islands. Just to focus on Martinique alone, having rejected massively (by a landslide 79.3 per cent) the proposed 'Article 74' which would have given the island greater autonomy from France in the referendum of 10 January, the Martiniquans nevertheless voted almost as resoundingly (68.3 per cent) on 24 January to endorse 'la création en Martinique d'une collectivité unique exerçant les compétences dévolues au département et à la région tout en demeurant régie par l'article 73 de la Constitution'.[15] The intricacies of Antillean politics, which the then French Overseas Minister Marie-Luce Penchard characterized as too local in character for most metropolitan French to follow,[16] are conveyed in the ambivalence of this outcome. After all, the OUI vote of 24 January would appear to the uninitiated to be about ensuring greater political autonomy from metropolitan France too, in this case by defining it as a 'collectivité unique', *despite* the fact that the Martinicans had in their vast majority voted against the adopting of 'Article 74'.[17] To sum up, it was a resolute No to becoming an 'overseas constituency ruled by Article 74 of the constitution'[18] but an almost as confident Yes to being a 'single constituency [...] ruled by Article 73 of the Constitution.'[19] The Martinican position on autonomy in relation to metropolitan

---

[15] This is the proposition which 68.3 per cent of the voters assented to on 24 January 2010, as reproduced on the French government website at: http://www.gouvernement.fr/gouvernement/guyane-et-martinique-second-referendum-le-24-janvier-apres-le-non-des-electeurs-dimanch.

[16] 'I think that many citizens of mainland France are not even aware that a referendum is scheduled to take place in French Guyana and Martinique [...] It remains a very local issue that is difficult for others to engage with.' ('Je pense que de nombreux métropolitains ne savent même pas qu'une consultation est prévue en Guyane et en Martinique [...] C'est quand même un débat très local, difficile à transposer.' Interview with Marie-Luce Penchard in *L'Express* no.3053, 7–13 January 2010, III of supplement entitled 'Martinique, Guyane. Les enjeux du référendum').

[17] The question posed in the referendum of 10 January was the following: 'Do you approve of the transforming of Martinique into an overseas constituency that will be ruled by Article 74 of the Constitution, equipped with a specific structure which takes its own interests within the Republic into account?' ('Approuvez-vous la transformation de la Martinique en une collectivité d'outre-mer régie par l'article 74 de la Constitution, dotée d'une organisation particulière tenant compte de ses intérêts propres au sein de la République?').

[18] 'collectivité d'outre-mer régie par l'article 74 de la Constitution.'

[19] 'collectivité unique [...] régie par l'article 73 de la Constitution.'

France is hence far from straightforward. Moreover, matters are not made simpler by the fact that some of the long-standing and high profile critics of Martinique's continuing French 'département' status including even Chamoiseau and Glissant himself were among those who voted *against* the adoption of 'Article 74' on 10 January. Chamoiseau, at the same time as insisting that he remains an 'indépendantiste', argued that 'Article 74' would have led to the 'fragilisation de la Martinique' and that it was hence for the best that it had not been adopted.[20]

Analysis of Glissant's views on the status of Martinique as both a cultural and economic neocolonial territory is valuable in terms of explaining the in-between position of the French Caribbean overseas 'départements'. In *Poetic Intention* (1969) Glissant tellingly on the one hand had expressed surprise at the fact that a value-system such as that of the West, founded on the ideas of individualism and property, had proved so remarkably successful and on the other hand had sought to dissociate himself actively from that legacy: 'what I am saying is that that history is not mine',[21] he retorted, stating that he had always felt more in sympathy with societies oriented more towards collectivism. Western history had hence imposed itself on him and others in the same context but he chose not to identify with the values it promoted. In *Caribbean Discourse* (1981), he writes in no uncertain terms of Martinique being both economically and culturally under the thumb of mainland France. The French Caribbean 'départements' suffer from 'one of the most pernicious forms of colonization: the one by means of which a community becomes *assimilated*' (CD, 5),[22] he argues. In economic terms, they exhibit a chronic lack of autonomy in relation to France. Class division in Martinique, as Glissant sees it, results from 'a powergame of economic interests steered by one dominant force, namely French market capitalism, which controls the system without entering into it as a « social actor ».'[23] The 'békés', that

---

[20]Chamoiseau made these points in an interview of 11 January 2010 with Catherine Pottier on 'France Info'.
[21]'je dis que cette histoire n'est pas la mienne' (*IP*, 39–40).
[22]'une des formes les plus pernicieuses de colonisation: celle par quoi on *assimile* une communauté'.
[23]'un jeu de conflits manipulés, orientés par un surdéterminateur qui décide du circuit sans y entrer comme "participant social": le capitalisme marchand français' (*LeDA*, 191).

is, the white owning class, remain in control of the means of production and hence determine the orientation of economic relations locally. Between government policy coming from the mainland centre on the one hand, and on the other, this class of 'passive beneficiaries of the system',[24] who in any case export profits out of the Caribbean, the economic life of the French Caribbean islands is decided, and not primarily to the advantage of the vast majority of their inhabitants. The islands remain colonies of sorts despite being French 'départments'. In a chapter entitled 'Monocolonialisme 1973–1979' Glissant explains the situation as he sees it thus: 'It is indeed the French citizen who finances the system, but what he is financing is French capital, of course a small amount of capital investment in relation to the global giants, our homegrown colonialists can only achieve a certain amount, but [...] the French citizen finances the gentle exploitation of the Martinicans to meet the interests of French capital investment.'[25] The consequence of this situation is that the Martinicans exhibit a state of 'morbidity', a sort of 'loser mentality'[26] resulting from the failure of generation after generation to overturn this iniquitous state of affairs.

In cultural terms, French Caribbeans today realize fully the hybrid nature of their identity, Glissant argues. They know they neither have to deny the African part of their make-up nor overstate it in reaction to the imposition of Western values (*DA*, 25). Their identity is truly in-between the Western and the non-Western, and hence, in so far as the West has become the leading paradigm globally, in-between a would-be universal and a type of local particularity which is fundamentally inassimilable to it. Hence Glissant's aforementioned belief in the potential for small countries to exist independently of larger nations; in his view this is the only way for an island like Martinique to free itself of a position of subservience in relation to a larger nation like France. Independence would facilitate the development of a local language,

---

[24]'profiteur[s] passif[s] du système' (*DA*, 193).
[25]the 'c'est bien oui le citoyen français qui subventionne le système, mais ce qu'il subventionne c'est le capital français, oh un petit capital au regard des monstres mondiaux, on a les colonisateurs qu'on peut, mais [...] le citoyen français subventionne au profit du capital français l'exploitation feutrée des Martiniquais' (*DA*, 207).
[26]'morbidité' (*DA*, 197), 'mentalité de vaincus' (*DA*, 198).

the use of creole having always been undermined by metropolitan France's economic pre-eminence.[27] The absence of a fully adequate language of their own is the reason why Martinican writers such as Glissant, Chamoiseau and Césaire before them, although cultivating 'a strategic relationship of resistance and subversion *to* the dominant language',[28] have almost always published in French and rather paradoxically, one might add, with prestigious Paris-based publishers like Gallimard and Seuil. How does one contest the supremacy of a neocolonial power using the language and intellectual heritage of that nation? This may seem like a performative contradiction and in many ways it undoubtedly is, as is particularly evident in the case of a book like Chamoiseau's entitled *Ecrire en pays dominé* (Gallimard, 1997). Why, as Walcott had objected at the time of the *Eloge de créolité* (*In Praise of Creoleness*), was this work not written and published in creole, one might ask? I believe that this objection certainly carries some weight and yet I think it is important to recognize that the ambivalent situation in which the Antillean writer and intellectual finds him or herself is such that s/he does not really have other realistic options. To publish in creole would be to address a much smaller and local audience. Moreover, why should even an independentist writer feel they have some obligation to write in creole when the vital years of education and cultural conditioning with respect to intellectual and literary history in their youth were all conducted in French? In short, the in-between position of the French Caribbean writer reflects the more broadly ambivalent position of French Caribbean citizens generally.

Salvaging universal values

We have discussed Glissant's staunch resistance to the universalist doctrine. We have also seen that this resistance originates in a trenchant rejection of French Republican universalist thinking and the importance of this latter in the brand of colonialism which the Caribbean islands like Martinique suffered at the hands of the

---

[27]Celia Britton, *Édouard Glissant and Postcolonial Theory* (University Press of Virginia, 1999), 36
[28]Ibid., 3.

French. In reality though, most if not all colonial projects, not just that of the French, propounded would-be universalist doctrines to greater or lesser degrees. The notion that one's own cultural values were not just superior to those of the communities being colonized but also transposable to other cultural contexts because worthy of being adopted by all was a necessary ideological justification for the act of appropriation at the heart of colonial projects. Moreover, as Glissant sees it, neoliberal-led economics-driven globalization is a present-day descendant of the colonialism of yore in its similarly universalizing ambitions. However, perennial philosophical doctrines often resist easy or blanket rejection; even if discarded in one context or other for the very best of reasons, they often resurface with renewed validity in the context of other debates. I think it is hence useful to our discussion to examine whether Glissant's blanket rejection of universalism is not too forceful; whether he does not deprive his thought of valuable universalist-type underpinnings. In short, does Glissant not throw out the baby of an aspiration to universally applicable values with the French Republican universalist and homogenizing globalist bathwater?

It is beyond the scope of a chapter of this length to discuss the relative merits of the various types of universalist doctrines which could be adopted as possible theoretical world views and political strategies today. I nevertheless propose to examine the views of three contemporary commentators in the ongoing debate about universalism, all of whom have published works on this topic in recent years. I believe that examination of these authors' views both facilitates a better understanding of the strengths and weaknesses of Glissant's position and allows for potential ways out of the universalism/particularism dichotomy. Caroline Fourest's *La dernière utopie. Menaces sur l'universalisme* (2009) offers a defence of the brand of universalism commonly associated with the French Republicanism mindset. Amin Maalouf, in *Le Dérèglement du monde* (*Disordered World*, 2011 [2009]), advocates a more internationally oriented brand of 'universalist humanism', Maalouf arguing that a position which takes account both of the 'universality of essential values' and the 'diverse nature of their cultural manifestations' is needed. Finally, François Jullien's *De l'universel, de l'uniforme, du commun et du dialogue entre les cultures* (2008) presents an original theoretical antidote to the ills of universalism on the one hand and the uniformizing tendencies of globalization on the other. Jullien argues that it is not the concept of 'difference' which should be opposed to universalism but rather that of the 'gap' (the 'écart'). Acknowledging gaps between cultures, as notably illustrated by the areas of conceptual disjunction between different languages, provides a vital basis for a genuine dialogue between them, that is to say a dialogue which is not tainted by the neo-imperialist ascendancy of one culture and language in relation to others.

The basis for Fourest's defence of Republican universalism is her scepticism of what she sees to be an increasingly invasive multiculturalist policy which, in her view, ultimately leads to showing tolerance towards the intolerant. Fourest wants to protect the French social model from a principally Anglo-American 'cult of difference'[29] which gives too much ground to extremist religious tendencies, so she argues. The French universalist model, with its accompanying insistence on secularism ('la laïcité'), permits a 'right to indifference'[30] which Fourest sees as much more effective in the fight against discrimination in all its forms. The right to indifference attempts to unite individuals and communities rather than focusing on what divides them because it does not cast a spotlight on those characteristics which they do not share. It is 'more idealistic'[31] than the Anglo-American model, but although it has often proven to be an expression of an 'an abstract conception of universalism',[32] this was only when in the hands of 'conservateurs' who did not want to recognize the demands of minorities.[33]

While Fourest is undoubtedly right to be concerned about the spread of religious extremism within Western societies, her defence of French Republican universalist thinking principally on this basis throws up some difficulties. Her analysis tends to overlook the problems which the French social model engenders or, when she does discuss these, to dismiss them rather summarily. Her reproving of 'conservatives' does little to mitigate the fundamental difficulty that French universalism, from its origins in Enlightenment thinking and the Revolution of 1789 to the present day, remains one of the

---

[29]Fourest (2009), 'culte de la différence' 11.
[30]Ibid., 63.
[31]'plus idéaliste' (Ibid., 64).
[32]'une conception abstraite de l'universalisme' (Ibid 65).
[33]Ibid., 65.

most abstract manifestations of the doctrine as far as application to real-world social and cultural issues is concerned. It is its remoteness from the real cultural specificities of diverse ethnic and religious communities which has long contributed to the feeling of exclusion which so many immigrant groups have long complained of in France. Fourest is also rather hasty in her dismissal of the Anglo-American multiculturalist model. While there can be no doubt that this social model throws up very real problems of its own, Fourest's apparent refusal to grant that it is in any important respect as successful as the French model conveys an attitude on her part that is verging on chauvinistic. Even Barack Obama, who Fourest praises for his attempts to bring people together above and beyond differences of race and culture,[34] ultimately falls short because he defends the public acknowledgment of different religious affiliations.[35] Fourest does not give a moment's consideration to the ways in which this attitude of Obama's might be defensible at the very least *in the American context*. Her universalist agenda obstructs acknowledging the specificity of socio-cultural contexts, and for this reason veers towards the unworldly abstraction of the 'conservatives' she claims to decry.

Ultimately, Fourest's defence of universalism reiterates traditional French Republican thinking and does little to answer the sorts of objections to it which members of minority immigrant and postcolonial communities have long made. There is not much room for the right to (not cult of) difference and to 'opacity' of the sort argued for by Glissant in the vision of French society defended by Fourest. In so far as the multicultural composition of Western societies is a fact, as Fourest herself acknowledges, and in the light of the reality that diasporic communities within Western societies are becoming increasingly paradigmatic of the social composition of our ever-globalizing world taken more broadly, this failure points to the conclusion that the case she makes for universalism is deficient in a number of important respects.

The topic of universalism is not the principal focus of Maalouf's *Disordered World* although he does propose a brand of universalism as part of a solution to the disordered state of the world today. On the one hand, Maalouf has long believed that universal values such

---

[34]Ibid., 110.
[35]Ibid., 244.

as democracy and the equal dignity of human beings cannot be sacrificed or compromised in the name of a declared respect for the particularities of cultures other than one's own;[36] acknowledging the right to cultural difference must not come at such a price. In this respect, his thinking conforms to the conception of universalism defended by Fourest. Yet on the other hand, the francophone Lebanese Maalouf's lengthy experience as an immigrant in France, and the equal ease with which he can exist in both Arab and European contexts, lead him to the view that it cannot be as simple as expecting peoples in diverse cultures and communities to assent to values presumed to be universal in the same way as each other. Cultural differences and the distance separating the languages associated with given cultures render the task of distinguishing that which is commonly shared from that which is not the same more complex than this. What route does Maalouf see out of the impasse which the difficulty of making such a distinction leads to? Cultural difference in different parts of the world being an incontrovertible fact, Maalouf proposes the concept of 'passerelles' ('bridges', literally 'footbridges') as a means of encouraging the identification of commonalities between different cultures. Bridges can only be built where there are areas of reciprocity between values. This concept would appear to be of a piece with Glissant's insistence that translation must be accorded pride of place in the twenty-first century. As no universal standard, either at the level of cultural values or of language, can legitimately be imposed by any one culture on others, the only way to proceed, Glissant argues, is by developing our capacities to understand all cultural others by placing more emphasis on the interfaces allowing communication between cultures.

François Jullien offers a nuanced and original take on the universalism vs. relativism/cultural particularism problem which, in its orientation and broad outlines, is of a piece with the Glissantian position while also perhaps offering a way out of Glissant's overvaluing of difference in relation to universals. Jullien initially makes a valuable distinction between the universal and the uniform. Whereas 'the universal is oriented towards

---

[36]Interview with Maalouf conducted by Egi Volterrani, December 2001, www.aminmaalouf.net. Also Maalouf (2009), 274.

the One';[37] the uniform is nothing but 'sterile repetition'[38] and the 'indefinite return of the same'.[39] The universal stands in opposition to the individual or singular whereas the uniform is antithetical to difference. This understanding of the uniform is for Jullien, as for Glissant, part of a broader argument about the negative effects of contemporary globalization. The uniform is the 'perverted double'[40] of universalism, and uniformization, or 'standardisation', 'has taken on an increased importance with the advent of globalisation'.[41]

Universalism, in spite of the negative uses to which it has been put historically, is thus presented by Jullien, theoretically at least, as more laudable than uniformization. Jullien highlights however the considerable extent to which the brand of universalism which has held sway in Europe since the French Revolution has been influenced by Kantianism: 'universality is conceived by Kant in an entirely rational, and hence abstract, way: Whether it be concerning action or knowledge, my relations with others or my knowledge of objects, only a universality posited as prior to all experience confers *legitimacy*.'[42] Moreover Kant's thought did not take into account the issue of cultural diversity at all, but conceived of human conduct as 'on a point of principle subject to the same law, the conceiving of this law itself being derived from that universality which is specific to *natural laws,* laws of which science discovered the logical necessity.'[43] The asocial and ahistorical character of Kantian universality is what led to a doctrine like human rights, or the rights of man, being the product of two abstract notions in Western thinking: that of a 'right' where the demands of the individual subject are stressed largely to the exclusion of duties towards others; and that of 'man' conceived of in isolation from his

---

[37]'l'universel est tourné vers l'Un', Jullien (2008), 31.
[38]'répétition stérile'.
[39]'retour indéfini du même' (Ibid., 31).
[40]'double perverti' (Ibid., 13).
[41]'a pris une importance accrue avec la mondialisation' (Ibid., 35).
[42]'qu'il s'agisse de l'action ou de la connaissance, de ma relation aux autres ou du savoir des objets, seule une universalité posée préalablement à toute expérience rend *légitime*' (Ibid., 22).
[43]'soumise par principe à la même loi, celle-ci étant elle-même conçue à partir de l'universalité propre aux *lois de la nature* dont la science a découvert la nécessité logique' (Ibid., 22).

context, and hence also in the first instance at least from the social and political dimensions of life.

Jullien's critique of the abstract, disembodied, asocial character of European, and subsequently Western, universalism is given further support by his discussion of contrasting conceptions of universal values which have long existed in other cultures, such as those of China, India and Islamic countries. The existence of other ways of conceiving of universals offers proof of the fact that universalism must be viewed as a historically and culturally conditioned phenomenon. If there are universalism*s* in the plural, there cannot be one definitive set of universally applicable principles which are valid for all. This has long been a Western delusion, one which Glissant rightly identifies as having been an indispensable support to the colonial project.

What conclusions does Jullien draw from the above observations? Problematic though a defence of universals in some ways is, Jullien does not want to dispense with them. Like Glissant and Maalouf, he does not see the abstract European brand of universalism as satisfactory. Moreover, universal*isms* generally should be jettisoned, he argues, because of their ideological character. Yet the idea of universal values should be retained as a regulatory idea (*idée régulatrice*): 'the universal will always continue to throw up the conditions of possibility of a common ground never totally immune to seeing its scope narrowing down and *turning in on itself*'.[44] Only universal values offer the prospect of finding common ground between the diverse peoples and cultures of the world. But what, then, of the manifold disparities between one cultural mindset and another? Jullien is more sceptical than Glissant of the idea that difference is a valid alternative to universalism. In view of the association made by French critics such as Fourest of difference with an overweening influence of anglosaxon thinking, and indeed by radical critics with postmodernism,[45] this scepticism on his part is undoubtedly an advantage.

It is at this point that Jullien proposes the 'écart' (the 'gap') both as an alternative to difference and as a way of getting beyond

---

[44]"[l'universel] ne cessera de dégager à nouveau, irrépressible, les conditions de possibilité d'un commun toujours menacé de se rétrécir et de se *replier*' Ibid 263.
[45]See, for example, Terry Eagleton's *The Illusions of Postmodernism* (Oxford: Blackwell, 1996).

the shortcomings of the universalist creed. It is an alternative which is in my estimation entirely compatible both with Glissant's insistence that each individual language and culture, however minoritarian they may be, are worthy of equal respect, and with Maalouf's desire to find bridges ('passerelles') between cultures. The gap is not as stark a concept as difference. It does not stand in opposition to the Same, but rather to that which is predictable, expected, and normative. By taking cognizance of the gaps between the thinking of peoples from different cultures (sinologist Jullien's principal points of reference are the French and Chinese cultures), notably through the conceptual disparities between languages, our cultural awareness is heightened. The one set of cultural and linguistic coordinates rebounds off the other in our thinking creating a productive tension which allows us to perceive the *unthought of* ('l'*impensé*'). For Jullien, this process is not so much about encouraging relativism as it involves *localising* given cultures, that is to say resituating them back in their specific historical and social contexts. No one culture should be permitted to extend beyond its context in an imperialistic manner. Rather, when we encounter two or more distinct cultures a process of evolving awareness is engendered in us, a fact which for Jullien has ethical and political implications: 'the *gap* is the concept of a cultural resistance which is also ethical and political.'[46] This cultural resistance results from the fact that we are less likely to think in a manner that coheres with the uniformized or standardized thinking which globalization today produces. Jullien's priority is encouraging genuine dialogue between different cultures and this cannot be achieved when one culture and language has ascendancy over others. Cultural difference cannot be rode roughshod over by the debased brand of English spoken that has become the lingua franca of the globalized economy. Like Glissant, Jullien consequently considers the practise of translation absolutely vital to preserving cultural specificity and diversity in our globalized world: 'Translation [...]', he argues, 'is the only possible ethical stance in our future "global" world.'[47]

---

[46]Jullien, 'l'*écart* est le concept d'une résistance culturelle qui est aussi éthique et politique.' 251.
[47]'La traduction [...] est la seule éthique possible du monde "global" à venir' (Ibid., 248).

CHAPTER FIVE

Glissant: postmodernist apologist for neoliberal-led globalization?

The generally sympathetic orientation of my reading of Glissant will by this stage already be apparent. I have indicated in preceding chapters that I believe that Glissant's works constitute a powerful response not only to French neocolonialism but also in more recent years a politically progressive counterstrategy in relation to contemporary globalization. The extent to which I believe Glissant's oeuvre of the last twenty years of his career can usefully inform and orient contestation of and resistance to globalization understood both in its politico-economic manifestations and, above all, in their cultural consequences will become clear in the remaining chapters of this book. In the present chapter, however, I would like briefly to discuss criticisms of Glissant which have been articulated notably by anglophone commentators in response to his writings from *Poetics of Relation* (1990) onwards. Contrary to my own reading, these commentators, some of whom writing from a radical standpoint, have objected to what they perceive to be a move away from politics in Glissant's work from around the turn of the 1990s onwards. From the time of *Poetics of Relation*, so the objection runs, a more pronounced influence of Deleuze in Glissant's thought led him to a position which was of a piece with the postmodernist outlook of the intellectual climate of the early

1990s and of postcolonial theory during that period. On this reading the politically committed Glissant concerned with a defence of the nation gave way to a politically emollient, even indifferent, Glissant whose theoretical writings gave expression to a postmodernist view which was complicit with the dominant trends characterizing our ever-globalizing world. As I will demonstrate in Chapter 6, the force of this attack has been undermined by the publication of a number of works by Glissant since 2007 the political content of which can be in no doubt. More generally, while it is undeniable that argumentation with a political orientation became much less prevalent in Glissant's publications since 1990, I will argue that a politically committed outlook is present, if in a only discreet manner in some texts, in the majority of Glissant's writings of the last twenty years of his life.

The 'post-political', 'postmodernist' Glissant

One of the most sustained attacks not just on the later Glissant but also on the direction postcolonial studies as a field took during the period widely coloured in Anglophone universities in particular by the trend known as postmodernism was made by Peter Hallward in his *Absolutely Postcolonial* (2001). This work was part of a broader, Marxist response to postcolonial studies in the Anglophone academic context from the mid-1990s onwards, notable purveyors of which included Aijaz Ahmad and Neil Lazarus. To limit our remarks to appraisal of Glissant, a number of commentators, such as Chris Bongie and Nick Nesbitt, have followed Hallward's lead in reproaching the later Glissant his supposed abandonment of political engagement.

The basis of Hallward's attack lies in the claim that Glissant, under the influence of Deleuze and Guatarri, aligned his thought to a 'singular' as opposed to 'specific' mode of thought, a distinction which Hallward himself characterizes as 'somewhat idiosyncratic'.[1] Favouring the singular, according to Hallward, involves severing discussion of postcolonial issues from the specificity of given

---

[1] Hallward, *Absolutely Postcolonial* (Manchester University Press, 2001), preface, xii.

cultural and historical contexts and from politics. In particular, Hallward laments the fact that the overtly independentist author of *Caribbean Discourse* appeared to abandon the insistence on the centrality of the nation which had been the 'pivotal concept'[2] of his earlier writings. The move from 'nationalism to post-nationalism'[3] which Hallward perceives in Glissant's latter work involves neglecting the fact that the nation, 'understood in a broadly Jacobin sense—the nation as made up of all those who, whatever their cultural origin [...] collectively *decide* to assert (or reassert) their right of self-determination',[4] was and indeed remains the only effective vehicle for progressive politics, as Hallward believes. The very nature of globalization, with its promoting of transnational flows of goods, peoples and cultures, runs counter to the integrity of nation-states and the idea of national sovereignty. In chime with this, argues Hallward, 'postcolonial theory has generally abandoned the concept of the nation for the sake of *cultural* hybridity and *cultural* mobility'[5] [italics Hallward's]; transnationalism is threatening the idea of nation just as culture is supplanting politics. Hallward thereby suggests that postcolonial studies has ceased to be the oppositional critical counter-discourse in the service of the oppressed which it once was, to become complicit with Western neoliberal-led globalization.

Chris Bongie, in his *Friends and Enemies: The Scribal Politics of Post/Colonial Literature* (2008), explicitly follows Hallward's lead with respect to Glissant's alleged post-political turn. In particular, Bongie's disapproval of what he perceives to be an excessive aestheticism in certain more recent works such as *La Cohée du Lamentin* (2005) and *Une nouvelle région du monde* (2006) characterizes his generally rather critical attitude towards the later Glissant. Glissant is accused by Bongie even of 'cynicism [...] when it comes to 'substantive politics and its necessarily partisan commitments',[6] Glissant's late work constituting a "guilty' recantation of the once trenchant political commitments

---

[2]Ibid., 74.
[3]Ibid.,. 127.
[4]Ibid., 127.
[5]Ibid., 129.
[6]Bongie, *Friends and Enemies: The Scribal Politics of Post/Colonial Literature* (2008), (Liverpool: Liverpool University Press, 2008), 328.

that constituted one half of his lifelong, modernist project.' Bongie continues: 'In taking this turn, late Glissant's work spectacularly confirms his lasting attachment to the other half of that two-faced project: namely, a faith in "aesthetic construction" [...] but that he now insists has no direct bearing on emancipatory politics.'[7] Glissant's latter-day project, then, so Bongie objects, 'is characterized by the concerted attempt to "desuture" [...] poetics from any and all oppositional politics of the sort with which he had once associated it'.[8]

As suggested above, it is perhaps an unfortunate coincidence that while Bongie's book must have been in preparation and shortly after its publication a number of unambiguously political texts by Glissant appeared. *Quand les murs tombent. L'Identité nationale hors la loi?* was first published in the left-wing newspaper *L'Humanité* on 4 September 2007 in response to the right-wing French government's creation of a 'Ministère de l'immigration, de l'intégration, de l'identité nationale et du Développement solidaire' in May 2007. *L'Intraitable beauté du monde. Adresse à Barack Obama* (2009), also authored with Patrick Chamoiseau, covers quite a broad range of social, historical and political topics. Moreover, as I will explain in Chapter 6, what is very evident in this latter work in particular is the extent to which Glissant sees substantive political issues and a certain kind of aestheticist outlook to be intertwined. The work *Mémoires des Esclavages* (2007) could also be cited, a work which coincided with Glissant having been allotted the task in January 2005 by President Chirac of setting the agenda for a future 'National Centre for the Commemoration of Slavery and its Abolition' ('Centre national consacré à la traite, à l'esclavage et à ses abolitions'). What these works all make plain is that any notion that Glissant had renounced all interest in substantive politics only to confine himself to some sort of other-worldy aestheticism simply cannot be given credence to.

Bongie's analysis of *La Cohée du Lamentin* does not take sufficiently into account that the concept of 'poetics' is not restricted to the standard aesthetic sense in Glissant's work, as I explained in Chapter 1. In one sense meant by Glissant 'poetics' encompasses not only aesthetics but also politics and ethics, suggesting a way of

---

[7]Ibid., 239.
[8]Ibid., 330.

apprehending the world as a totality not just as it presently is but as it could be. It is undeniable that there is some conflation of the aesthetic sense and this other sense of the term in Glissant's writing and this makes it difficult to ascertain with clarity what exactly is being claimed in certain passages. Nevertheless, what is certain is that any notion that references to poetics are to be understood in the limited artistic sense is to be resisted. For instance, when Glissant claims that an enormous insurrection of the imaginary is an important part of the struggle against globalization, Bongie infers that what is being designated is a process of aesthetic enlightenment.[9] What we are faced with, he concludes, is an aesthetic choice, 'not primarily or necessarily a political choice.'[10] Yet the imaginary for Glissant, although vital to a poetic outlook, is not severed from political concerns. On the contrary, it is crucial to envisaging an alternative *political* future. In a similar vein, Bongie argues that *La Cohée*, in its 'hyper-aestheticizing tendencies',[11] often gives the impression that the poetics of relation is 'sufficient unto itself and, as a consequence, that it is not politicians, or people armed with principles, who will be of most help to us in our dealings with the forces of globalization and Empire but poets.'[12] Once again, Bongie appears to assume a strict separation of the political and aesthetic spheres, in a manner and to a degree, one might add, that is revealing of anglophone assumptions about the separation of art and politics; the continental tradition has not tended to make such stark distinctions. Hence an emphasis on poetics of relation on Glissant's part is ultimately tantamount for Bongie to getting lost in art-related issues and notably poetry, this latter understood rather questionably as the height of other-worldly abstraction.[13] Whereas poetics in the sense meant in the formulation 'poetics of relation'

---

[9]Ibid., 335.
[10]Ibid., 336.
[11]Ibid., 338.
[12]Ibid., 337.
[13]In *L'Imaginaire des langues* (2010), in an interview conducted at the time of the publication of *Philosophie de la Relation* (2009), Lise Gauvin homes in on the fact that Glissant had in that work argued that the poem is 'the only dimension of truth, permanence or deviance that links up the presences of the world' ('la seule dimension de vérité ou de permanence ou de déviance qui relie les présences du monde' [104]), a claim which does not appear to concord with the everyday assumption that poetry is divorced from worldly concerns.

is anything but aestheticism conceived as cut off from real-world concerns. It does indeed incorporate an aesthetic outlook but is by no means limited to aestheticism and secondly, even that dimension which does involve aestheticism does not involve conceiving of this latter in the anglophone compartmentalized and largely otherworldly manner.

In so far as the theoretical basis for the claim that Glissant's work took a post-political turn from around the turn of the 1990s onwards originates in the view that his interest in Deleuzian thought in this period took greater prominence, I propose to briefly examine the claim that Deleuze's thought implies apoliticism and an alignment with postmodernism. I in no way seek to contest the value of the Marxist critique of the field of postcolonial studies with respect to this latter as it existed in anglophone universities in the 1990s; a general questioning of the orientation of the field of the sort initiated by such as Lazarus and Hallward was timely and much needed. However, the view that a Deleuzian influence on the field specifically was the basis for an adherence on the part of Glissant among others not just to the postmodernist mindset but also, by that same token, to a complicity with neoliberal-led globalization, is in my view highly problematic. To argue this convincingly, one would need to be able to claim authoritatively first of all that Deleuze's thought is by and large of a piece with, if not an actual theoretical expression of postmodernism. Second, assuming one succeeded in doing this, one would have to be able to offer plausible evidence that the Deleuzian influence in Glissant's work coloured his later output in its large part to such a significant degree as to transform his vision and outlook into a postmodernist one and then, on that basis, into a position which was globally sympathetic to globalization. This is no easy task and is in my view fundamentally misguided.

Critical commentary on Deleuze is noteworthy, as Reidar Due points out in a politically neutral study devoted to the philosopher, in part for 'the lack of agreement among scholars about the nature and direction of Deleuze's thought.'[14] Whereas some critics have interpreted Deleuze's philosophy as abstract and divorced from practical relevance, others have tended towards presenting it as

---

[14] Reidar Due, *Deleuze*, (Cambridge: Polity, 2007), 4.

applicable to practical experience. Due adds: '[m]ost commentators disagree sharply on the further issue: is Deleuze a political philosopher? Some say that he is, that his philosophy is conducive to certain kinds of political action and analysis, whereas others deny this, claiming that his ontology is such that it rules out any such consequences for action.'[15] Interestingly, moreover, a number of commentators who are of a politically radical persuasion disagree quite dramatically on this very issue. Hallward, who has himself devoted a study to the work of Deleuze is decidedly of the view that the philosopher's work can have little bearing on matters political. Nicholas Thorburn, by contrast, in a study entitled *Deleuze, Marx and Politics* (2003) is keen to present Deleuze's philosophy as of a piece with and of use to radical political thought. As is Thomas Nail who, in his *Returning to Revolution: Deleuze, Guattari and Zapatismo* (2012), sees in the ideas of Deleuze and Guattari an inspiration for revolutionary alter-globalization movements today. Deleuze and Guattari formulated 'political concepts most consonant with the leaderless and networked horizontalism that characterizes today's return to revolution practically demonstrated by Zapatismo, the alter-globalization movement and the Occupy movement.'[16]

In Hallward's view, 'the truth is that Deleuze's world is indifferent to the politics of this world. A philosophy based on deterritorialization, dissipation and flight can offer only the most immaterial and evanescent grip on the mechanisms of exploitation and domination that continue to condition so much of what happens in our world.'[17] In what would appear to be a backhanded compliment, given his own political radicalism, Hallward concludes that Deleuze was an 'inspiring' philosopher but that 'those of us who still seek to change our world and to empower its inhabitants will need to look for our inspiration elsewhere.'[18] Hallward is careful not to assimilate Deleuze to postmodernism as such in this work and he is surely right not to do so as such an ascription throws up

---

[15]Ibid., 6.
[16]Thomas Nail, *Returning to Revolution: Deleuze, Guattari and Zapatismo*, (Edinburgh University Press, 2012), 3.
[17]Peter Hallward, *Out of this World. Deleuze and the Philosophy of Creation* (London: Verso, 2006), 162.
[18]Ibid., 164.

a difficulty which is also present in the case of Glissant. Whatever parallels could arguably be established between the ideas of a continental or continental-descended postcolonial thinker and those of postmodernists, the contexts in which their ideas were formulated were very significantly different. It should not be forgotten that although postmodernist theory is generally thought to have begun in France with Jean-François Lyotard's *The Postmodern Condition: A Report on Knowledge* (1979), by the time that it came to prominence in the anglophone world, and notably in American academic and intellectual circles, its emphases had changed quite significantly. The sorts of celebrations of hybridity and difference, for example, present in the writings of postcolonial theorists who came under the influence of postmodernism in North American universities were almost entirely absent in the French context. Postmodernism, in its fully fledged form, just like postcolonial studies, became an Anglo-American creature, unmoored from its French points of origin. In the north American context postmodernism reflected a culture which gave priority to communities over collectivities, to cultural relativism rather than universally applicable values and social agendas, and to attempts to reduce state power supposedly in favour of promoting individualistic and locally based interests.

In his book *French Theory: How Foucault, Derrida, Deleuze & Co. Tranformed the Intellectual Life of the United States* (2008 [2003]), which incidentally was originally published in French, François Cusset set out in broader terms the ways in which theoretical writings produced by French thinkers underwent a transformation when they were adopted in the American context. This book on 'the *American* invention of *French* theory' [italics Cusset's] addresses 'the American identity of French Theory, or the way it has been displaced and reconstructed to confront specifically American questions'. It does this 'by raising the issue of a "denationalization" of concepts, or of what Pierre Bourdieu would call "a structural misunderstanding", and even by pondering the strange feedback effect of a recent return of French Theory *to France*, where it is now coming back undercover, under the disguise of an American type of threat against France's age-old abstract universalism.'[19] A paradoxical state of affairs indeed! It would be

---

[19]François Cusset, *French Theory: How Foucault, Derrida, Deleuze & Co. Tranformed the Intellectual Life of the United States* xiv (originally published

beyond the scope of this book to discuss the fortunes of French Theory in US academic discourse in any detail; suffice it to say that Cusset's thesis is a much needed reminder of the dangers inherent in assimilating theoretical paradigms originally conceived in France to the intellectual trends which grew out of them in the anglophone world. As in the case of what came to be known as 'postcolonial studies', 'theory' (often classed diversely as philosophy, sociology, psychoanalysis, or anthropology in France) took on a new life in the United States. Henceforth, the tail would be wagging the dog, and dwarfing it in sheer size and influence moreover. There were positive spin-offs, postcolonial studies being a case in point: an area of enquiry which essentially came into existence as a new academic discipline and would henceforth have to be taken seriously as such by the Western academic establishment (a trend which regrettably would take many years to take root back in France). Nevertheless, and nowhere more so than in the area which came to be known as 'theory', these positive implications came at a price, namely that the discourses in question inevitably came under the pervasive influence of the US American mindset and preoccupations and were exported around the world's academic circuits in that guise, partly because the English language was the international lingua franca and not French.

To return to Deleuze specifically, the contrast between Hallward's reading and Nail's study is particularly striking in that Nail's reading is diametrically opposed to Hallward's, despite their general political orientation being along similar lines. Nail reminds us that Hardt and Negri put Deleuzian thought centre-stage in radical left theoretical works such as *Empire* (2000), *Multitude* (2004) and *Commonwealth* (2010) and that their concept of 'multitude', constituting as it does a theory of revolutionary potentiality or 'difference-in-itself', is a descendent of Deleuze and Guattari's philosophy. Slavoj Žižek saw in Deleuze's thought the theoretical foundation of today's anti-global left in his *Organs without Bodies: Deleuze and Consequences* (2004), Nail also reminds us. Nail is keen to follow in these theorists' footsteps and argues that Deleuze and Guattari's most original contribution to the history of political philosophy is their 'non-foundational theory of revolution

---

as *French Theory: Foucault, Derrida, Deleuze & Cie et les mutations de la vie intellectuelle aux Etats-Unis* [Editions la Découverte, 2003]).

(without state, party, vanguard or representation).'[20] Deleuze and Guattari 'never gave up on the belief that a worldwide revolution could emerge from the smallest of political experiments without the representation of the state, party, vanguard or proper class consciousness',[21] he argues.

Whatever the merits of Nail's, Thorburn's and others' claim that Deleuze's thought is compatible with radical political thought and activism, their arguments do make it harder to accept unquestioningly Hallward's view that it was the Deleuzian influence on Glissant which stripped his thought of the political commitment which had been central to it hitherto. Certainly Bongie's thinly veiled broadsides aimed at later Glissantian aestheticism seem very largely misguided not least because Glissant was a poet and novelist as well as theorist throughout his career, not just during the last ten to fifteen years of it. The concept of poetics, just like that of relation, had been present in *Poetic Intention* (1969) yet these aestheticist proclivities had not impeded Glissant in his trenchant support for Martinican independence from France at that time. What Bongie does not address as thoroughly as the matter merits is the complexity of acknowledging that a later Glissantian work like *Une nouvelle région du monde* (2006) may indeed foreground (although by no means exclusively so) aestheticist preoccupations and yet that they perhaps detract in no way from a continuing commitment to certain radical political agendas on Glissant's part. Aesthetics and politics never were an either/or binary for Glissant and nor are they in his later publications.

The case Nail et al. make for Deleuze as inspiration to political radicals invites reflection on the possible validity of the counter-hypothesis to that proposed by Hallward in *Absolutely Postcolonial*. What if the greater influence of Deleuze in Glissant's work from around the turn of the 1990s onwards, far from being synonymous with a retreat from political radicalism, was in fact just a new way of conceiving of that radicalism? The case I will make in Chapters 7 and 8 will involve the claim that Glissant's Relation, far from being some sort of apology for neoliberal-led globalization, in fact

---

[20]Thomas Nail, *Returning to Revolution: Deleuze, Guattari and Zapatismo* (Edinburgh University Press, 2012), 10.
[21]Ibid., 4.

constitutes a counter-narrative of globalization, rather in the manner in which Gilroy referred to the 'black Atlantic' as a 'counterculture of modernity' in his seminal work of 1993. Glissant's horizontal, rhizomatic world of relational networks might perhaps reflect the leading characteristics of globalization but the goals Glissant ascribes to it are entirely different. Moreover, in his *Philosophie de la Relation* (2009), Glissant explicitly rejects the accusation that he has abandoned the idea of the nation:

> Nobody is claiming [...] that the notion of the nation has been become obsolete. The way it discreetly brings things together is necessary to human groups in order that they can frequent the places they live and the landscapes they create on a daily basis, and in order that connections be established between these and other places and landscapes. It is not the connections within a given society that are outmoded, nor the way that others are collectively viewed, but that traditionally guaranteed focus, which dictated the iron law of relations between states, and which would force me to accept that my way of being in the place I inhabit should be considered the first to be 'universally' valid, and that the way I relate to others in the world hence takes place exclusively in this way.[22]

This passage makes explicit a view which is left implicit in many of Glissant's other later works, namely that he is not hostile to defending the idea of the nation but rather to the chauvinist nationalism of colonialism and neocolonialism. This antipathy is the basis for his rejection of universalist agendas and for his consequent embracing of the idea of difference, albeit a subtly contrasting conception of difference to that promoted in Anglo-American societies.

---

[22]Nul n'entend [...] que la dimension de la nation est désormais hors jeu: sa secrète corrélation (progressive ou stupéfiante), est nécessaire aux collectivités humaines pour fréquenter les lieux qu'elles habitent et les paysages qu'elles suscitent jour après jour, et pour les relier aux autres lieux et aux autres paysages: ce qui est caduc, ce n'est pas la liaison dans une collectivité, ni le regard commun dévolu aux autres, c'est cette visée traditionnellement assurée, qui a dicté la loi de fer des relations entre Etats-nations, et qui imposerait que ma manière d'être dans mon lieu serait la première "universellement" valable, et qu'ainsi ma fréquentation du monde ne s'accomplirait que par cette manière et elle seule. (Glissant *Philosophie de la Relation* [2009], 41).

The necessary 'opacity' of cultures, multilingualism and translation

Whichever side one takes in the debate concerning Deleuze, the claim that Glissant's later thought might be complicit with globalization meets one major theoretical obstacle as well as a number of concomitant arguments which also problematize such a categorization. As briefly explained in Chapter 1, Glissant argues for the right to opacity of all cultures, a claim which stands diametrically opposed to any notion that it is acceptable that cultures be streamlined or homogenized in line with a dominant or majoritarian culture such as American culture today. Moreover, Glissant's advocacy of the right to opacity dates back to *Poetic Intention* (2010 [1969]) at least, and is a constant in his thought until his very last publications, a fact which puts into question the idea that the texts of the late 1980s, as Hallward argues, and *Poetics of Relation* (1997 [1990]) in particular, mark a watershed moment after which Glissant cast his hitherto committed political stance to one side.

Hallward devotes little time to discussing the concept of opacity in his account of Glissant, a fact which is perhaps not coincidental given his keenness to present the later Glissant as largely indifferent to politics.[23] In his brief appraisal of the concept he objects that Glissant presents opacity in somewhat different terms in *Poetics of Relation* (1997 [1990]) from in previous works. Henceforth opacities can coexist and are less dependent on the particular qualities of the elements which compose them (*PR*, 204), Hallward points out. To suggest as Hallward does on the basis of a somewhat obliquely formulated one-sentence statement of Glissant's that the concept of opacity has mutated is somewhat implausible. Glissant does indeed write that 'Opacities can coexist and converge, weaving fabrics. To understand these truly one must focus on the texture of the weave and not on the nature of its components.' (*PR*, 190)[24] However, this statement immediately

---

[23]Hallward, 78–79.
[24]'[d]es opacités peuvent coexister, confluer, tramant des tissus dont la véritable compréhension porterait sur la texture de cette trame et non pas sur la nature des composantes' (*PR*, 204).

follows the claim in the immediately preceding sentence that opacity is 'subsistence within an irreducible singularity' (*PR*, 190).[25] Hence it cannot be that the coexistence or even confluence of opacities implies their dissolution. Indeed to make such an inference would be to misunderstand the central concept of creolization as Glissant defines it. Glissant repeatedly insists, in works after 1990 as in earlier works, that creolization involves two or more cultural phenomena coming into contact, their meeting producing unexpected results, but that the individual phenomena fully retain their own individual identities. Creolization, Glissant points out in numerous places, is not the American-style cultural melting pot and is hence not synonymous with cosmopolitanism as this is understood in anglophone countries.

My own view is that the concept of opacity is presented in a consistent manner from *Poetic Intention* through to Glissant's later works. Regarding its appearance in *Antillean Discourse*, opacity as developed in this work is, as J. Michael Dash puts it, a 'dynamic and subtle' notion: '[o]n the one hand it is contrasted with the dangerous lure of universal culture. On the other, it attempts to distance itself from the false opacity of ideological folklorism or the romanticising of cultural essence and authenticity.'[26] Opacity in Glissant's sense is neither obscurity nor sectarianism; it is not about perceiving one's own culture as exclusive of others but about protecting it from subsumption in the invasive neo-imperialist cultural influences from outside which would seek to coopt it. It stands opposed to the drive for transparency, not in the commonly used contemporary sense of accountability, but in the sense of comprehensibility. The insistence that the other's culture should be fully comprehensible to oneself usually involves a refusal or failure to engage fully with that other culture on its own terms. If the other is to be immediately comprehensible to oneself then he or she will most likely have to make compromises, altering or distorting his/her own cultural meanings in order to be understood by the other. The 'right to opacity' which Glissant insists on is hence a demand that one's own culture, however minoritarian it may be, should be accorded full respect. It is in this sense that Glissant 'believe[s] in

---

[25]'la subsistance dans une singularité non réductible' (*PR*, 204).
[26]Dash, *Édouard Glissant* (Cambridge University Press, 1995), 143.

the future of small countries'.[27] Glissant is of the view that ensuring that small countries can enjoy political independence from larger federal-type political structures is an effective way of preserving the specificity of their cultures. The following caveat should be borne in mind however: Glissant nevertheless did not argue for independence at all costs, hence his having voted against greater autonomy from France in the 2010 referendum because he judged the moment and circumstances inopportune. Moreover, it was the colonial inheritance above all that he was opposed to, not federal political structures of all types per se.

In the light of Glissant's defence of small countries the claim that he abandons the idea of the nation in favour of celebrating transnational networks is highly problematic. It is my contention that it is a fundamental misreading of the political orientation of Glissant's later thought taken as a whole. The horizontal and rhizomatic conception of reality and identity which Glissant promotes undoubtedly does involve celebrating transnational ties but it conceives of these as part of a counter-tendency to the dissolving of cultural specificities wrought by neoliberal-led globalization. As such it is an extension of a tendency present in the earlier work which Glissant produced in opposition to French neo-colonialism and which, for such as Hallward and Bongie, predated his supposed 'post-political turn'. In *Poetic Intention*, opacity is defined as 'the resistance of the other' and is 'fundamental to our knowledge of the other'.[28] In *Caribbean Discourse*, Glissant was preoccupied with the question of 'to what extent [...] Martinicans have constructed a particular thought-world, to what extent has a counter-poetics developed in the face of the threat of successful colonization ('colonization réussie').'[29] Colonialism was a paradigmatic instance of transnationalism par excellence and was in this respect a predecessor, albeit a more noxious predecessor, to globalization. The transnational designs of colonial powers, in Glissant's view, required a 'counter-poetics', an oppositional poetics which had everything to do with cultural politics and, in this sense of the term 'poetics', much less to do with aesthetics in the strict sense of the term. In the period post-1990, this counter-poetics is in

---

[27]'croi[t] à l'avenir des petits pays' (*IBM*, 42–43).
[28]'la résistance de l'autre' and is 'fondamentale de sa connaissance' (*IP*, 175).
[29]Ibid., 143.

my view transposed and extended by Glissant to a new context in which transnationalism is the order of the day, that of globalization in its contemporary form. We will examine this present-day counter-poetics in more detail in Chapter 8 in particular.

Glissant's insistence on the right to opacity, and hence on a cultural politics of resistance to all forms of political, economic and cultural hegemony, is closely associated in his work with a defence of individual languages and of a multilingual world. The imposition of a language by majoritarian or hegemonic cultures on minoritarian, non-hegemonic or subjugated cultures has proved to be one of the most effective ways of guaranteeing the continuing subordinacy of these latter, Glissant believes. The francophone Caribbean has long been kept subordinate to France by the continuing use of the French language in the islands. Glissant's insistence on opacity however has nothing to do with the sort of inward-looking nationalism which came to the fore in 2016. The Glissant of the 1990s and 2000s believed it was the widespread use of the English language which posed the biggest threat to the diverse cultures of the world. 'It is true that the leveling effect of Anglo-American is a persistent threat for everyone and that this language, in turn, risks being transformed into a technical salesman's Esperanto' (*PR*, 112),[30] he observed. The only remedy to this, Glissant argued, was to continue to promote the use of languages other than English in international communications and transactions of whatever sort. The world is multilingual and multicultural and it must remain so. The only way to ensure that it does however is to promote the practice of translation:

> What every translation suggests in essence, via the passing from one language to another that is intrinsic to it, is the preeminence of all the languages of the world. And translation for this very reason indicates and offers us proof that we must conceive in our imaginations this totality of languages.[31]

---

[30]'Il est vrai que se maintient pour tous la menace de l'égalisation par l'anglo-américain, lequel risque à son tour de se transformer en un espéranto du technico-commercial' (*PR*, 126).

[31]'Ce que toute traduction suggère en son principe, par le passage même qu'elle ferait d'une langue à l'autre, c'est la souveraineté de toutes les langues du monde. Et la traduction pour cette même raison est le signe et l'évidence que nous avons à concevoir dans notre imaginaire cette totalité des langues' (*IPD*, 45).

This statement clearly promotes the idea that each and every language is deserving of full respect, but it also points in another direction. For Glissant, the diverse languages of the world, although distinct, form a totality which is a concomitant phenomenon to a cultural totality comprised of interrelationships between diverse phenomena. As early as his first theoretical work Glissant had hypothesized: 'I conjecture that there will perhaps no longer be any culture without all cultures',[32] a remark which, as it was made in 1956, was striking in its prescience and opened the way for the full-blown embracing of transnational networks in later works, notably from the turn of the 1990s onwards. In the *Entretiens de Baton Rouge*, a series of interviews conducted in 1990–1, Glissant would claim, with reference to writing specifically, that 'a writer today formulates his oeuvre in one language, but in the presence of all the languages of the world'.[33]

As regards translation specifically, Glissant believes that it is only via the translation of each language into other languages that the multiplicity of the phenomena making up the world can be preserved (*IPD*, 45). The translator's role is not a passive one moreover as the act of translating is intimately connected with cultural processes of creolization and with Relation: 'The language of the translator functions like creolization and like Relation in the world, that is to say that language produces unpredictable outcomes.'[34] The work of the translator is a constitutive part of a process of creolization, bringing together different cultural worlds into new configurations. Translation hence brings together totalities which are in and of themselves distinct from each other but which, in their diverse and complex combinations, reaffirm the multiple and interpenetrative nature of the cultures of the world:

> Translation today is practised like a bringing into contact of totalities that one should always be careful to point out are not totalitarian. So, we do not only bridge the gap between one

---

[32]'Je devine peut-être qu'il n'y aura plus de culture sans toutes les cultures' (*SC*, 13–14).
[33]'[u]n écrivain aujourd'hui conjecture son oeuvre dans une langue, mais en présence de toutes les langues du monde' (*EBR*, 84).
[34]'Le langage du traducteur opère comme la créolisation et comme la Relation dans le monde, c'est-à-dire que le langage produit de l'imprévisible' (*IPD*, 45).

language and another but enter into the mysteriousness of a multirelation in which all the languages of the world [...] tread paths together which are all echos. Echoes of multiplicity [...] all translation henceforth enters into the rhizome of imaginary representations.³⁵

Multilingualism is for Glissant one of the modes of the imaginary (*TTM*, 26), and translation is a vital part of the creation of rhizomatic, that is horizontal, transcultural networks. However there is another sense of the term multilingualism that is employed by Glissant and which designates an *awareness* of the existence of languages other than one's own rather than necessarily a direct engagement with such languages, either through knowledge of them or via translation. 'Multilingualism does not presuppose the coexistence of languages or a knowledge of several languages but the presence of the languages of the world when speaking or writing one's own.'³⁶ 'No language can exist outside the chorus of other languages',³⁷ writes Glissant in a similar vein in *Quand les murs tombent. L'Identité nationale hors la loi* (2007). It is in this sense of multilingualism that one writes in the presence of all the languages of the world. The different languages of the world historically have been and remain so interconnected, Glissant believes, that writers today cannot but be aware of the existence of other languages when writing in their own languages. During the colonial era writers were monolingual. The French and British conceived of their languages in absolute terms such that, even in cases where certain writers did know foreign languages, nevertheless when they sat down to write the uses to which they put their own language expressed a monolingual outlook (*EBR*, 137). This can no longer be the case and multilingualism, moreover, is for Glissant central to

---

³⁵'traduire s'exerce aujourd'hui comme une mise en rapport entre des totalités dont il faut toujours prendre soin de dire qu'elles ne seraient pas totalitaires. Alors, nous ne franchissons pas seulement la distance d'une langue à l'autre, nous entrons dans le mystère d'une multirelation où toutes les langues du monde [...] trament ensemble des chemins qui sont autant d'échos. Des échos de la multiplicité. [...] toute traduction entre désormais dans le rhizome des imaginaires' (*CL*, 143).
³⁶'[L]e multilinguisme ne suppose pas la coexistence des langues ni la connaissance de plusieurs langues mais la présence des langues du monde dans la pratique de la sienne' (*IPD*, 41).
³⁷'Aucune langue n'est sans le concert des autres' (*QMT*, 24).

the interconnective, relational mindset which is the predominant one today: 'Multilingualism is for me a force that is constitutive of Relation',[38] Glissant comments.

It will by now be clear that multilingualism is absolutely central to the vision Glissant puts forward for an alternative world today, that is to say a world which includes the network-based and transnational interconnectedness which is commonly associated with globalization and yet which seeks to reroute this tendency in more ethically and politically defensible directions. Relationality on an international scale, or what Glissant terms 'multirelation' ('la multirelation'), cannot be guaranteed by the existence of one dominant world-language which everyone is supposed to speak but rather by 'the widest possible proliferation of languages, and a proliferation of languages in Being'.[39] This multirelation is for Glissant entirely of a piece with and indeed a necessary precondition for his ideal of the 'Whole-World': 'The future of the Whole-World is not linked to that of a single language, be it a dominant language or a language that is artificially created. The future of the Whole-World is linked to the multiplicity of languages',[40] Glissant sums up in an interview of 2005.

---

[38]'Le multilinguisme est bien pour nous une force constitutive de la Relation' (*EBR*, 125).
[39]'une démultiplication totale des langues, et une démultiplication des langues dans l'être' (*EBR*, 89).
[40]'Le devenir du Tout-monde n'est pas lié à celui d'une langue unique, que ce soit une langue dominante ou une langue construite artificiellement. Le devenir du Tout-monde est lié à la multiplicité des langues' (*IL*, 82).

CHAPTER SIX

Glissant's latter-day political commitments

In this chapter we will examine a number of works which appeared in the latter years of Glissant's career and whose content was either unambiguously of a political nature or carried pronounced political implications. I have already indicated that I do not believe that the publication of these works marked some sort of 'return to politics' on Glissant's part. Such an assessment would involve the sort of separation of the political, ethical and cultural spheres which so much of Glissant's work intrinsically challenges. To conclude from certain works prior to 2007 in which politics did not figure prominently that Glissant had cast aside radical political agendas only then suddenly to reawaken to the need for them is implausible. Many of those preceding works do in any case contain content with strong implications for politics, such that even in the lengthy passages in which Glissant's focus is non-political there is no reason to suppose that he has ceased to hold political convictions which are every bit as committed as they had been previously. Any assumption along the lines that theoretical or literary writing, or passages within theoretical or literary works, which say nothing or little about the manifold problems generated by capitalism and/or imperialism are, *by that very omission*, to be admonished, viewed as somehow inadequate or even complicit with the forces of political reaction is properly insupportable. The debate about committed writing has a long history which I will not recount here,[1] but in the twentieth century one of the most important legacies of that debate was the demonstrable failure of attempts to impose the criterion of explicit political commitment on literary writers. This is not to say that committed literature is inevitably less aesthetically successful than non-committed literature. The novels of Paul Nizan,[2] for example, attest to the aesthetic viability of combining radical politics with literary aims. Rather it is to defend the idea that a certain autonomy of the cultural sphere from politics proper or even political thought must be accepted as valid.

There have always been and still are quite significant numbers of writers and philosophers who never thought that what they were producing needed to have any bearing on political issues. Radical thinkers and critics have quite rightly reproached them for what is often a certain naivety about political and social issues. Politics, so these critics justly object, will find its way in through the back door, texts speaking the political even at precisely those moments when they seem furthest removed from it. The case the Sartre of *What Is Literature?* (1947) famously made against the 'Art for Art's Sake' movement in the nineteenth century exemplifies this tendency. On the other hand, there are also numerous examples of literary authors and philosophers whose political sympathies were well to left of the political centre but who did not voice their politics in any direct or explicit way in their works. When philosopher and erstwhile political theorist Maurice Merleau-Ponty resolved to cease expressing his support publically for Marxism from 1950 onwards and to publish on exclusively philosophical topics, it did not mean that he consequently became a political reactionary. Nor did it mean that a later work such as the posthumously published *The Visible and the Invisible* (*Le Visible et L'Invisible* (1964)) could be fairly dismissed as a mere reflection of the ideological values of bourgeois democracy. The relationship between culture and politics,

---

[1] I have discussed this issue at some length in my book *The Early Sartre and Marxism* (Lang, 2008) and in the following article: 'Reaching the Public via Literary Commitment: The Development of a Revolutionary Literature in the Writings of Paul Nizan', in *The Irish Journal of French Studies*, no.10, Special Issue 'Intellectuals and Public Opinion: A Transhistorical Perspective', 2011, 61–76.
[2] *Les Chiens de garde* (Rieder, 1932), *Le Cheval de Troie* (Gallimard, 1935), *La Conspiration* (Gallimard, 1938).

as the debates about committed art and philosophy throughout the twentieth century demonstrated, is much more complex than this.

It is perhaps the complexity of this issue which leads certain radicals, even today, to defend positions which are somewhat reductive of the cultural sphere. Hence Glissant's aestheticism for Bongie, as we have seen, is *by its very nature* evidence that Glissant had become politically disengaged and totally unconcerned with real-world issues. Hallward's stance in his *Absolutely Postcolonial* is more nuanced but is nevertheless not entirely convincing either. Hallward opts in this work rather idiosyncratically on the one hand to disculpate literary writing very largely from political responsibility while on the other accepting to judge theoretical writing, at least in the case of Glissant and other postcolonial theorists, on the basis of whether it is or is not explicitly compatible with a left political agenda. '[W]e must abandon any attempt to prescribe [...] a particular political agenda for art and literature', he argues. '[I]t is time to recognise that the evaluation of literature is essentially indifferent to politics as such.' Writers 'invent new ways of using words' provoking people to think and 'these new ways of using words may have an indirect political effect, but there is no theoretical justification for claiming that they *should* always have such an effect.'[3] This argument is largely unobjectionable in and of itself, but Hallward claims to be advancing it on the basis of a desire for a strict separation of culture and politics. One might wonder however why theoretical writing for Hallward, unlike literary writing, is apparently to be evaluated in line with criteria set by a political agenda. Or at least, *some* theoretical writing is. Glissant's *Poetics of Relation* (1990) is rejected as little short of a betrayal of the harder-nosed positions of *Caribbean Discourse* (1981), but the oeuvre of Deleuze, which Hallward reads as entirely apolitical as we have seen, is treated respectfully, albeit in a somewhat backhanded manner.[4] Glissant's *Poetics of Relation* is not treated so charitably, even though the reason he

---

[3]Hallward, *Absolutely Postcolonial. Writing Between the Singular and the Specific* (Manchester University Press, 2001), preface, xx.
[4]In *Out of This World. Deleuze and the Philosophy of Creation* (2008) Hallward concludes that '[f]ew philosophers have been as inspiring as Deleuze. But those of us who still seek to change our world and to empower its inhabitants will need to look for our inspiration elsewhere' (164).

is to be castigated is allegedly that he came under the influence of Deleuze. By the time of *Poetics of Relation* Glissant is claimed to have abandoned the 'specific' in favour of the 'singular', but this distinction only thinly veils Hallward's real underlying agenda which is to admonish postcolonial theorists, Glissant among them, for moving away from the radical political agendas of years gone by. Judging by Hallward's paradoxical attitude to the philosophy of Deleuze, it is unclear whether he situates theoretical writing in the cultural or the political spheres. On the one hand, he concedes that apolitical philosophy can be accepted as such on condition that one accepts that it is some sort of diversion from real-world concerns. On the other, in the hands of a postcolonial thinker like Glissant theoretical writing is to be evaluated according to criteria set by a radical political agenda.

Hallward hence adopts stances with respect to the cultural sphere that are non-reductive and functionalist by turns. By any measure of judgment, it would have to be conceded that theoretical writing *must* be able to be categorized as being in the sphere of culture rather than that of politics *to some degree at least*. But insofar as theory and philosophy can be thought of as cultural discourses Hallward adopts an ambivalent attitude with respect to the criteria which can be used to assess their value: he employs non-political and politically oriented criteria by turns. The problematic nature of his position is revealing of the immensely complex task which attempts to define culture in relation to politics broadly conceived, and vice versa, attest to. In practice, the separation of politics and culture which Hallward in principle at least defends is difficult to enforce. For instance, one might object that it must surely still be valid to criticize a piece of literary writing on political grounds just as one could see genuine value in philosophical writing in which no discernible political leanings can be identified whatsoever. We would nevertheless perhaps do well to keep in mind Merleau-Ponty's objection to Sartrean 'committed writing' as set out in *The Adventures of the Dialectic* (1955), the nub of which was that Sartre's position, which involved politicising the cultural sphere, ran the risk of compromising in the process both politics *and* literature. 'To recognize literature and politics as distinct activities', Merleau-Ponty concludes, 'is perhaps finally the only way to be as faithful to action as to literature […] Literature and politics are linked with each other and with the event, but in a different way, like two layers of a single symbolic life or history.'[5]

Hallward's position, in principle at least, concords with that of Merleau-Ponty on this issue but in practice he apparently wishes to remain faithful to the post-war Sartrean idea of politically committed thinking, in other words the infusing of politics into the cultural sphere, at least in so far as theoretical writing can be said to fall in this latter category. It is worth remembering in this regard that Sartre's own position with respect to political commitment evolved significantly. The conception of committed writing of the immediate post-Second World War years for which Sartre is best known and which notoriously saw him holding Flaubert and Goncourt responsible for the repression which followed the Paris Commune simply because they did not write anything against it, is not in fact representative of the ways in which Sartre conceived of the relationship between culture and politics throughout his career as a whole. His monumental existential biography of Flaubert, *The Family Idiot* (1970), demonstrates a much more sensitive understanding of the relationship between culture and its socio-politico-historical context. Moreover, by this time, Sartre had 'come to see the imagination of language as the essential medium of inter-subjective communication' and '[i]t is the evolution in his ideas on the nature of linguistic communication which [...] enabled him to commit writers such as Flaubert and Mallarmé.' For the Sartre of *The Family Idiot*, it is via the imaginary that Flaubert demoralizes the bourgeois reader, exposing him or her to the corrosive effect of his ironic nihilism. Yet, this act is a form of commitment because, for Sartre, despair can serve as a basis for subjective existential reawakening.[6] The key point is that for the Sartre of 1970, even Flaubert's and Mallarmé's writing could be associated with the concept of literary commitment. Commitment was hence not to be only linked with explicitly and overtly politicized texts and positions.

---

[5] Maurice Merleau-Ponty, *The Adventures of the Dialectic* (Northwestern University Press, 1973, trans. Joseph Bien), 201.
[6] Christina Howells, *Sartre The Necessity of Freedom* (Cambridge University Press, 1988).

Mémoires des esclavages (2007)

As previously mentioned, in 2005 Glissant was asked by President Chirac to preside over the setting up of a new 'National Centre for the Commemoration of Slavery and its Abolition' ('Centre national consacré à la traite, à l'esclavage et à leurs abolitions') which was to be incorporated into the new Museum of the History of Immigration as of 2007. Setting aside momentarily Glissant's activities as a theorist and writer, it is worth noting at the outset that this appointment is not just an indication of the extent to which Glissant was highly thought of, including in French political circles, but also offers evidence as to Glissant's level of commitment to ensuring that the legacy of slavery was handled with due seriousness in official French channels. The setting up of the Centre followed on from the path-breaking Loi Taubira of 2001 which officially declared slavery a crime against humanity. However, as Glissant points out in *Mémoires des Esclavages*, the Loi Taubira had itself been the outcome of pressure campaigns spanning a number of years. Glissant had signed a declaration along with Chamoiseau and Wole Soyinka in 1998 explicitly stating that slavery had been a crime against humanity, and hence had publically lent his support to the campaign to obtain an acknowledgment through official channels of the evil nature of slavery. *Mémoires des Esclavages*, a work which grew out of Glissant's experiences while presiding over the creation of the Centre, was published in 2007 and contains an 'Avant-propos' written by the then Prime Minister Dominique de Villepin. However if one were to judge the work on the basis of its political content, these facts about the circumstances in which it came about and the type of support it received are evidence that Glissant was at the time occupying a public function with clear political implications. The legacy of slavery has always been a topic of some importance not just for communities in former French colonies like Glissant's home island Martinique and other Caribbean islands but also for immigrant, often formerly colonized, communities living in mainland France. Whatever the explicit political content of the book might be, presiding over the creation of the Centre hence involved shouldering a responsibility with clear social implications and Glissant, having been selected for the task, accepted this role. *Mémoires des esclavages* cannot be separated from this social role which Glissant's involvement in this project implied. In a myriad of ways, moreover, *Mémoires* is testimony to the due seriousness with which Glissant intended to accomplish his mission. Glissant states that he sees the principal aim of the Centre as involving transforming the nature of critical thinking and the corpus of materials for study with respect to transatlantic slavery such that aspects of this phenomenon which have hitherto remained obscure can be revealed more fully (*ME*, 147). Comparative studies are valuable but insufficient for this task and should be augmented by an emphasis on what Glissant calls 'transversalities'. Such transversalities should facilitate finding new orientations for the study of slavery and enable us to come up with new areas where valuable crossovers between one set of phenomena and another are possible (*ME*, 149). The Centre should be headed by a director and assistants to coordinate programmes of research and teaching, and new findings made by researchers connected to the Centre will be published regularly, Glissant points out. This activity will ensure greater visibility for the various areas of enquiry promoted by the Centre, which will accord a significant place to research into modern-day forms of slavery (*ME*, 150). In some cases, enslaved clandestines' lives are at serious risk and the study of their experience should in part be about trying to combat the causes of their enslavement. Also, the consequences of slavery in contemporary institutions, modes of thought, and ideology formation is an angle worthy of greater exploration by researchers at the Centre, Glissant continues (*ME*, 151). As for the Centre's Archives, an essential project will be identifying other such sources of archival material concerned with slavery which have a similar orientation and whose overarching research topics focus on the plurality of places in which slavery existed. The Centre's day to day organized activities should be oriented first and foremost towards young people, employing a range of pedagogical approaches. The principal objective here should be to work together on new areas of research concerning slavery, by way of regular exhibitions and presentations of the work of centres, museums, memorials and institutes devoted to slavery around the world. This work will yield comparative studies and the bringing together of work from different contexts such that they are mutually illuminating (*ME*, 153). The adult visitors to the Centre will be invited to participate in the creation of archives devoted to different historical periods of slavery, namely the transatlantic and the modern periods, and would work with documentation gathered from individual benefactors or families. Members of the Centre will work with such people to help them unearth more information about the documents which are in their possession (*ME*, 154).

Glissant sums up his plans for the Centre thus: 'The national centre has not been conceived of as place for lamenting the past but as a place buzzing with relation [...] with exchanges of knowledge and with solidarities between people, which are what are most lacking in the world, at least in the relations between the sensibilities of different peoples.'[7] It is hence clear that the Centre is to play not only a commemorative role but also is to take an active one in French and francophone societies today, informing and educating but also bringing individuals together. It is, as Glissant sees it, to play a social role in creating links and the relations of solidarity between social groups which are lacking today.

Quand les murs tombent. L'Identité nationale hors la loi? (2007)

As mentioned previously Glissant, in partnership with Chamoiseau, decided to respond in a swiftly penned published text to the French government's creation of a 'Ministère de l'immigration, de l'intégration, de l'identité nationale et du Développement solidaire' (Ministry for Immigration, Integration, National Identity and Collective Development). *Quand les murs tombent* contains in-depth discussion of the concepts of identity and national identity, and of the question of whether repentance is or is not appropriate and necessary to atone for the enslavement and colonization of others, or for genocides. Other than these themes, the text reiterates theoretical preoccupations to be found in many of Glissant's works such as his advocacy of 'worldliness' ('mondialité'), multiplicity and diversity, as well as emphasizing the dangers inherent in US economic and cultural hegemony. In so far as this text was a direct

---

[7]'Le Centre national est conçu non pas comme un lamentarium mais comme un lieu vivant de relation [...] d'echange de connaissances et de solidarités, ce qui manque le plus au monde, au moins dans les rapports des sensibilités des peuples' (*ME*, 157).

ripost to the newly elected French government's creation of a completely new ministry of which Glissant disapproved it is clear that its very publication was a political act. It was meant to challenge a new trend which its authors firmly believed to be reactionary and dangerous for French society, and was hence controversial and provocative, especially in the light of the intellectually and literarily high-profile status of its two authors.

In what follows some of the central arguments in *Quand les murs tombent* will be summarized, all the opinions expressed hence being those of Glissant and Chamoiseau. Identity we are told is not fixed and static. Identity is a way of being in the world and identities exist in relation to each other. Exchanges and exchanging between individuals and cultures hence lie at the core of the concept of identity understood in cultural terms, and any kind of collective or group identity by its very nature can only be open and receptive with respect to other cultural identities. This open character of identity does not mean that identities are not rooted; roots however are not to be understood as exclusive of each other but rather as constantly coming into contact with other roots. 'Changing whilst exchanging means being fulfilled in the highest sense of the term and not losing oneself.'[8] This is the case for individuals as it is also for nations. Consequently, when a given community welcomes foreigners and accepts their differences and opacities it is not the case that it will be denatured. On the contrary, the presence of cultural others is a positive addition to the host community.

The attempt to designate what a specific cultural or national identity is as if it were a determinate, autonomous entity can only lead to a mistakenly inward-looking perspective, Glissant and Chamoiseau argue. Only in instances where the very existence of a nation-state is threatened by outside forces is it necessary and useful to invoke the idea of a determinate national identity to bring people together. The idea advocated by right-wing nationalists that the cultural identity of France is undermined by the presence of immigrants, is hence a gross overstatement. Such nationalists can only think of trying to erect walls between cultures but fundamentally fail to understand the very nature of cultural identity of which relationality is such an important

---

[8]'Changer en échangeant revient à s'enrichir au haut sens du terme et non à se perdre' (*QMT*, 19).

dimension. Putting up walls is also a means of preventing poor or poverty-stricken immigrants from getting on in Western societies. However, such walls do not exist to block the transnational flows of capital, products, technologies and standardizing technologies which characterize globalized capitalism. There is hence, Glissant and Chamoiseau suggest, one rule for the well to do or wealthy and one rule for the poor. In reality, the relationship between the West and the non-Western countries from which its immigrants originate is much more porous than Western nationalists think. Post-colonial communities bear the scars of past suffering at the hands of Western colonizers but they were also westernized along the way. The West developed and emphasized certain values and modes of thinking which had already begun to germinate in other cultures; reason, individuality, human rights, and gender equality were all encouraged in Western first-world nations. But the West did not just appropriate the non-Western world; colonial nations themselves underwent changes as they came into contact with the countries they colonized, partly because, as Glissant and Chamoiseau put it 'brute and blind force expose he who wields it to unassailable weaknesses. In appropriating the world, the West was also appropriated by it'.[9]

Repentance, Glissant and Chamoiseau argue, cannot be demanded but it can be received and understood if proferred. To demand that the descendants of perpetrators of crimes against humanity repent is not necessarily productive and diminishes those making that demand; of greater value is reassessing the histories and legacies of human tragedies such as slavery in order to draw conclusions. However, Glissant's and Chamoiseau's position runs counter to the idea that the proferring of official apologies for past crimes serves no useful purpose at all, as Nicolas Sarkozy was clearly to suggest in the now notorious speech of 2009, authored by Henri Guaino, which he gave in Dakar, Senegal. Moreover, the act of repenting for past crimes against humanity aggrandizes the nation which offers an official apology, and repentance need not be associated with Christian or moralistic repentance, the authors argue.

---

[9] '[l]a force brutale et aveugle livre celui qui l'exerce à d'imparables faiblesses. En prenant le monde, l'Occident s'est aussi fait prendre par lui.' (*QMT*, 14).

'Worldliness' ('mondialité') and an acceptance of diversity offer a way out of the rigidity of fixed and limiting national identities. All forms of collective identity today should be conceived of as open-ended. National identity is not grounded by the presence of a single unitary root. However, this is not synonymous with saying that what Glissant and Chamoiseau call 'identities-relation' are not rooted at all. It is rather that their roots stretch out to meet up and join with other roots coming from elsewhere. Exchange and cooperation become the watchwords in such a situation, countering tendencies towards sectarianism and authoritarianism. Interestingly, true diversity is identified by Glissant and Chamoiseau with the imaginary: 'True diversity is only to be found today in our imaginary representations'.[10] This is an essential feature of Glissant's conception not just of diversity but also of political change and will be discussed later in this chapter.

Manifeste pour les "produits" de haute nécessité (2009)

It should be noted at the outset that this text, like the preceding one, is not attributable to Glissant alone as in fact the names of no less than nine francophone Caribbean authors, academics and activists[11] names appear on the cover. However there is good reason to suppose that Glissant was the text's principal author given both his seniority and stature in relation to the others and also the themes of poetics and utopianism which are interwoven into the argument. What is striking in relation to the two texts just discussed dating from 2007, and all the more so Glissant's earlier output, is the directly political content of quite a number of passages in the *Manifeste*.

The *Manifeste* was written in the context of a social protest movement in the French Caribbean against government policy accused of not doing enough to ensure equal treatment for the

---

[10]'La vraie diversité ne se trouve aujourd'hui que dans les imaginaires' (*QMT*, 15).
[11]Ernest Breleur, Patrick Chamoiseau, Serge Domi, Gérard Delver, Édouard Glissant, Guillaume Pigeard de Gurbert, Olivier Portecop, Olivier Pulvar and Jean-Claude William.

overseas 'départements' (counties). 'Any social advancement can only be brought about via *a political experience* which draws on structuring analyses of what has taken place',[12] that is to say in relation to the political history which preceded that social progress. In this regard the matter of the continuing economic power enjoyed by the 'békés' in the Caribbean territories is mentioned. The problem of the pricing of products, though, 'is inscribed into a logic of a market capitalist system, which has become extended across the whole planet'.[13] Consequently it is necessary for Caribbeans to aim for autonomy at the level of the essential products, that is, food products and energy provision. But this process requires a simultaneous challenging of the market-led world order:

> The other great necessity is then to get involved in radically contesting the capitalism of today [...] and to place the foundations for a non-economically oriented society, in which the idea of development and of continual economic growth would be put to one side in the interests of people's fulfilment; in which employment, salaries, consumption and production would be sites for self-development and the perfecting of human values.[14]

The character of this rejection of market-led capitalism is strongly reminiscent of the early Marxian idea of creative labour, namely the view that labour can and should be a site of creativity as opposed to alienation and exploitation, and that there ought to be the possibility of ensuring that through labouring human fulfilment can be achieved. As such Glissant's position is best

---

[12]'Toute avancée sociale', writes Glissant, 'ne se réalise vraiment que dans *une expérience politique* qui tirerait les leçons structurantes de ce qui s'est passé' (*MPHN*, 4).
[13]'est inscrit dans une logique de système liberal marchand, lequel s'est étendu à l'ensemble de la planète' (*MPHN*, 6).
[14]L'autre très haute nécessite est ensuite de s'inscrire dans une contestation radicale du capitalisme contemporain [...] et de jeter les bases d'une société non économique, ou l'idée de développement à croissance continuelle serait écartée au profit de celle d'épanouissement; ou emploi, salaire, consommation et production seraient des lieux de création de soi et de parachèvement de l'humain (*MHN*, 7).

understood as descending in important respects from the ethical humanist Marxist tradition's reflections on the nature and possibilities of labour.

In this text, the gap between the satisfaction of basic material needs and the aspiration to a greater sense of self-fulfilment is bridged by the idea of poetics. The imaginary is vital to poetics in that it allows us to project forwards to aspirations which go beyond the mundane or prosaic. Glissant is not of course referring to aspirations to greater wealth or material acquisition but to 'self-fulfilment, where the currency is dignity, honour, music, singing, sport, dance, reading, philosophy, spirituality, love and free time put in the service of our great inner desires (in short, poetics).'[15] Indeed poetics is conceived of as being almost by definition anti-capitalistic by Glissant, that is to say the very antithesis of capitalist ethics (a phrase which in France would be considered an oxymoron by many even today). To lead one's life 'constantly elevating oneself in the direction of what is noblest and most demanding, and hence towards what is the most fulfilling [...] amounts to living one's life, and life itself, in the complete fulness of poetics.'[16] Moreover, if we can all thus project beyond the prosaic 'these institutions which are so arrogant and powerful today (banks, transnational companies, hypermarkets, healthcare manufacturers, mobile phone companies...) could not withstand it.'[17] Poetics is the route to collective emancipation from the shackles of subjugation at the hands of market-led capitalism. Moreover, this emancipation would also be of a piece with a more ecologically friendly outlook and approach to policy-making. Such an ideal is utopian, Glissant concedes, but a collectivist political project must feed off such aspirations (*MPHN*, 11).

---

[15]'un epanouissement de soi, la ou la nourriture est de dignité, d'honneur, de musique, de chants, de sports, de danses, de lectures, de philosophie, de spiritualité, d'amour, de temps libre affecté a l'accomplissement du grand désir intime (en clair: le poétique)' (*MPHN*, 3).

[16]'dans l'élévation constante vers le plus noble et le plus exigeant, et donc vers le plus épanouissant [...] revient a vivre sa vie, et la vie, dans toute l'ampleur du poétique' (*MPHN*, 7).

[17]'[r]ien de ces institutions si arrogantes et puissantes aujourd'hui (banques, firmes transnationales, grandes surfaces, entrepreneurs de sante, téléphonie mobile...) ne saurait ni ne pourrait y résister' (*MPHN*, 8).

L'Intraitable beauté du monde. Adresse à Barack Obama (2009)

Written in the period characterized by an atmosphere of post-election euphoria, this text celebrates Obama as a personification of creolization and hence his election to the US Presidency which Glissant sees as a genuinely progressive step forwards for humanity. As diversity is to be found in Obama's own background and incarnated in his person, he is well placed to preside over the multicultural and multiplicitous nature of our complex world, Glissant argues. Glissant goes further, strongly suggesting that Obama's election allows for the political incarnation of a poetics of relation to come about:

> What is a Poetics of Relation *when it is lived out principally in the context of politics? It appears, Sir, that you have indicated this to us. Once that transformations, sharing, exchange and intermixing have taken place in the imaginary sphere, it is first and foremost the will to never try to turn back, [...]the determination to find other solutions be they intellectual or material, [...] the pleasure of looking for and finding other places for meeting and deliberating [...]. What we are claiming is that these reflexes born out of poetics are and constitute a politics.* (italics in Glissant's)[18]

Obama's election to the highest office in US politics and hence to a position of pre-eminence on the world stage is hence presented as the real-world political manifestation of Glissant's own theoretical world view. A poetics of relation hereby finally materializes on the political stage, Glissant suggests, with the arrival of a political

---

[18] *Qu'est-ce qu'une* Poétique de la Relation, *exercée dans le champ du politique principalement? Il semble, monsieur, que vous nous l'ayez indiqué. C'est d'abord, une fois que les mutations, de partage, d'échange, de mélange, se sont opérées dans les imaginaires, la volonté de ne jamais revenir en arrière, [...] la détermination à trouver d'autres solutions, [...] l'obstination à ne rien imposer par la force, soit spirituelle ou intellectuelle ou matérielle, [...] le plaisir de chercher et de trouver d'autres lieux de rencontre et de délibération [...]. Nous disons en effet que ces réflexes nés de la poétique sont et constituent une politique* (IBM, 17–18, italics in Glissant's).

leader who incarnates not just the creolized identity that is the only way out of his own country's age-old identitarian problems but also the processes of creolization which are the only way forward for humanity as a whole the world over. Relation must be lived and engaged with actively, not merely undergone. It is thus, moreover, that Relation can come to incarnate and spread beauty, a concept which Glissant presents as intrinsically inimical to exploitation, crime and domination (*LBM*, 28):

> There is no beauty in solitary recollections of the past, in fundamentalisms, unshared national Histories, ethnic cleansing, the negation of the other, expulsions of emigrants and rigid certainties. No more beauty in racial or identitarian essence. No beauty in industrial capitalism, in the hysteria of finance, or the madness of the markets and of hyperconsumerism. (italics in Glissant's)[19]

Obama's outlook on the world does however come in for gentle criticism in this work in the following respect. Glissant reminds us that Obama believes in the United States' capacity to lead the world '*yet the peoples of the world [...] have no calling other than to enter into Relation, to find fulfilment through sharing and to build their identities through a process of exchange*' (italics in Glissant's)[20] Moreover the financial crisis has confirmed the structural weakness of the United States. The crisis, Glissant argues, was not a distortion but revealed the intrinsic absurdity of the system itself. '*We believe in the future of small countries, of places which escape the implacable logic of globalisations*' (italics in Glissant's).[21]

---

[19]*Il n'y a pas de beauté dans les mémoires solitaires, les fondamentalismes, les Histoires nationales sans partage, les épurations ethniques, la négation de l'autre, les expulsions d'émigrés, la certitude close. Pas plus de beauté dans l'essence raciale ou identitaire. Pas de beauté dans le capitalisme de production, dans les hystéries de la finance, les folies du marché et de l'hyperconsommation* (IBM, 28–29, italics in Glissant's).

[20]'*[o]r les peuples [..] n'ont pas de vocation autre que celle d'entrer en Relation, de s'enrichir au partage et de ne se construire qu'à l'échange*' (IBM, 39, italics in Glissant's)

[21]'*Nous croyons à l'avenir des petits pays, des lieux qui échappent à la logique impitoyable des globalisations*' (IBM, 42–43, italics in Glissant's).

The supposed cultural dominance of the United States in today's world is 'both real and imaginary'[22] because the first victim of that hegemony is the English language itself which has become much more limited and functional, the very opposite of the way languages should exist in the 'Tout-monde'. Moreover, there should be more languages not less, hence resistance to homogenizing trends is important. 'Only diversity can win out over Empires',[23] Glissant observes. The unpredictable character of poetics of Relation is to be protected and celebrated, and *'the Whole-World is sensitive to the warmth of utopias, the oxygen of dreams, to the delightful meanderings of a poetics [...] It puts us in a position to anticipate that new region of the world that we will enter all together via so many different routes.'* (italics in Glissant's)[24] The 'nouvelle region du monde' is in part an ideal of beauty which is at one and the same time that of aesthetics and that of a progressive collective political project.

Returning to themes discussed in *Mémoires des esclavages*, Glissant touches briefly on the question of reparations—reparations rather than repentance—for slavery. 'Those who agree to paying reparations for the damage done by slavery aggrandize themselves', writes Glissant taking a slightly different tack from in the earlier work, 'and those who request or demand them compromise themselves',[25] from which we can infer that Glissant does not believe that financial reparations are a high priority. However, Sub-Saharan Africa is the one exception to this rule. Given the deleterious effect of slavery on African countries the West has a debt to repay to the Africans and this is a commitment which must be honoured. Sub-Saharan Africa must be acknowledged as a top priority among all the high-priority situations needing attention around the world.

---

[22]'à la fois réelle et imaginée' (*IBM*, 42).
[23]'C'est la diversité seule qui triomphe des Empires' (*IBM*, 44).
[24]*[l]e Tout-monde est sensible à la chaleur des utopies, à l'oxygène d'un rêve, aux belles errances d'une poétique [...] Il nous met à même de pressentir cette nouvelle région du monde, ou nous entrerons tous ensemble, par tant de voies et de recours différents*' (*IBM*, 48, italics in Glissant's).
[25]'Celui qui consent des réparations aux dommages escalavagistes se grandit et celui qui en demande ou en réclame se rabaisse' (*IBM*, 29).

Philosophie de la Relation (2009)

Some of the more detailed theoretical issues notably concerning the relationship between politics and theory are discussed in this lengthier work published in the same year as *L'Intraitable beauté du monde*. 'What is [...] a philosophy of Relation?' begins Chapter 14. 'An impossibility were it not a poetics', comes the swift reply.[26] Relation, then, is in its very nature tied up with a prospective vision for how the world could and should be, with what it could and ideally would become. This prospective vision is at once a philosophical outlook and potentially a political project: 'Specific poetics which come about in the world are achievable political projects everywhere'.[27] As we have seen, Glissant believes that in the person of President Barack Obama philosophy finds its appropriate and much needed instantiation in the political sphere.

Glissant argues that Relation is not in and of itself an ethical doctrine. It creates different poetics and brings diverse phenomena together. It is up to us to inscribe our ethical vision in Relation, a point which is explained in a passage the wide-ranging implications of which make it worthy of quotation in full:

> Relation does not posit any of our moral principles, it's up to us to write them into it, via a very individual effort of both mind and our imaginary representations of the world. Moral behaviours are suffering from no longer being set by stories that we have told ourselves, but rather growing directly out of aesthetics (starkly rigid vision or imaginary representation of the world), that we experience, collectively or in a more direct way in chaos most commonly.
>
> Aesthetics [...] points towards an ethics, exhorts us to define moral behaviours, and on the other hand puts us in a position to shape the finalising of artistic creations, marks of and witness to the interlacings of the world.[28]

---

[26] 'Qu'est-ce, [...] une philosophie de la Relation? Un impossible en tant qu'elle ne serait pas une poétique' (*Philosophie de la Relation*, 82).
[27] 'Les poétiques particulières survenues au monde sont des politiques réalisables partout' (*Philosophie de la Relation*, 85).
[28] 'La Relation n'infère aucune de nos morales, c'est tout à nous de les y inscrire, par un effort terriblement autonome de la conscience et de nos imaginaires du monde.

From this last paragraph it becomes clear that when Glissant discusses aesthetics he is designating two different phenomena depending on the given context in which the subject of aesthetics is raised. On the one hand, the term 'aesthetics' takes the meaning of standard usage, that is, it refers to matters pertaining to art of one description or another. Yet there is another sense, which links up with the use of the term 'beauty' which Glissant applies to discussions of political conjunctures in *L'Intraitable beauté du monde*. In this sense, aesthetics are understood as entirely of a piece with an ethical outlook, in other words with a vision for how we wish to lead our lives and for the course which we believe of our world should take now and in the future.

Looking back to the first paragraph, the point is clearly made that in so far as ethics are for Glissant derived from this type of aesthetic vision, in which the utopian ideal of beauty acts as a regulative ideal, they require projection via the imaginary. The aesthetic regulative ideal can only be grasped as goal via an imaginary projection beyond the mundane and prosaic features of our everyday world both in its immediate and local manifestations and in so far as it is instantiated in the political systems which manage the day to day and year to year running of our societies. Politics today in the narrow party political sense is lacking progressive vision, Glissant believes. Reactionary political forces like right-wing nationalist parties have occupied the visionary space in Western political systems today but they only have disreputable political agendas to offer. An ideal of beauty must be retained at all costs if Western societies are to recover and have a chance of reinstating positive, ethically defensible, political agendas. This ideal can only be strived for by way of an imaginary projection beyond our immediate circumstances.

Les conduites morales peinent à ne plus se régler a partir d'histoires que nous nous serions racontées, mais à émaner directement de l'esthétique (vision reche ou imaginaire du monde), que nous vivons, ensemble ou directement, en chaos le plus souvent. L'esthétique [...] augure d'une éthique, pousse à définir les conduites morales, et d'autre part nous met à même de façonner les achèvements de l'art, marqueurs et témoins des entrelacements du monde' (*Philosophie de la Relation*, 73–4).

PART THREE

Envisioning the twenty-first century otherwise: utopianism, anarchism and the critique of neoliberalism

CHAPTER SEVEN

Globalization and its critics: neoliberalism, alter-globalization and contemporary anarchism

This third and final part of the book will initially put the work of Glissant to one side to discuss the context and political conjunctures to which the radical dimensions of his political thinking are inevitably a response. The guiding master narrative of our age, at least since the end of the Cold War, has been globalization and the nature of this phenomenon will be an initial focus of our attention. Since the turn of the 1990s globalization, in essence a set of economic arrangements founded on the transnational circulation of goods, assets and cultural products in the broadest possible sense of that term, has known many vicissitudes. It has met with resistance, both of ethically and politically laudable varieties and of reprehensible types as such that embodied in extreme right-wing nationalist parties and ideologies. At the present time, even a very sympathetic commentator would have difficulty arguing that globalization is in a healthy state.[1] Initiated by and modelled on an economic

---

[1] Zanny Minton Beddoes underlines the difficulty of being optimistic in the current climate in his 'A liberal's lament', in *The World in 2016* (published by *The Economist*), 16–18.

model and on institutional procedures devised in the United States, globalization is suffering from quite a number of deeply rooted systemic problems many of which are inevitably interlinking. The financial crisis of 2007–8 grew out of problems caused by financial deregulation and related speculation on mortgages in the United States but its effects affected the whole financial system worldwide and, concomitantly, had profound knock-on effects for national economies. As countries struggle to keep down expenditure in order to repay huge loans, growth has stagnated, first in the developed Western world but then subsequently in the emerging economies, making the danger of a second financial crisis a real one. At the 2014 annual World Economic Forum conference held in Davos inequality of incomes was singled out as a major cause of economic stagnation and instability.[2] Indeed there is a general consensus that the gap between the extremely rich, the world's top 1 per cent, and the rest, that is, 'the 99 per cent' as they have come to be known, has been consistently widening ever since globalization in the form we know it today came into existence as a set of economic and trading relationships. To these factors can be added the long-term consequences of the arguably peripheral but in reality very economically consequence-laden foreign policy blunders made by the US Republican Party during the Presidency of George W. Bush (2000–8). The illegal, neocolonial occupation of Iraq in particular proved to be immensely costly both in lives and money, while nevertheless enriching big business oligarchs in the United States who obtained the vast majority of the contracts for the reconstruction of a country which the United States' own military had destroyed.[3] What took place was in effect a transfer of funds from ordinary American taxpayers to American big business and arms manufacturers via an artificially created theatre of war in the Middle East. The United States national economy took a big financial hit over many years while its top 1 per cent got richer,

---

[2] This highlighting of inequality in official channels coincided with the slowing of growth in the emerging BRICS economies and the realization that this stagnation was affecting the economic buoyancy of the global economy as a whole. Influential commentator Joseph Stiglitz's *The Price of Inequality* (London: Penguins books, 2013 [2012]) also cast a spotlight on the problem of inequality and its wider consequences.

[3] See Naomi Klein, *The Shock Doctrine: The Rise of Disaster Capitalism* (London: Penguin, 2007).

a fact which contributed significantly to the increasing fragility of the financial system in the build-up to the financial crisis of 2007–8. Moreover, as has become evident since 2013, the disaster that the American occupation of Iraq proved to be sowed the seeds for one of the most pressing challenges the United States and other Western nations faced in many years, namely the challenge posed to the West by a new, more organized and powerful brand of Islamic fundamentalism incarnated notably in ISIS, otherwise known as Daech, an organization initially thought up by principally Iraqi captives incarcerated in a US-run prison south of Baghdad. Radical Islamism of this newer variety has also been developing and proliferating outside of the Middle East such that it has begun to pose a genuine ideological challenge to the West's continuing hopes that its political ideals and values can serve as a model for others. This had not been the case with earlier brands of Islamism, contrary to the view propagated by the Anglo-American political class in the years 2000–2008. 9/11 led to the US government tightening controls on civil liberties at home via measures such as the Patriot Act (2001), and to the development of a burgeoning and immensely profitable homeland security industry, but in reality an Islamist organization such as *Al Quaeda* only ever possessed an extremely limited capacity to challenge Western ideological dominance. Daech, Boko Haram and their affiliates have been turning this situation around in recent years at the level of the ideological and day-to-day political stranglehold in which they have trapped the peoples they rule over, the growing influence they exert on disaffected and in particular young Muslims, and the effectiveness of their terrorist strategies within Western nations. In short, radical Islamism has come to look like a genuine threat in the last few years, and this is partly due to the West's excessively antagonistic stance towards the Muslim world in the years prior to the election of Barack Obama to the US Presidency in 2008.

The immense complexity of the present war situation in Syria is owing to many factors, including disagreement over the future of Bachar Al-Assad's regime and the future of territories held by Daech for some years and now recently liberated. While there has been international consensus about the need to degrade and destroy Daech, the matter of whether Al-Assad must go has remained hotly contested. It looks likely that the resolution of the Syrian conflict, if a lasting one can be found, will involve considerable financial investment if the military campaigns which are already underway are to be conducted over a period of many years. This reality will similarly impact on the still fragile Western economies in the years to come and may hence obstruct full economic recovery or, worse still, contribute to those nations descending once again into financial crisis. If one adds to all of these problems the strictures which environmentally sustainable policies will impose on governments, as outlined and agreed at the COP21 conference held in Paris in December 2015, then it is clear that the way ahead both for the West, but also for the world economy which remains in many ways dependent on its structures, is going to be far from straightforward.

An examination of the social protest movements, known variously as the 'anti-' and 'alter-globalization' movements, which have grown up in response to the deficiencies of globalization will follow an analysis of its origins and characteristics. These movements, which ultimately coalesced under the broad banner of what came to be known as the Global Justice Movement (GJM), subsequently morphing into what Cristina Flesher Fominaya calls 'global waves of protest',[4] has itself proved challenged at a number of levels. Its diverse composition has been a strength, at least when viewed from the standpoint of democratic ideals and allowing for a broad range of opinions, but has not always allowed for the greatest political effectiveness. Chapter 7 will conclude in a more in-depth examination of a certain strand of thought and activism to be found in the GJM which I believe is both of particular intrinsic interest and which links up in important respects with the later thought of Glissant, namely a specific brand of contemporary anarchism known variously as 'post-anarchism' and 'radically non-ideological anarchism'. It is not my intention to drag Glissant's politics posthumously into a camp which he never expressed any explicit affiliation to, but nevertheless to indicate the myriad of ways in which his theoretical positions share common ground with this tendency in order both to sharpen our understanding of the political content of Glissant's later writings and to highlight an approach which offers valuable strategies for countering the hegemonic nature of neoliberal-led globalization. Glissant shared with the

---

[4]Flesher Fominaya, *Social Movements and Globalization* (Basingstoke: Palgrave, 2014), 80.

activists of the GJM a profound sense of disillusionment about the capacity of existing political elites to follow progressive political agendas today and bring about long-term positive developments. In the light of this disillusionment, the anarchist tradition of political thought offers valuable alternative strategies via encouraging alternative, less hierarchical approaches to the political structuring of society. A key area of common ground which would seem to invite a *rapprochement* between Glissant's later thought and 'non-ideological' anarchism is a tendency to uphold utopianism as a viable strategy for thinking about our collective political futures. Chapter 7 will conclude with an analysis of this linkage, paving the way for further reflection about what sort of political strategies can viably be adopted today in the light of the failings of neo-liberal-led globalization.

The latter discussion will be our principal preoccupation in Chapter 8 where we will ultimately address the question of whether an alternative kind of politics genuinely is possible, if so what that might be, and finally in what ways Glissant's thought coheres and can valuably contribute to it. We will argue that in spite of the immense difficulties involved in engaging in meaningful action in the direction of progressive political agendas in the world today, be it because of post-financial crisis budget slashing or owing to the more pressing threat than ever before posed to Western values by Islamic fundamentalism, there nevertheless remains important political terrain which can be claimed by alter-globalization groups. Progressive agendas cannot be allowed to be eternally sidelined by the political class on the grounds that austerity measures are the only way to pay off the debts which nation-states found themselves saddled with in the wake of the financial crisis of 2007–8. Nor can progressive political agendas be shelved entirely on the grounds that the West has a common enemy in the form of Islamic fundamentalism and must quell all internal self-questioning in the name of unity. Unity in the face of an adversary both as intransigent and as intrinsically inhumane as the militaristic Islamic fundamentalist groups which have been proliferating over the last few years will it seems be necessary. Just as it would be unwise for residents in a jointly owned property to fall out over the colour of their residence's outside paintwork when proven problems of land subsidence threaten the very structural integrity of the building in the near future, so it is judicious to pull together in the interests of combating an adversary with whom no dialogue is apparently possible and whose credo is brutality and the oppression of the populations it rules over. However, when viewed in the perspective of recent history, the situation is more complex than this and requires a more subtle response. In light of the fact that since the early 2000s at least the West, and notably the United States, has significantly exacerbated the problem of fundamentalist Islam via the vigorous pursuit of highly dubious policy decisions in the Middle East, in reality the neoliberal-led agenda which has presided over the globalizing economy is in part responsible for the predicament the West is currently facing. Indeed it is partly due to structural problems and badly chosen priorities in our own system that we currently face such staunch opposition from certain quarters. To say this is not to attribute an ounce of credibility to the agendas pushed by the Islamic fundamentalist groups. Rather, it is to assert forcefully that in spite of the pressing need to respond in a unified and firm manner to the threat posed by radical Islamist groups, it remains vital that critical thinking about the failings of our own system continues to take place. Working to rethink our priorities in such a way that a fairer system guaranteeing greater equality and social justice can be aspired to has to be part of a longer-term agenda to defend the post-enlightenment liberal values of tolerance and social justice which we hold dear. The longer term battle cannot be won with 'hard' power but requires the sort of more persuasive, because more convincing, economic, cultural and political agendas which are typically associated with 'soft' power. The West can only regain the respect of others if it can demonstrate that it is making efforts to set an example once again that is worth following. To return to my earlier metaphorical example, while it would not be judicious to fall out over the paintwork in a time of crisis, pointing out that there are serious flaws in the construction of the property's foundations and construction *would* still be worth pursuing because it could help to reduce the chances of other long-term problems further down the line. In short, the *way* that the West resolves the problems emanating from the fallout from the financial crisis on the one hand and the *way* that it and its increasingly influential associates (and notably in recent years Russia) address the present menace that is Islamic fundamentalism on the other is just as important as finding effective strategies for addressing these chronic problems in the short term. It is with this in mind that in

Chapter 8 we will examine what Glissant's thought, in conjunction with certain strands of alter-globalization thinking, has to offer in terms of contributing to alternative agendas and perspectives.

Neoliberal-led globalization: free-market deregulation, neo-imperialism and growing inequality

In this section of the chapter we will set aside discussion of Glissantian thought specifically in the interests of examining the context in which and in response to which it was formulated more broadly. I have indicated in previous chapters that I believe that Glissant's later thought, notably in its political content, offers a progressive counternarrative to the overarching paradigm of our time, namely globalization. It has been argued, and in my view the claim is very convincing, that the thought underpinning oppositional movements of thought or countertendencies often contain many of the ideas commonly associated with the paradigms they oppose.[5] This is the case in Glissant's later oeuvre indeed to the degree that in places the uninitiated reader could be forgiven for thinking that in his discussions rhizomatic identities, creolization, the value of difference, just to name a few of his most central theses, Glissant is offering an apology for globalization in its present form rather than a critical reading of it. It is clear however that this is not the case in reality and it is hence of great value to our present analysis to assess what the leading characteristics of globalization are, why, how and where it came into being as the dominant economico-socio-cultural paradigm of our time, and what prospects it would appear to offer for the future.

Globalization in its present-day form cannot be properly understood if its origins are not traced to the reconstruction of national economies and the accompanying construction of a new agenda for international relations in the post-Second World War years. With much of Europe in ruins and in need of a considerable

---

[5]S. A. Hamed Hosseini, *Alternative Globalizations. An Integrative Approach to Studying Dissident Knowledge in the Global Justice Movement* (Oxon: Routledge, 2010), 206.

amount of financial assistance, the United States emerging economically strong from the Second World War, and the seeds of a new Cold War germinating between the United States and the Soviet Union, a number of essential measures reconfirming the United States as the leading Western power can be identified. The post-war years witnessed the creation of the United Nations and the Bretton Woods institutions: the World Bank and International Monetary Fund. Starting in 1948, the Marshall Plan provided the financial backing for the reconstruction of Western Europe. The post-war years would prove to be the beginning of a new period of economic prosperity in the West which was to extend with a good degree of consistency through until the 1970s. The United States's size and the fact that its mainland had been spared from attack during the Second World War, among other factors, soon confirmed it as the natural leader of the West, a concept which had always been somewhat imprecise but which was given greater conceptual clarity in the second half of the twentieth century by dint of the presence of only one serious geo-political rival, the USSR, whose geographical location was eastern by comparison.

Whatever the relative merits and drawbacks of American leadership and unmatched supremacy in relation to other Western nations from the end of the Second World War onwards, there can be little doubt that the United States's greater influence both economically and in the sphere of international relations ensured that the principal institutional frameworks and economic arrangements in what in the West was dubbed the 'Free World' were instigated and set in accordance with American values, practices and ideological priorities. Free-market economics, commercial competitiveness and consumerism were presented not only as a necessary accompaniment to political liberalism but as its twentieth-century incarnation, the 'laissez faire' free-market system being thought of as by and of its very nature the incarnation of democratic principles when contrasted with the Soviet system's command economy and restrictions on individual liberties. By the mid 1970s, however, the situation had changed significantly. The Cold War, embellished by the nuclear arms and space races, was still ongoing but the Eastern block was suffering significant structural problems which would ultimately lead to its own collapse over a decade later and the West was undergoing a major economic downturn in the wake of the oil crisis of 1973.

The period which followed is characterized by victories for the advocates of right-wing agendas in the United States and the United Kingdom. The Reaganite Republican Presidency, with Thatcher's Conservative government following suit, vigorously pursued a free-market agenda involving giving free reign to the private sector and cutting back state expenditure. During the same period, and in conjunction with these policy orientations, the initially Keynesian agenda of the financial branches of the Bretton Woods institutions, the World Bank and the IMF, were being confidently revamped in the image of a pronounced brand of free-market economics. In her book *The Shock Doctrine: The Rise of Disaster Capitalism* (2007), Naomi Klein highlights the considerable influence on US economic policy both at home and abroad which the mindset of the Chicago School of Economics and its leading light Milton Friedman exerted. Friedman argued that the New Deal and Keynesianism had got the United States off on the wrong track. His influential work *Capitalism and Freedom* (1962) provided a blueprint for free market-led policymaking which ultimately was not only substantially to inform the neoliberal agenda but also the neoconservative movement which would ultimately achieve full political ascendency during the Presidency of George W. Bush (2000–8). Whereas Keynesianism and social democracy had involved a compromise between the state, business and labour, Friedman advocated private ownership and greater autonomy from state legislation for big business. As early as the 1970s, the policies of the IMF and the World Bank had been the object of staunch criticism from anti-capitalist campaigners, but by the 1980s they were increasingly tightly harnessed to the right-wing Republican agenda.[6] These Bretton Woods institutions had been set up originally to ensure the maintaining of economic stability and growth internationally, but increasingly promoted the extension of the US Republican free-market agenda of deregulation to the international context. 'The colonization of the World Bank and the IMF by the Chicago School was a largely unspoken process', observes Klein, 'but it became official in 1989 when John Williamson unveiled what he called 'the Washington

---

[6] Klein, *The Shock Doctrine*, 163. The superior size of the US economy gave it more influence over IMF and World Bank policy than any other nation and its agendas tracked those of the US government quite closely.

Consensus'. This was a list of economic policies that he said both institutions considered the bare minimum for economic health' and these policies included an insistence that all state-run enterprises should be privatized, and that barriers stopping foreign firms from trading should be removed. All in all, the Washington Consensus was a blueprint for setting as an international standard 'Friedman's neoliberal triumvirate of privatization, deregulation/free trade and drastic cuts to government spending.'[7] 'With the demise of the bipolar order' following the end of the Cold War 'the emergent "Washington Consensus" could be spread to every corner of the globe, unrivalled and unimpeded as never before.'[8]

Prior to this, recommendations were handed out by the World Bank and IMF as an accompaniment to the allocation of financial loans transformed, via the introduction of 'structural adjustment' programs from 1983 onwards, into an insistence on compliance with free-market ideology. 'For the next two decades, every country that came to the fund for a major loan was informed that it needed to revamp its economy from top to bottom.'[9] Free-market economics was becoming the leading paradigm not just for the economies run by right-wing parties in anglophone countries but for all national economies henceforth which needed help from international institutions. Globalization as we know it today was, in its nascent form, being both nurtured and shaped by neoliberalism. Marshall McLuhan's now well-known phrase 'the global village'[10] was becoming more and more true, and the mode of economic operation of that village was being determined to an ever greater degree by US economic policy.

References to the United States as enjoying neoimperial status throughout the 1990s and much of the 2000s are fairly commonplace, and this preeminent status was resoundingly confirmed by the collapse of the USSR from 1989 onwards. It is beyond the scope of this book to discuss the manifold factors which

---

[7]Ibid., 163.
[8]Ruth Reitan, *Global Activism* (Oxon: Routledge, 2007), 2.
[9]Ibid., 144.
[10]Marshall McLuhan famously made a case for the world being a global village in works such as *The Gutenberg Galaxy: The Making of Typographic Man* (University of Toronto Press, 1962) and *Understanding Media: The Extensions of Man* (New York: McGraw Hill, 1964).

led to this collapse. The fact is though that with the disintegration of the United States' main ideological and military rival, the United States emerged as the unchallenged world superpower and, in comparison to the 1970s and even the early 1980s, the whole ideological terrain of world economic policy shifted to the right. The traditional right/left political divide became increasingly blurred, especially in anglophone countries where the political left, where it still genuinely existed, was increasingly forced to choose between adopting right-wing policies or being castigated by the right-wing largely monopoly-owned press to the point that electoral failure was an inevitability. Tony Blair's successful courting of Rupert Murdoch from 1995 onwards is well known, and it is noteworthy that many years after leaving office herself Margaret Thatcher, in a rare moment of insight, was to observe very accurately that the finest achievement of her political career was Tony Blair and New Labour.[11] When a political seismic shift takes place that is so great that the opposing party ends up adopting the policies of the party in office then it is clear that the whole terrain on which the political process is taking place has shifted.

El-Ojelli and Hayden, in their *Critical Theories of Globalization* (2006), state that they favour a 'broad and open conceptualization of globalization', citing in particular Held and McGrew's (2002) focus on 'growing world connectedness'[12] and Michael Mann's focus on globalization's extension of social relations across the globe.[13] Setting aside the fact that the vital dimension of economic *rapports de force* is overlooked in both of these definitions, there is obvious validity to such characterizations of globalization and the transnational dimension which they draw attention to was a parallel development to the emergence of the socio-cultural phenomenon known as postmodernism which pervaded Western societies notably in the 1980s and 1990s. Perry Anderson in *The Origins of Postmodernity* (1999) points out that it was from the 1970s that the term 'postmodern' came into usage in the field of the arts where it was used to designate a break from the tenets of modernism. Its

---

[11]http://conservativehome.blogs.com/centreright/2008/04/making-history.html Thatcher made this remark in 2002.
[12]Chamsy El-Ojelli and Patrick Hayden, *Critical Theories of globalization* (Basingstoke: Palgrave Macmillan, 2006) 13. Get ref from El-Ojelli&H.
[13]Ibid., 13. Ditto

influence subsequently extended to fields of academic theory[14] and ultimately spread such that it became an expression of overarching cultural sensibility in advanced capitalist society. Postmodernism expressed a scepticism of grand historical narratives in favour of smaller, non-hierarchized narratives, a preference for surfaces in relation to depth, a questioning of enlightenment-derived notions of progress and elitist distinctions between 'high' and 'low' culture, and criticism of the modern tendency to assume that meaning and identity are stable. Difference as opposed to universals was vaunted, as were otherness and contingency in contrast to sameness and cohesion.

Whatever the intrinsic merits and drawbacks of postmodernism, it is not difficult to see how this attitude of mind could have been perceived as an expression of Western complacency when viewed from the perspective of non-Western societies, many of which were struggling or worse economically in the 1980s and 1990s. One doesn't have to look as far as war-torn or poverty-stricken, even famine-stricken, nations to see that the kind of modish, resolutely middle-class brand of non-conformism to which the postmodern mindset corresponded notably in the United States was not a lifestyle that was likely to have universal appeal around the globe. And yet even postmodernism, which in some ways could be viewed as an internal critique of Western neoliberal hegemonic tendencies, was going global along with a raft of other Western cultural and institutional practices as well as ideological agendas. This anti-universalist anti-establishmentarianism was itself posing as a would-be new universal as was the vaunting of difference which lay at the heart of the US 'melting pot' model of multiculturalism.

It was from roughly the turn of the 1990s that the term 'globalization' came into common parlance to describe this fundamentally neoliberal-directed configuration of international trading relationships. Moreover, with the USSR out of the way, the Republican Presidency of George H.W. Bush did not take long to vaunt the desirability of a New World Order, that is to say a world whose geopolitical direction was not only 'new' but was also to be directed in a largely unilateral and unipolar manner by the New

---

[14]Lyotard, *The Postmodern Condition* (1979), Baudrillard, *Simulacra and Simulation* (1981), Frederic Jameson, *Postmodernism, or the Cultural Logic of Late Capitalism* (Durham, NC: Duke University Press. 1991).

World, that is, North America. The war the United States waged to liberate Kuwait from the US's former ally Saddam Hussein in 1991 offered it an opportunity to flex its muscles as a self-appointed world policeman, a logic which it would try to push further, although ultimately much less successfully, a little over a decade later at the time of its invasion and occupation of Iraq. On this latter occasion, the limits of the real capabilities of the United States when it came to forcing other nations to bend not just to its military might but also to its political will became very apparent.

The latter years of the twentieth century saw the ascension of the neoconservative right to a position of preponderant influence within the Republican Party. Democratic President Bill Clinton was subjected to one costly smear campaign after another as the Republicans were planning a return to the White House which would ultimately transpire in suspicious circumstances in 2000 when the outcome of the election ultimately was decided in the State of Florida where Republican candidate George W. Bush's brother Jeb Bush was Governor. George W. Bush won by a margin of only 537 votes but accusations of serious irregularities in the voting process cast a long shadow of doubt over the legitimacy of this victory. Some 36,000 newly registered voters mainly from ethnic minorities and low-income communities had been refused the right to vote because their names had never been added to the voter rolls by Florida's secretary of state Kathleen Harris who was presiding over the state's election process while coincidentally being herself an active member of the Bush Jr. state-wide campaign committee.

The apex of neoconservative thinking in the late 1990s was the Republican foreign affairs think tank Project for the New American Century (PNAC), the whose members included Dick Cheney, Donald Rumsfeld, Jeb Bush, Paul Wolfowitz, Richard Perle and Francis Fukuyama.[15] This group advocated maintaining a strong military capacity, pursuing a bold foreign policy which allowed for the promotion of American interests abroad, and promoting the idea that the United States had global responsibilities and should naturally be the world's leading nation. In the latter regard, the long-term strategy of the PNAC group was to turn the post-Cold

---

[15]Fukuyama was famously to expand the eminently neoliberal-sympathetic thesis that the 'end of history' had now been reached. With the United States having become the unchallenged world leader no further mutations would be necessary or desired.

War unipolar moment into a unipolar era: the first century of the new millennium was to be an American century in the sense that the adoption of American values would be encouraged throughout the world. Achieving greater homogeneity worldwide was thought to make dealing with problems of nuclear proliferation and 'rogue' states easier. However, bringing about such a state of affairs required trying to anticipate where threats to American interests might materialize, be they in the form of rogue states or potential challengers for the title of world leader, and taking steps to counter those threats before they became unmanageable. North Korea and in particular Iraq were from the outset considered by PNAC members to be in need of 'regime change' and of potentially requiring pre-emptive action. Unlike his brother Jeb, George W. Bush was not a member of the PNAC group but the preeminent roles played by Cheney and Rumsfeld in his administration meant that government policy closely tracked the objectives and priorities which the neoconservative PNAC members had set out. Upon his taking up the US Presidency, the toppling of Saddam Hussein was from the outset an objective of George W. Bush's administration.

The event that came to be known simply as 9/11 offered Bush and his associates the pretext they needed to invade and occupy Iraq in 2003. This pretext was in reality a very unconvincing one as it quickly became clear first of all that the Iraqis had not been behind 9/11 at all and secondly that Iraq did not possess the nuclear capability which the Americans and British governments claimed they did. The majority of the international community at the United Nations was consequently opposed to the invasion. The Bush administration however pressed ahead, naively believing as they claimed to that the American troops would be welcomed by the Iraqis as liberators, and hoping that other Muslim states in the Middle East would follow suit. Neither of these hopes were borne out in the facts and the United States found itself quagmired in a protracted occupation of Iraq (2003–2011) which was to be costly both in American soldiers' lives and American taxpayers' money, not to mention (and they rarely were in official channels) Iraqi civilian and military lives.

During this period the economically emerging nations known as the BRIC (Brazil, Russia, India, China, and from 2010 BRICS following the inclusion of South Africa) were continuing to grow in strength, the most meteoric of which, China, had been growing at an unprecedented rate since the 1980s. All the indicators were pointing to significant shifts in the global economic balance of power. In a work published as relatively early as 2002, historian Emmanuel Todd was arguing that '[t]here is no reason to denounce or become hysterical about the emergence of an American empire that in reality, and only one decade after the breakup of the Soviet Union, is going through its own disintegration.'[16] Seen in this light, American neo-imperialism in the Middle East, contrary to all appearances, was not an instance of a superpower offering a demonstration of its supremacy, but conversely the rather desperate attempt of a hegemon on the wane to find a new oasis at which to drink in order to halt the process of inevitable dehydration and demise; the oasis in question provided crude oil, a natural resource which the US economy required in huge quantities at the time. The American economic decline thesis which I am supporting has been advanced by numerous commentators. Even as sympathetic a commentator to US hegemony as Niall Ferguson conceded in a work of 2004 on the topic that US imperialism was looking very fragile: '[T]he global power of the United States today – impressive though it is to behold – rests on much weaker foundations than is commonly supposed.' The United States, continued Ferguson, is an empire but the Americans do not know how to manage it properly. 'Consequently, and quite regrettably', concludes Ferguson, 'it is quite conceivable that their empire could unravel as swiftly as the equally "anti-imperial" empire that was the Soviet Union.'[17] Dambisa Moyo, in *How the West Was Lost* (2011), offers:

> three main reasons why the West has seen its substantial advantage erode; an erosion whose pace is accelerating with every passing year.
> First, through blinkered political and military choices, the West (principally the US) has successfully managed to alienate the very emerging countries with whom it now competes. [. . .]
> Second is what Thomas Friedman describes as the 'flatness of the world'—the lowering of transport, communication and

---

[16]Emmanuel Todd, *After the Empire: The Breakdown of the American Order* (London: Constable and Robinson, 2004 [2002]) 21.
[17]Niall Ferguson, *Colossus. The Rise and Fall of the American Empire* (London: Penguin, 2004).

manufacturing costs, which has made the transfer of technology easier. [...] [Technological and governance] advantages once held in Western monopoly have, over time, dissipated, and will certainly continue to do so.

[Third], over the last fifty years, the most advanced and advantaged countries of the world have squandered their once impregnable position through a sustained catalogue of fundamentally flawed economic policies.

It is these decisions that, along the way, have resulted in an economic and geopolitical see-saw, which is now poised to tip in favour of the emerging world.[18]

Moyo's conviction that the US-led West will be overtaken by the emerging economies and notably China is a long-term prediction based not just on the present situation but on an analysis of the leading economic trends of recent history, and the last few decades in particular. These indicators, as the oligarchs comprising the American political and business elites have known for some time, have been pointing in the direction of the United States being on a medium- to long-term fall from grace since at least the early 2000s and the seeds of decline had been sown much earlier.

Peripheral but ultimately central to the United States' fall from grace were the plans of the National Security Agency (NSA), initially hatched in the early 2000s, to monitor and stock the entire world's internet traffic, a fact which came to light when disaffected NSA agent Edward Snowden disclosed thousands of classified NSA documents to the non-coopted media in May 2013. What initially looked like a sideshow to the more profit-oriented projects of the homeland security industry soon became an integral part of the narrative of US neo-imperialism. Revelations to the effect that not only the communications of ordinary citizens were being monitored but also those of many heads of state around the world confirmed that the United States was not prepared to let go of its role as self-appointed world policeman without a struggle. But such efforts were not simply proof of the US's technological supremacy; they were yet another symptom of a hegemon on the wane desperately trying to claw back some purchase on the situation. It is tyrannies and totalitarian

---

[18]Dambisa Moyo, *How the West Was Lost. Fifty Years of Economic Folly – And the Stark Choices Ahead* (London: Penguin, 2012 [2011]), Preface, ix.

states which try to monitor citizens' every communication, not democracies. Upon the fall of Colonel Gadhafi in 2011, which had been orchestrated by the West not simply to protect the Libyan people but just as importantly 'to thwart Gaddafi's attempt to create a gold-backed African currency to compete with the Western central banking monopoly',[19] the Western media expressed its customary outrage at the discovery that Gadhafi had instigated a system for intercepting his citizens' every email communication. Less than two years later we discovered that the world's leading nation and self-proclaimed incarnation of democracy and political liberty was doing the same but on a considerably more ambitious scale.

Moyo published the words cited above in 2011, by which time the economically cataclysmic event that was the financial crisis of 2007–8 had taken place. The advent of this financial disaster and its medium-term aftermath reconfirms the thesis presciently advanced by Todd at a time – the early 2000s – when to all outward appearances US hegemony had looked unassailable: the American empire was suffering serious structural problems and was in decline. It is common knowledge today that the financial crisis of 2007–8 was very largely created in the United States due to the proliferation of a high number of toxic financial products, and notably subprime mortgages, in the financial system. Finance capitalism and its derivatives had gone completely awry. The logic of financial deregulation in the interests of ensuring ever larger profits for the elites had been pushed to its extreme limit and the system reached breaking point. When the contagion spread beyond the United States it soon became apparent that there was a serious risk of the whole financial system on an international scale imploding. Falling back on a strategy that goes all the way back to the Rothschilds in the late eighteenth century, central banks used large injections of public money which would have to be paid off by taxpayers in order to bolster up a now manifestly corrupt banking system comprised of banks which were judged 'too big to fail', meaning that if they did go bankrupt the whole system would collapse. As has happened so often in Western history, taxpayers were being used to maintain the elites in the opulence to which they were accustomed: it soon became apparent that significant sums

---

[19]https://www.intellihub.com/declassified-emails-reveal-nato-killed-gaddafi-stop-libyan-creation-gold-backed-currency/.

of the money were still being channelled into financial bonuses for bankers as they always had been.

In the aftermath of the financial crisis the age-old system of debt repayment, a mainstay of the financial system since its inception, became one of the overarching master narratives of our era in the West. Nation-states had to borrow large sums of money in order to stay afloat and have consequently been trapped in a spiral of debt repayment, the reality of which only reconfirmed the fragility of the West as global leader in relation to the emerging economies. Perhaps paradoxically, in view of the fact that they were the architects of the crisis, the US and UK economies ultimately rebounded faster economically than did the economies of the eurozone. Eurozone countries such as Spain, Ireland and in particular Greece suffered painful economic consequences. In fact Germany was the only eurozone state which can be said to have maintained economic buoyancy and equilibrium, a fact which led to irritability on the part of some German citizens with respect to the other European nation-states which they believed they were obliged to keep bailing out at their own cost. In 2011, there was a real fear that the euro currency would collapse entirely, a fear which is still rekindled periodically, the most recent example being the case of Greece in 2015. Keeping Greece in the union involved yet more compromises from other states in the eurozone, but forcing Greece out would have generated even deeper-seated problems.

Periods of protracted economic downturn commonly have political knock-on effects. This was certainly the case following the Wall Street Crash of 1929 which led to the Great Depression, a recession which even Milton Friedman acknowledged was essentially generated by the US central bank, the Federal Reserve.[20] It was the spread of the Depression to Europe which proved to be the decisive factor in the rise of far-right nationalism and most notably Nazism in Germany in the 1930s. Since the financial crisis of 2007–8 we have similarly witnessed the rise of extreme right-wing groups and parties. In Britain and France for example, Ukip and the National Front commonly place the blame with the European Union as well as with the usual scapegoats, namely foreign immigrant communities. A nationalist reflex movement gained strength as a response to the

---

[20] Milton Friedman and A. Schwartz, *A Monetary History of the United States 1867–1960* (Princeton: Princeton University Press, 1963).

perception that transnational political structures were undermining national sovereignty and autonomous decision-making about economic as well as political matters. What radically separates these critics of globalization from their left-wing counterparts is their focus on political and identitarian as opposed to economic issues. Whereas the French National Front directs its spleen at supranational policy-making and cultural others the Alter-Globalization Movement emphasizes the ways in which neoliberal-led globalization is first and foremost a set of economic arrangements which Western elites, and notably Anglo-American Western elites, have put in place in line with ideological and cultural values aimed at extending their own sphere of influence to the world as a whole.

Political decision-making, sociologist and theorist Alain Touraine argued nearly twenty years ago, had become increasingly technocratic, that is to say conducted by politicians either with no real room for manoeuvre, such were the pressures exerted on them either coming from beyond their own national boundaries or, more recently, owing to the budget restrictions imposed by national debt repayments. Or, as Touraine argued, decisions were being determined by teams of experts in one area of policy or another who were not democratically elected and whose expertise did not equate with having an overarching political vision.[21] As I have argued, and I will continue to explore this thesis in the remainder of this book, Glissant is similarly dismayed at the lack of any genuinely progressive political agenda. As Todd puts it, it seems that 'the idea of "progress" must be filed away along with other expired concepts'.[22] The absence of progress in the post-enlightenment sense which also informed political liberalism is, moreover, the central reason why Glissant upholds utopianism as a regulative ideal; utopianism offers a vision for the future that is otherwise lacking, one which may be unattainable but which can at least orient our moral compass. As the situation stands at present, the feeling shared by more and more citizens of nation-states in the globalized economy is, as Zygmunt Bauman puts it, that of being on a pilotless plane;[23] the moving

---

[21] Alain Touraine, *Pourrons-nous vivre ensemble? Egaux et différents* (Fayard, 1997), 61.
[22] Todd, *After the Empire*, 25.
[23] Zygmunt Bauman, *Globalization: The Human Consequences* (Cambridge: Polity, 1999).

landscape that is neoliberal-led globalization appears very much to them to be lacking in clear orientation and direction. Among other difficulties, this throws up problems of accountability, or more precisely a perceived lack thereof, as government leaders, sometimes justifiably and sometimes not, shoulder off the blame for one biting austerity measure or another onto circumstantial factors beyond their control. Such a decline in genuine accountability is also one of the factors which fuels support for extreme political groups as citizens feel impelled to protest via the ballot box about the fact that manifesto promises made some years earlier have not been kept.

If our media pundits are to be believed, the worst of the financial crisis is far behind us. The way the US and UK economies have rebounded in particular would on the face of it vindicate the choices of our centre-right and right-wing policy-makers, at least to some degree. The financial system which we endorse and live by may degenerate into crisis periodically but it can also be restored to its previous buoyancy, so one might conclude; capitalism is not perfect but it fundamentally works. There are reasons for suspecting that such an optimistic reading of our present situation is doubtful, especially when it is viewed in longer-term and historical perspectives. There can be little doubt that the system was severely shaken in 2007–8 and that it continues to harbour many quite fundamental structural problems. The recovery even in the United States and the United Kingdom is more fragile than it appears and has been thus far achieved in part at the cost of deep cuts to social expenditure. Austerity has precluded the possibility of growth notably for much of Europe and in the UK has merely widened an already considerable disparity between the wealthier and the poorer sections of society. The undermining of public services and the increasing disintegration of the social fabric in the UK is no small price to pay and can hardly be called an instance of successful policy-making. As we have been seeing with the successes in recent years of right-wing nationalist groups like Ukip, such policies do not come without a heavy price tag attached to them.

There are other arguably even more significant indicators that the situation the global economy finds itself in today is a matter for serious concern. While the halt in significant economic growth at home has proven to be a containable problem, the economic slowdown of the emerging economies known as the BRICS from 2010, and then more significantly from 2013 onwards has raised the spectre of another major financial crisis. It was following the slowdown of the BRICS that those in the upper echelons of the Western-run international financial institutions such as the IMF and the World Bank began to take full cognizance of the fact that growing economic inequality – a state of affairs which has been a key feature of contemporary globalization since its very inception – was a fundamental problem impeding growth and, by the same token, obstructing the possibility of the global economy being restored to a healthier condition. Since 2011 inequality has been a central item on the agenda at the World Economic Forum held annually at Davos and former World Bank Chief Economist turned alter-globalization campaigner Joseph Stiglitz examined the problem in detail in *The Price of Inequality* (2012). It is perhaps significant that thinking about tackling inequality should have become a priority only when it became clear that ever-increasing disparities in wealth were bringing growth worldwide to a standstill such that even the wealthiest top 1 per cent were facing serious profit losses.

The challenges which lie ahead are numerous and have the potential to throw up significant difficulties which could adversely affect the global economy, and they will have to be played out in the context of two major overarching longer-term issues, namely the campaign against Islamist fundamentalism on the one hand and the increasingly acknowledged necessity to take steps to reduce global warming. The COP21 conference held in December 2015 in Paris constituted an important step in the direction of international cooperation on an issue which has been rapidly becoming the grand narrative of our era, as is suggested by the title of Naomi Klein's book *This Changes Everything: Capitalism vs. the Climate* (2014) on the topic. With the world being faced with the ever-pressing problem of sizeable demographic increases, on top of the continuing fragility of the global economy, the challenges posed by the necessity of promoting environmentally friendly policies seem only the greater.

Social protest movements vs neoliberalism and neoliberal-led globalization

In this section the social protest movements which have opposed neo-liberal capitalism and more recently globalization will be examined as a prelude to assessing what sort of strands of alter-globalization thinking Glissant's later thought links up with. The present account, like of the previous section, will work on the assumption, first, that on balance neoliberal-led globalization has been generative of greater rather than less inequality around the world. This is not to say of course that it has had no positive effects. We are not claiming that there are no instances in which the kinds of developments which its advocates equate with progress (the dissemination of new technologies, higher levels of connectivity via the internet, or financial loans aimed at building market economies and so on) can indeed be considered to be positive developments. It is also the case that the last twenty years have witnessed, within the structures of the globalized configuration, the rise of emerging economies such as the BRICS, China's economic ascent in particular having been quite exceptional. To argue that examples of growth of this sort are in and of themselves regrettable would be disingenuous. Nor would it be reasonable to measure up neoliberal-led globalization to the yardstick of absolute perfection; no political or economic system is beyond reproach. Our conviction is nevertheless that globalization has generated more unfairness overall than it need have done and that it ought to be a concern of those citizens in countries which can impact on the course Western and global economics take henceforth to try to redirect it.

The roots of contemporary protest movements lie in the 'new social movements' (NSMs) of the 1960s and 1970s: the student movement, civil rights campaigning, as well as feminist and environmentalist movements. These became influential in the latter years of the 1960s and remained such throughout the 1970s but began to decline in the 1980s. As S. Hamed Hosseini puts it, '[t]he so-called anti-globalization movement has not been created *ex nihilo*. Rather [...] it has ideological-experiential roots in both the so-called new Left middle class (such as green, identity-based, welfare and cultural movements [...])' and 'old Left movements (socialism, unionism, and anarchism)'.[24] As far as neoliberalism's dominant influence on Western economics is concerned, there had been protests against the policies of the IMF and the World Bank stretching back to the 1970s, but it was not until the early 1990s that diverse groups and networks began to coalesce into what was come to be known a few

---

[24]Hamed Hosseini, *Alternative Globalizations*.

years later as the 'anti-globalization movement' (AGM). It was also labelled diversely as the 'movement of movements' and the 'alter-globalization movement' and was later to take the title of Global Justice Movement (GJM). A landmark event in the following period was the Zapatista uprising of 1994 in Mexico where a new brand of anti-capitalist protesting surfaced. The uprising began on 1st January 1994, the day that the North American Free Trade Agreement (NAFTA) came into force. Hundreds of thousands of people rose up against the Mexican state and organized themselves into libertarian-inspired federated communes. This anarchist-inspired act of political autonomousness inevitably met with repression from the Mexican state but it did demonstrate that it was possible to set up types of socio-political organization that constituted a valid alternative to the existing structures that were subordinated to prerogatives set by neoliberal capitalism.

A notable development was the creation of ATTAC (Association for the Tobin Tax for the Aid of Citizens) in 1998 by the left-wing French newspaper *Le Monde Diplomatique*. Nearly a decade later ATTAC was to have become an umbrella organization bringing together numerous groups that were spread across European Union countries and was to have 80,000 members worldwide. However the most significant turning point moment in terms of galvanizing the AGM was the 'battle of Seattle' of 1999 when protesters converged on Seattle at the time of the World Trade Organization's Ministerial Conference. The negotiations were overshadowed by massive street protests outside the hotels and the Washington State Convention and Trade Center with, at the lowest estimate, 40,000 protestors involved. Seattle set a new precedent in that henceforth the big meetings of the AGM would take place as counterparts to major international conferences. The annual meeting of the World Economic Forum in particular would from 2001 onwards have an alter-globalization counterpart in the form of the World Social Forum (WSF). The WEF's meetings have been taking place every year in Davos, Switzerland, since the 1970s. Since 2001 the WSF has similarly met every year although at diverse locations. However, the WSF tends to be scheduled for January, which is the same month as the WEF. This parallel scheduling as well as the proximity of the name World Social Forum to World Economic Forum sends out a clear signal however: that the WSF is the progressive and ethically friendly counterpart to the WEF.

The first meeting of the World Social Forum took place in January 2001 in Porto Alegre, Brazil. This location was to remain the venue in 2002 and 2003, but in 2004 Mumbai was chosen, in 2005 it was Porto Alegre again to be followed in 2006 by three venues in tandem, namely Caracas (Venezuela), Bamako (Mali) and Karachi (Pakistan). To give some idea of scale, the 2002 WSF had 60,000 attendees and over 12,000 delegates representing 123 countries. The WSF includes a wide range of groups and hence quite contrasting perspectives: ATTAC, Focus on the Global South, the Brazilian Worker's Party, and Alliance for a Responsible, Plural and United World are just a few of those who have participated. Over the years, the WSF has also attracted an impressive array of prestigious plenary speakers: Noam Chomsky, Adolfo Pérez Esquivel, Joseph Stiglitz, Naomi Klein and Evo Morales just to name a few. What all the participating groups share is the desire to campaign for an alternative future, that is a future not dictated by a free-market, profit-oriented agenda set by neoliberal-led globalization. They advocate an alternative, counter-hegemonic approach to globalization, hence the oft-used slogan in WSF meetings, 'Another World is Possible'.

The WSF has remained one of the most constant presences on the alter-globalization movement's agenda. Otherwise, as the decade following 2000 went on, and in the light of the force of protest about the Iraq war, GJM activity specifically started to lose some of its momentum. It became closely linked to the anti-Iraq war protest movement but to some extent was subsumed by it, losing some of its own distinctive focus. Flesher Fominaya argues convincingly that since the financial crisis of 2007–8 we have witnessed numerous and very contrasting social protest movements such as Iceland's 'Saucepan Revolution', the Arab Spring, and the Spanish *Indignados*, and that although links can be charted between them they don't really constitute one global movement. Flesher Fominaya prefers to refer to these and other trends as a 'global wave of protest' and argues that it is this sort of configuration which has to all intents and purposes occupied the space which had previously been that of the GJM.[25] She offers four explanations as to why this 'global wave'

---

[25] Cristina Flesher Fominaya, *Social Movements and Globalization* (Basingstoke: Palgrave, 2014), chapter 7.

emerged: 'the global financial crisis as definitive contextual factor'; 'the development of oppositional political cultures of reistance'; 'specific transnational diffusion processes'; and 'the creative use of ICTs and other forms of media'.[26] The so-called Arab Spring, it must be conceded, is however a rather special case as populations in a number of Arab nations overthrew authoritarian rulers. Ultimately, Flesher Fominaya asks whether the most recent global wave of anti-austerity and pro-democracy movements we have witnessed is 'a continuation from the GJM or a new wave?',[27] concluding the former: 'There is a continuity of actors, social movements, activist networks, master frames and participatory repertoires of deliberation from the GJM to the current wave.' We are now in the specific context of the aftermath of a major financial crisis but it is 'long-established political opposition cultures' that are being 'remobilized'. Moreover, the GJM had been pointing up the flaws in the financial system which ultimately led to the financial crisis for some time prior to it taking place.[28] The way that the movement is manifesting itself is different today, then, but essentially the same basic preoccupations are shared across the board, as was the case with the GJM. Moreover, '[p]erhaps the clearest, yet intangible, outcome of this wave of mobilizations is the politicization of civil society'.[29]

To return to the years of the AGM and the GJM, although the composition of these movements was very diverse, Steger, Goodman and Wilson argue that there were a number of values and concepts which were broadly assented to, among which the following: transformative change, participatory democracy, equality of access to resources and opportunities, social justice, universal rights, global solidarity and sustainability.[30] Moreover, five central claims came to the fore: (1) 'Neoliberalism produces global crises'; (2) 'Market-driven globalization has increased worldwide disparities in wealth and wellbeing'; (3) 'Democratic participation is essential for solving global problems'; (4) 'Another world is possible and is

---

[26]Ibid., 185.
[27]Ibid., 186.
[28]Manfred B. Steger, James Goodman and Erin K. Wilson, *Justice Globalism. Ideology, Crises, Policy* (London: Sage Publications, 2013), 88.
[29]Ibid., 46.
[30]Steger, Goodman and Wilson, *Justice Globalism*, 27–43.

urgently needed', the basis of which is the idea of a 'concrete utopia', with the anti-capitalist movement in the meantime being a sort of 'enacted utopia'[31]; and (5) 'People power, not corporate power!' Over the years in which the GJM was developing, mobilizing and gaining in strength a shift in perspective from a 'national imaginary' to a 'global imaginary' was perceptible.[32] Moreover, the movement was made up of networks of diverse groups who saw 'collective identity as being based on a recognition of difference'.[33] To give just two examples, the group Focus on the Global South made the concept of 'deglobalization' a central operative concept informing programs on such as alternative regionalism, climate and justice, and peace and security. Grassroots Global Justice (GGJ) conversely has defined itself as a "movement-building' organization, an alliance of locally or issue-specific networks.'[34]

Of the intellectual contributions to the debate about anti- or alter-globalization, those of Joseph Stiglitz, and Hardt and Negri, are worthy of special attention. Stiglitz was chief economist and vice president of the World Bank from 1997–2000 and publically took the side of the AGM, a move which ultimately led him being pressurized into resigning from his post. Since that time, he has published many important books analysing the shortcomings of globalization, the financial crisis and its aftermath, and the problem of inequality (see Bibliography). He has nevertheless been criticized in some quarters for suggesting that the AGM's/GJM's hostile attitude to the global financial regime per se amounts to unproductive oppositionalism. Steger, Goodman and Wilson counter Stiglitz's objection by claiming that 'justice globalists hold coherent ideological commitments that allow them to produce constructive alternatives to global financial arrangements based on neoliberal principles of deregulation, privatization and financialization.'[35] Whether this gets entirely to the heart of the matter is open to debate. Those 'constructive alternatives' would have to be examined in some detail and, in any case, Stiglitz has nevertheless made

---

[31] Laurence Davis and Ruth Kinna, *Anarchism and Utopianism* (Manchester: Manchester University Press, 2009), 216.
[32] Ibid., 56.
[33] Flesher Fominaya, *Social Movements and Globalization*, 69.
[34] Ibid., 71.
[35] Steger, Goodman and Wilson, *Justice Globalism*, 87.

clear that he takes a highly critical view of the *way* our financial system has been operating; he believes things should be done very differently, just as his critics do. It would appear that once again the issue of the role and status accorded to utopian ideals in the GJM's opposition to neoliberal-led globalization is an important criterion for judgment, and we will make this our focus in the latter part of this chapter as well as in Chapter 8.

Hardt and Negri struck a chord with the publication of *Empire* (2000), a work which sold well and soon became influential. It was followed by other works including *Multitude: War and Democracy in the Age of Empire* (2004) and *Commonwealth* (2009). By the time *Empire* appeared, Antonio Negri was already known for his long-standing involvement in Marxist political groups and for avocating the idea of autonomism which encourages social groups to take charge of organizing themselves independently of any central party structure. As such, autonomism shares common ground with certain strains of anarchism, and stresses everyday resistance at local levels and its potential to force through changes in the organization of the capitalist system. In the work of the same name, Hardt and Negri situate the development of Empire as having been between the first Gulf War and the war in Kosovo. A key specificity of the concept of Empire – which is written with a capital 'e' – is the idea of a form of imperialism which is no longer centred on nation-states as it had been previously. Empire is a postmodern construct created and fostered by the elites, is oligarchical, and transcends traditional boundaries as well as imposing universals. Hardt and Negri also discuss issues relating to resistance to Empire which they concede is difficult. They introduce the concept of the 'multitude' by which are designated citizens around the world who, from their local contexts, increasingly participate in networks which connect them up with other groups. These citizens can be unwittingly or knowingly complicit with Empire but they also have it within their power to resist it by constructing a counter-Empire, an alternative organization of global flows and exchanges. I shall argue in Chapter 8 that what I consider to be a counternarrative of globalization in the later work of Glissant can in some ways be seen as a parallel theoretical development to this concept of a 'counter-Empire'.

I would now like to give consideration to an area of critical debate in the secondary literature with respect to the ideological orientation(s) of the Global Justice Movement which I think is of particular significance. The issues thrown up in this discussion go to the heart of the debates and disagreements which animated the socialist and communist left throughout the twentieth century and are hence of particular significance in terms of our situating and understanding the GJM as part of a long tradition of anti-capitalist activism. I believe that these issues also inevitably remain pressing ones today in the context of what Flesher Fominaya calls the 'global wave of protest' of the last few years. This latter tendency, encompassing as it does a generalized unhappiness with the way that the globalized economy has been functioning, is in some ways even less ideologically homogenous than was the GJM. The sizeable increase in numbers of citizens the world over who have been expressing their sympathy with an alter-globalization agenda have nevertheless rendered the GJM's specific political priorities more uncentred because more dispersed.

The area of critical debate I referred to above concerns the ideological make-up of the GJM and more precisely the matter of which fundamental orientations can be identified within it, over and above the diversity of the specific interests of the various groups which compose it. Ruth Reitan makes a distinction between '"reformist" NGOs and more "radical" or direct action social movements and networks',[36] which would suggest a conceptual homology with, or at least descendence from, the division in the socialist movement which ran from the nineteenth century through a good portion of the twentieth century between groups which sought to bring about progressive change from within the capitalist system on the one hand and groups which conversely believed that the system was completely rotten and had to be rejected and overthrown before any effective socialist politics could be achieved. It was precisely this debate, for example, which had led to the split in the French Socialist Party in 1920 and the creation of the Bolshevik-inspired Communist Party. The British Labour Party took the same line on this issue as the French Socialists, hence its long-standing commitment to a social democratic agenda. Flesher Fominaya makes a similar distinction between groups within the GJM which remained affiliated to the institutional left and those which she labels 'autonomous movements'. The latter employ a

---

[36]Ruth Reitan, *Global Activism* (Oxon: Routledge, 2007), 8.

network form of organization and communication which allows for the integration of and interaction between multiple issues and identities, and for a connection between local, national and global levels of action. The networks employed can regenerate and evolve and activist members tend to see collective identity as being based on a recognition of difference and diversity. The political subject is seen as having multiple overlapping identities. Activists in such networks want to do politics differently and do not want to seize, control or even participate in national power structures. They also consider themselves independent from trade unions and NGOs, not just political parties. Some of these groups even initiated 'Autonomous European Social Forums' as an alternative to the official European Social Forums (part of the World Social Forum).[37] Clearly this latter group exhibits quite radical libertarian anarchist tendencies. We will discuss contemporary anarchist thought in the next section of this chapter, but the brand of it which we will argue has something to offer alter-globalization thinking today is not as staunchly resistant to all forms of political and hierarchical structures per se as this.

S. A. Hamed Hosseini proposes a useful even if not in every respect entirely convincing take on the reformism/radicalism distinction. Following Goodman (2002) he argues, like Reitan and Flesher Fominaya, that on one side of the equation there are the reformists who hope to bring about positive change from within official institutional and party political structures. On the other side however, he identifies a 'revitalised version of socialist internationalism with radical aspirations.'[38] This latter tendency, for Hamed Hosseini, cannot be reduced to either the old 'revolutionary' template of years gone by, nor even to the reform/revolution binary at all: it is a tendency 'within the current global resistance oriented towards redefining and redirecting global processes in alternative ways that cannot be identified with either radical particularism, or reformist cosmopolitanism'. It 'attempts to rebuild global governance and transnational relations not just through institutional reforms but also predominantly through the plural participation of grassroots from below in transnational solidarity networks and autonomous plural public spheres. It is an ideological attempt in developing alternative globalizations [...] It aims to put the totality of

---

[37]Flesher Fominaya, *Social Movements and Globalization*, 69.
[38]Hamed Hosseini, *Alternative Globalizations*, 82.

globalization on a genuinely democratic tack by transforming global relations'.[39] 'Like reformist cosmopolitanism it is internationalist in ambition, but is not based on a proposition of the possibility of "one emancipatory subject" or even on one institution-based reformist model for our increasingly complex world. Neither is it based on the ignorance of localities and people's identities on the ground. The alter-globalization mode of contention does not see an indispensable antagonism between *universal* norms and the particular demands for autonomy.'[40] And nor does it see antagonism between other dualisms such as unity versus diversity, material versus postmaterial and so on.[41] On the basis of this account it is hard to see exactly how the 'revitalised version of socialist internationalism with radical aspirations' which Hamed Hosseini distinguishes from reformism within the GJM manages to escape the traditional reform/revolution binary altogether. However, as we shall see in Chapter 8, his argumentation here is part of a broader and illuminating reading of and vision for the alter-globalization movement. Hamed Hosseini is of the view that the alter-globalization outlook (which he rightly favours to the anti-globalization perspective) 'can provide a challenge to all predominant modes of social knowledge', and that it has a capacity to 'develop a new historical subjectivity that is able to balance the dualities, and inclusively accommodate lines of social polarization such as class, gender, race and so on'.[42] Clearly Hamed Hosseini is keen to get beyond the restricting binaries of years gone by and we will temporarily postpone more in-depth discussion of his theory until the next chapter.

Anarchism, utopianism and social protest movements

In this section I hope to illuminate further some of the leading tendencies of the alter-globalization movement as it has manifested itself in the Global Justice Movement and in the years which have

---

[39] Ibid., 82.
[40] Ibid., 84.
[41] Ibid., 86.
[42] Ibid., 86.

followed the financial crisis of 2007–8 by way of a discussion both of political anarchism and of utopian thinking. By the same token, this discussion will I believe inform the appraisal of what the later Glissant's political thought has to offer us in our present-day situation in Chapter 8. I would from the outset like to allay any concerns that my intention is to argue that Glissant was in fact an anarchist of some description. I do not believe this to be the case. The hope he expressed in his *Adresse à Obama. L'Intraitable beauté du monde* (2009) that Obama might have had the possibility of setting the world back on a politically fair and just course suggests that he thought that it was still possible at least to conduct a progressive agenda within the existing political system. Moreover, he never explicitly stated that he had any affiliation to political anarchism and so it is not my intention to artificially create one. However, anarchism, like Marxism, is a tradition of political thought as well as a set of actual political practices which means that it is possible to chart lines of filiation between political ideas which do not present themselves explicitly as anarchist and elements of anarchist doctrines. And there are good reasons to do precisely this in the case of Glissant. First, the later Glissant's politics are strongly characterized by their utopianism and there is a direct and well documented line of filiation between utopian thinking and the anarchist tradition; an exploration of possible connections between Glissant's utopianism and that of anarchism would hence seem to be called for. Secondly, a number of other key aspects of Glissant's later thought also bear evident similarities to anarchist thought and politics: an emphasis on horizontal, cross-cultural networks as opposed to vertical power structures; a profound scepticism of all hierarchical thinking in the political sphere; a scepticism of institutionalized political systems and of systematic thinking; a dislike of any project to impose universal values and norms; and a belief in the capacity of local-level politics to bring about positive change.

Like Marxism, socialism and liberalism, anarchism has a long history and it is not my intention to attempt to recount that history in detail. Nevertheless, I think that a few general observations may be useful as a prelude to the analyses that are to follow. As Ruth Kinna points out:

> The attraction of modern utopian theory to anarchism can be explained as a response to Marx's anti-utopianism, famously

captured in his refusal to consider recipes for the cookbooks of the future on the grounds that socialism would be shaped by the inevitable crisis of capitalism [...] For Steven Lukes, this position was contradictory. Marx and Engels could hardly claim ignorance about the form(s) socialism was likely to take while also claiming insight into the development of history. Their mistake was to downplay the implications of their thought.[43]

According to Lukes, then, Marx and Engels were in reality much more utopian in their aspirations than they themselves conceded, but they veiled their utopianism in a shroud of scientificity. Historical materialism, they believed (and notably Engels in his later years), was a science of history which offered certitudes about the way history was to develop. According to this view, the collapse and overthrow of capitalism and its replacement by a socialist society were facts of history, not just a theory. Consequently there was no need to hold utopian ideals.

Hence utopian thinking among anarchists from the nineteenth century onwards was in part a reaction against Marxism.[44] This is not to suggest that anarchism has always implied utopianism as 'there is a strong anti-utopian trend in modern anarchism'[45] too, but simply to highlight that there are well established precedents of utopian thinking within the anarchist tradition. As regards the origins of contemporary anarchism, May '68 is often cited as an important turning point moment. 'Anarchism then rode on the coat tails of the new social movements, before poststructuralism and radical ecology sharpened its relevance to contemporary politics'[46], writes Giorel Curran. More recently, opposition to globalization explains the renaissance of anarchism to a good degree, but there are complex and varied other factors including: the fracturing of the left pre- and post-1989; the end of communism and the

---

[43]Ruth Kinna, 'Anarchism and the Politics of Utopia', in Davis and Kinna, *Anarchism and Utopianism* (Manchester University Press, 2009), 224.
[44]An attempt to make up for what Lukes perceives to be a lacuna in Marx's thought would be made by William Morris in his *News from Nowhere* (1890).
[45]Kinna, 'Anarchism and the Politics of Utopia', 221.
[46]Giorel Curran, *21st Century Dissent. Anarchism, Anti-Globalisation and Environmentalism* (Basingstoke: Palgrave Macmillan, 2006), 2.

fragmentation of the left which this induced; and the success of the latest phase of capitalism, namely neoliberal globalization.[47] Uri Gordon explains the hiatus in the history of anarchism thus:

> The anarchist movement as we see it today in advanced capitalist countries is not a direct genealogical descendant of the nineteenth- and early twentieth-century thread of libertarian-socialist militancy, which was effectively wiped out by the end of the second world war. Rather, the mainspring of today's anarchism can be found at the intersection of other social movements whose beginnings were never consciously anarchist – including radical ecology and feminism, black and queer liberation, and the anti-neoliberal internationalism launched by movements in the global south, most celebrated of which are the Mexican Zapatistas.[48]

What, then, of the points of intersection between alter-globalization movements of today, utopianism and anarchism? Saul Newman explains the connection between the first two of these phenomena thus:

> It is possible to see the anti-capitalist movement as a deliberately utopian politics: its slogan is, after all, 'another world is possible'. However, I would suggest its utopianism is more like [...] a form of politics that affirms a kind of radical disruption of the current order through the invoking of the idea of an alternative, without at the same time setting out what this alternative actually is (this is perhaps its weakness as well as its strength). The slogan 'another world is possible' functions in this sense as an 'empty signifier' [...] it suggests a kind of alternative empty horizon that can take different shapes and be interpreted by different people in different ways.
> [...]
> Moreover, the anti-capitalist movement represents a kind of 'enacted utopia' which might be seen in its massive demonstrations, and different and innovative forms of protest and direct action—tactics which involve not only confrontations,

---

[47]Ibid., 3.
[48]Uri Gordon, 'Utopia in Contemporary Anarchism', in Davis and Kinna, *Anarchism and Utopianism*, 261.

but also theatre, alternative speeches, parody, *détournement* or cultural subversion, street parties or festivals. Of particular interest is the reclamation of physical spaces by groups such as Reclaim the Streets'[49]

For Newman, this point of intersection between alter-globalization and utopianism is best expressed as a form of contemporary anarchism. Anarchism, he argues, is 'increasingly presenting itself as the radical politics of the future [...] because many of its ideas about decentred and non-hierarchical forms of politics seem to be reflected in contemporary global anti-capitalist struggles', Newman adds. 'Indeed the strength of anarchism lies partly in its strong utopian dimension: in its belief in another kind of society- based on egalitarian and non-authoritarian relationships- is possible.'[50] Nevertheless, Newman does not accept the utopian dimension of contemporary anarchism or of the alter-globalization movement uncritically: 'While a utopian dimension to radical and emancipative politics must be retained, I have suggested that it must also be rethought.' Radical political utopianism must remain seen as a 'disruption of the current order which, at the same time, emerges from *within* the current order, and which introduces a moment of radical indeterminacy and unpredictability in which anything is possible. Rather than a society of the future, utopia is an *event* which takes place in the present.'[51] Utopia for Newman, then, appears to lie in the very unpredictability of the present which, in its indeterminacy, throws up opportunities for positive change by allowing us to cast off old certainties and the passive acceptance of inequalities.

In her book *21st Century Dissent. Anarchism, Anti-Globalisation and Environmentalism* (2006), Giorel Curran's focus on the point of intersection between anarchism and the anti-globalization movement leads her to consider in a more specific way which variety of contemporary anarchism is the best suited for the task. She concludes that many of today's campaigners against neoliberal-led globalization are in reality 'post-ideological anarchists'.

---

[49]Saul Newman, 'Anarchism, utopianism and the politics of emancipation', in Davis and Kinna, *Anarchism and Utopianism*, 216.
[50]Ibid., 210.
[51]Ibid., 218.

This variety of anarchism is a brand of 'post-leftism', which Curran argues is 'a broad response to the post-1989 political climate in which contemporary dissent is situated.'[52] Bob Black has often been identified as an advocate of post-leftism, which 'is not so much an ideological position as a political principle that underpins much new anarchism.'[53] In his *Anarchy After Leftism* (1997) 'Black labels post-left anarchism "type-3 anarchism" – a decidedly non-ideological form of anarchism that he claims is neither individualist nor social in its entirety' although it has roots in the anarcho-individualist tradition. Rather than a 'school or movement – organizations they would oppose in any case – post-leftism repositions individuals and autonomous insurrectionist acts at the centre of their transformational politics'.[54] Otherwise put, post-leftist anarchism is a way of doing left-wing politics after the collapse of the radical left in official, institutional politics in Western societies. It offers a space for activists which they otherwise very largely lack.

As Curran points out, there are anarchists – notably social anarchists – who have been very critical of 'post-anarchism', berating what they see as 'new anarchist 'posturing'- post-leftist, poststructuralist, post-ideological, or otherwise- dismissing it all as pretentious bluster. Social ecologist and eco-anarchist Murray Bookchin does just this. In doing so he resurrects the long-standing tension between individual and social anarchism.' Bookchin (*Social Anarchism or Lifestyle Anarchism: An Unbridgeable Chasm* [1996]) laments the turn to individualist anarchism, which he sees as a capitulation to neo-liberalism. He claims it is 'egotistical anarcho-individualism preoccupied with "polymorphous concepts of resistance" such as "[a]d hoc adventurism, personal bravura, an aversion to theory ... celebrations of theoretical incoherence (pluralism), a basically apolitical and anti-organizational commitment to imagination, desire, and ecstasy, and an inherently self-oriented enchantment of everyday life". [...] For Bookchin it is the very integrity of anarchism that's threatened'; the needs of the individual must be interwoven with the needs of the collective.[55] Whether or not the groups making up the alter-globalization

---

[52]Curran, *21st Century Dissent*, 32.
[53]Ibid., 33.
[54]Ibid., 33.
[55]Ibid., 45.

GJM can be fairly charged in the way Bookchin had thus charged postanarchism some years previously requires analysis, and it is worth noting that Bookchin's assessment was forcefully dismissed by Black. At one level, Bookchin's critique was a case of an 'old-school' thinker rejecting newer tendencies which he saw as undermining of the tradition, although this fact does not in and of itself invalidate its substance. Nevertheless, at least as far as the GJM is concerned – and the linkage between its groups and post-ideological anarchism can by no means be identified as existing across the board, nor be taken for granted – the charge of 'egotistical anarcho-individualism' would not appear to be applicable. The groups making up the GJM often approach alter-globalization from varied perspectives but do not laud the individual over the collective. Diversity cannot be taken to be synonymous with incoherence, and the activities of the GJM as well as the continuing annual meetings of the World Social Forum cannot be fairly accused of amounting to a rejection of all attempts at political organization.

It is a feature of our era, moreover, that ideological leftism is hard to advocate convincingly because very difficult to mobilize in practical political terms. It is impossible to argue credibly that our contemporary era is a productive one for left-wing political agendas. The budget-slashing, debt-repayment agenda which is the lot of so many national governments today effectively rules out the possibility of pursuing a policy of increased financial investment in social services, housing for the poorer sections of society, let alone leisure activities and culture. Even where centre-left governments have been elected in recent years, they have not been able to pursue such an agenda successfully. Of course, if our Western societies were to undergo massive restructuring then there is no doubt that there would be more than enough wealth to make such an agenda viable. Such restructuring has always proven difficult however, even when there might have been a will to push it through, because the workings of the global financial system are such that no one nation or set of nations can afford to jeopardize its economic position in a competitive market. 'Raise taxes for the rich and they will take their capital elsewhere', is the common response to any serious calls for wealth redistribution, and the renationalization of privatized industries certainly does not figure highly on many governments' list of priorities. Capital and investments exist essentially in an international rather than national context, a fact which has made the attempts of the rich to avoid paying taxes on their assets and profits almost systematic, as even a cursory glance at the sheer number of firms whose headquarters are listed as being in offshore tax havens confirms. Globalization thereby limits the power of political decision afforded to individual nation-states to a much greater degree than previously, if one compares today's world with that of the 1950s and 1960s. It subjects most economic activity, and consequently much social policy, to the vicissitudes of the global free-market.

For these reasons, it is unfair to berate so-called post-ideological leftism for being inadequate when it comes to promoting a genuinely socialist agenda. In a world in which such an agenda is largely impossible in official political channels, activists are faced with a choice between inaction or alternative forms of political action. The GJM and its associated annual conference the WSF has offered an opportunity for groups that are pursuing such alternative types of activism to meet, coalesce and reflect collectively on strategies for countering the more regressive tendencies of neo-liberal-led globalization. The alter-globalization movement, then, brings together organizations which exist independently from each other into a collective space in which they can gain strength through dialogue. It is composed of diverse groups with specific focus-issues and agendas, not of agglomerations of rebellious individuals whose thinking is inchoate, unreflective and disorganized. While I think Curran's assimilation of their activism to post-ideological anarchism is a line of reflection that is worth pursuing, a number of caveats need to be borne in mind. First, it is far from being the case that the individuals and groups making up the GJM would have all accepted the post-anarchist categorization. Secondly, although the problems facing institutional leftism today must be conceded, I do not entirely share Curran's almost exclusively positive assessment of the 'post-ideological' character of the variety of anarchism she supports. When she claims that 'it is a politics that rejects the stranglehold of ideology and draws from a broader political canvas',[56] she appears to be unduly disparaging of 'ideological' politics as it is far from being the case that political agendas with clear ideological leanings are necessarily or always limiting. Ideology can also bring people

---

[56]Ibid., 230.

together and make effective political action possible. Were it the case that a genuinely socialist as well as ecologically responsible agenda had serious chances of succeeding on a global scale today, that agenda would be a preferable one to contemporary post-leftism, whether it was more ideological than the latter or not. Post-ideological leftist anarchism, then, may be the best, or one of the best, strategy/ies available in a context that is inhospitable to progressive politics, but should not necessarily be assumed to be the culmination or apotheosis of over a century and a half of radical left political thought and activism. That said, I agree that it does display qualities which were absent from left-wing politics and which any left agenda would do well to incorporate henceforth. There is certainly value in the fact that 'post-ideological politics in general, and a post-ideological anarchist politics in particular, do not proffer perfect models of dissent or singular visions of the good society' but encourage 'the principles of autonomy and the practice of a non-hierarchical democratic politics.'[57] This dimension of alter-globalization activism will be explored further in the next chapter.

---

[57] Ibid., 230.

CHAPTER EIGHT

A poetics of resistance and change: Glissant, a maître à penser for twenty-first-century dissident thought?

We have examined in some depth the theoretical underpinnings to Glissant's critical stance with respect to contemporary globalization, rejected radical critiques which suggest that his later thought reflects or is inadvertently complicit with globalization, and examined the political content – in places explicitly radical political content – of some of his later writings. We have also discussed some of the leading trends working in the direction of encouraging changes to the way globalization functions such that it gains in social justice and fairness. In this eighth and final chapter of this book we will, among other things, assess what sort of place can be accorded to later Glissantian thought in the context of such protesting against globalization and also, what sort of guide Glissant can hence be for the alter-globalization movement. It is our conviction that the later Glissant can be such a guide, or more precisely one 'maître à penser' among others. To hold that Glissant could ever offer the one, single example that the alter-globalization movement needs to follow would be both unrealistic and undesirable: it would be to foreclose on the diversity and multiplicity that characterizes the alter-globalization movement's component individuals and groups and it would be to reintroduce a strong dose of hierarchical thinking the likes of which Glissant's thought runs counter to. I suggested in Chapter 7 that the anti-hierarchical, because heterogeneous and often ideologically open-ended character of the Global Justice Movement and the World Social Forum means that their component strands bear significant resemblances to certain currents of contemporary political anarchism. This certainly does not amount to claiming that *all* the participants in the alter-globalization movement are 'post-ideological', 'post-leftist'anarchists, nor that Glissant can or should be placed in either or both of these categories. It is to make the more limited claim that our understanding of the GJM and the WSF is enhanced if we establish a thematic link between the nature of their organizational structures and those of contemporary 'post-ideological' anarchism, and that establishing such a link also enables us to gain a better insight into the fundamentally anti-establishmentarian orientation of Glissant's political thinking. It is not just Glissant's radical and anti-hierarchical latter-day political orientations which bear similarities to post-ideological anarchism but also the pronounced utopian dimension of his thought. In both cases, utopian idealism is actively incorporated into an agenda for progressive political change not as a concrete blueprint for action but as a regulative ideal, that is to say as a set of ideals and objectives which guide values and objectives in the present, protecting the political agenda from ever-pressing encroachment by the limitations which real-world politics impose.

It will by now be clear that the type of questioning of contemporary globalization which we are referring to is not 'anti-globalization' as such but 'alter-globalization'. The GJM encompassed both tendencies but the latter is the more progressive of the two. The desire to oppose globalization entirely in the hope that it can be reversed such that the world reverts back to a *pre*-globalized economic and cultural condition is implausible. It is also a desire which certain elements of the GJM paradoxically had in common with the nationalist extreme right. Alter-globalization conversely seeks to redirect globalization so as 'to rebuild global governance and transnational relations not just through institutional reforms but also predominantly through the plural participation of grassroots from below in transnational solidarity networks and autonomous plural public spheres.'[1] Alter-globalization therefore accepts that globalization is here to stay but seeks to orient it in more ethically justifiable directions and indeed to harness its positive aspects such as transnational flows, sophisticated communication systems and internationalism at various levels in order to achieve that goal. Glissant's vision of an ever-more creolized and creolizing world in which the diverse communities of the world, while remaining true to their own languages and identities, interact with each other through horizontal communication networks is of a piece with this vision. Globalization, under the impetus of neoliberalism, has in recent decades only reinforced and accentuated the tendency of capitalism to generate asymmetries. With the world's top 1 per cent getting still wealthier inequality has been and remains a growing problem, and one which even the economic growth of certain nations traditionally associated with the underprivileged global south is not doing much to remedy. For growth often does not translate into a better spread of wealth within any one nation and the meteoric rise of China and India has not ensured a higher standard of living for the vast majority of their citizens. The location of the asymmetries has been changing but marked asymmetries they remain. The alter-globalization agenda seeks to encourage a rejigging of the cards such that it becomes possible to envisage a future beyond that imposed by the capital accumulation of the top 1 per cent. The economic asymmetries of our world cannot be eradicated but they can be reduced for the benefit of those masses of citizens around the globe who continue to live in poverty. To employ a metaphor which will be familiar in our digital age, alter-globalists believe that global capitalism can be reconfigured, that it is not too late to reorient the trajectory on which the vessel which we inhabit increasingly interconnectedly is set. They believe, moreover, that the very future of our planet, or at least of human life on it, depends on such a process of reconfiguring.

As mentioned in Chapter 7, Hardt and Negri's concept of the 'counter-Empire' served as a powerful theoretical tool for the GJM when it came to conceptualizing opposition to neoliberalism's imperial ambitions. Movements of dissident knowledge and

---

[1] S. A. Hamed Hosseini, *Alternative Globalizations. An integrative approach to studying dissident knowledge in the global justice movement* (Oxon: Routledge, 2010), 82.

political practice benefit greatly from the introduction of oppositional counterdiscourses and Hardt and Negri's notion of a 'counter-Empire' suggested a force which could potentially meet and push back that of neoliberalism in the interests of the greater common good. The multitude, so they argue, have the capacity to join together via international networks and build an alternative set of social arrangements. Building on my observations about Glissant and Gilroy in Chapter 2, I would argue that the counternarrative of globalization which I believe Glissant's later thought offers can profitably be compared with Gilroy's idea that the 'black Atlantic' constituted a 'counternarrative of modernity'; in *The Black Atlantic* (1993) Gilroy argued that black cultures in the modern era were expressive of a counterculture which challenged the hegemonic discourse and ideology of the majoritarian white communities. In a similar vein, 'counter-Empire' coheres with Glissant's ideal of communities around the world protecting their own distinctive cultures from assimilation and yet building new identities and solidarities through creolizing processes and horizontal networks. Clearly the two conceptions are not identical but they do fit the one into the other. The preserving of a given culture's opacity at a local level, that is, irreducibility to the influence of larger majoritarian cultures, is a necessary step in the direction of presenting a meaningful alternative to the imperial designs of those majoritarian cultures. At the risk of appearing incorrigibly Western, talk of counternarratives and countercultures might invite cross-referencing with Alain Badiou's conviction that in today's world it is vital that what he calls the 'communist hypothesis' be kept alive. In a work of the same name, as indeed in an earlier work *The Meaning of Sarkozy* (2010) Badiou argues that the idea of communism, divorced from its real-world instantiations in the twentieth century, can serve as a rampart against the ever-increasing encroachments of neoliberal economics; the communist hypothesis helps us to continue believing that a different type of collective organization of society is possible, 'communism' being an Idea with a regulatory function in the Kantian sense of the term, not an actual political programme.[2]

I should indicate that it is not my intention to suggest that all the ills of today's world can be put at the door of neoliberalism,

---

[2] Alain Badiou, *The Communist Hypothesis* (London: Verso, 2015).

nor that there is nothing worse than neoliberalism. There certainly are other models of society which are on balance less defensible overall in terms of ensuring fairness and humaneness. Moreover, to blame the West for all the world's structural problems today would paradoxically be to reassert a pre-eminence which for some years now has been much less real than it previously was. My point is rather to criticize the fact that the success of neo-liberalism in the Anglo-American context has led to the West contributing massively to its own long-term structural decline. This might not seem such a bad thing to many outside of Western nations, nor indeed to some of the more progressive voices within them. If the West is economically, politically and morally bankrupt, so the reasoning might go, why not look elsewhere for political and economic models to follow? Such a conclusion does not seem unreasonable. However, the crux of my argument is rather that in its discrediting of the West, notably since the war against and occupation of Iraq, neoliberalism has also by implication invited a rejection of so many progressive political values and socially oriented policies which had previously been the genuinely progressive contribution of the West to the modern history of humanity. I am certainly not speaking of colonialism, and capitalism, though a motor for change as Marx acknowledged, has always been riddled with defects. I am speaking rather of post-enlightenment values of tolerance, the defence of human rights, civil liberties, universal suffrage, advances in employment legislation, and the struggle for gender equality. Neoliberalism has discredited not just itself but much more and even, for some in the world today, the West itself and everything it stands for, a state of affairs which is deeply regrettable.

S.A. Hamed Hosseini, in his book *Alternative Globalizations. An integrative approach to studying dissident knowledge in the global justice movement* (Oxon: Routledge, 2010), presents one of the furthest-reaching, most persuasive and convincing accounts of the alter-globalization movement and its possibilities for bringing about constructive change. Hamed Hosseini offers a detailed and conceptually sophisticated analysis which it would be beyond the scope of the present chapter to do full justice to; I will limit my remarks to discussion of certain salient points made by Hamed Hosseini before focusing in particular on his notion of 'accommodative consciousness' which I consider to be particularly valuable to understanding the alter-globalization mindset. Stating his preference for alter-globalization in relation to anti-globalization, Hamed Hosseini rightly suggests that the underpinnings to this mode of thought can only be understood *relationally*, that is to say in relation to the context in which they have germinated: 'The counter-hegemonic bases of dissident knowledge must be examined in terms of the movement's confrontation with the ideational bases of dominant ideological discourses.'[3] It is not, however, as simple as alter-globalist thinking developing in opposition to a dominant ideology which it opposes. The relationship of the former to the latter is much more dialectical and mediated than such a binary opposition would suggest: 'Since movements are not isolated from their historical context, and they have been mainly socialized within the same cultural system, they usually borrow many discursive elements from the enemy's ideology.'[4] Alter-globalization, then, can only be understood in relation to the phenomenon of globalization itself and the way that it is conceived of and presented by those who advocate and direct it. Being a product of the same cultural context it uses many of the same concepts which it nevertheless subverts. This manner of conceiving of alter-globalization is intrinsically convincing and also valuable to our understanding of what I am calling Glissant's 'counternarrative of globalization'. Later Glissantian theory draws significantly on concepts which we have come to associate habitually with globalization itself, but the orientation of his theoretical positioning seeks to subvert their logic. Glissant extends the creolizing processes formerly associated with the Caribbean context to the international context and this would appear to be a theoretical expression of the transnational flows of cultural values commonly thought of as characterizing globalization. He stresses horizontal networks of communication, a preoccupation which resembles closely the ever-growing tendency today in the direction of undermining traditionally vertical political power structures. There is an increasingly generalized mistrust of authority in today's world, be it that of the political class or of other institutions such as the medical and teaching professions as well as the banking sector. Such a generalized mistrust of so many other areas of accredited knowledge is a cause for concern. In our age of online social networks, subjective opinion, drawn from not

---

[3] Ibid., 71.
[4] Ibid., 72.

always reliable information sources, is increasingly substituting more and more for knowledge derived from formal education and professional expertise. Glissant's transnational concept of creolization and advocacy of horizontal communication networks are ambivalently positioned when it comes to the questioning of vertical structures. On the one hand, Glissant does want to subject those structures to profound questioning. He would not condone the gradual erosion of all forms of authoritative knowledge but would not either be against the questioning of the authority of those financial and political elites which set and manage the agenda for the globalized economy. But above all he wishes to encourage the growing trend to see progressive political change as requiring alternative, local-based strategies involving transnational networks of communication; such strategies are indispensable to the retention and pursuit of genuinely progressive political ideals today. As such, his thought both draws on but also at the same time redirects or reconfigures contemporary trends commonly associated with globalization; Glissant wishes to harness some of the leading features of the globalized configuration but in order to put them in the service of another world view.

Hamed Hosseini highlights 'three fronts in which the global justice movement ideationally confronts dominant ideologies: confronting the globalization of neo-liberalist ideology; a post-September 11 new imperialist discourse in international relations; and consumerist values.'[5] He perceptively presents the alter-globalization tendency as an attitude of mind, not just as a politics in the narrow sense. Alter-globalization involves 'dissident knowledge' and this can constitute 'a challenge to all predominant modes of knowledge' in that it has the capacity 'to develop a new historical subjectivity that is able to balance the dualities, and inclusively accommodate lines of social polarization such as class, gender, race and so on'. Hamed Hosseini calls the cognitive dimension of this vision 'accommodative cognition'[6] or 'accommodative consciousness'. This latter, which Hamed Hosseini considers an 'ideal-mode of thought', is defined as

1. transcending the polarity of *soft-praxis* versus. *hard-praxis* and its associated intellectual dualisms that are rooted

---

[5]Ibid., 72.
[6]Ibid., 86.

in the 1970s–1980s controversies between modernists and postmodernists, structuralists and poststructuralists, Marxists and post-Marxists

2. going beyond the incompatible conceptions of social differentials – around issues like gender, race, cultural identity [...] – in establishing a flexible solidarity based on a collaborative inclusion of the Other into the definition of Self
3. understanding the "complexity" of globalization processes, and the world system in terms of their unevenness, contradictions, and multidimensionality; this is associated with systemic conception of particular events in relation to the main globalization processes without overlooking their specific socio-cultural contexts.[7]

Accommodative consciousness is an 'anti-reductionist mode of social thought'[8] encouraging an integrative vision as opposed to one characterized by binaries and polarities. An integrative vision, or indeed integrative visions in the plural, are beneficial for many reasons. They help: to affirm collectivities although without sacrificing individualities; to challenge the system as a whole ideologically without ignoring identities; and to target redistributive and material issues without refraining from recognition of lifestyles and post-material concepts.[9] Accommodative consciousness is conceived of by Hamed Hosseini as going beyond the reform/revolution dichotomy of years past in left-wing political struggles, a point about which I remain sceptical, as I indicated in Chapter 7. I am neither persuaded that we are presently in such a resoundingly post-ideological age (if we are in one at all – the resurgence of the nationalist extreme right would suggest not) nor that there is such a specificity to locally based international solidarities that the reform/revolution dichotomy can be either completely transcended or entirely sidelined. It is worth remembering that in the early twentieth century the debate between socialists and communists about whether progressive change could be brought about from within the existing system was not a stark choice between grudgingly

---

[7]Ibid., 92.
[8]Ibid., 118.
[9]Ibid., 118.

accepting the long-term continuing existence of capitalism on the one hand, and refusing to accept this and working to ensure its possible overthrow it by physical force on the other. The difference was one of strategy rather than contrasting ultimate goals: the socialists sought the ultimate defeat of the capitalist system as ardently as did the Bolshevik-inspired communists but believed that this objective could be achieved more convincingly by progressive change in the direction of socialism from within the existing political system. Alter-globalists today similarly often do not think in stark binary terms of reform or revolution, as Hamed Hosseini points out. It is not for this reason, however, that the dichotomy can be said to have been definitively superseded such that it should never be thought useful again. To remove it from political discourse as a choice that can be made is, in my view, implicitly to comply with the logic of self-styled 'post-ideological' neo-liberal hegemonic discourse which propagates the doctrine known as TINA (There is No Alternative [to global capitalism]).

This reservation about Hamed Hosseini's argument notwithstanding, his theory is perspicacious in offering a much-needed basis and blueprint for collective political action in today's struggle to transform contemporary globalization into a fairer, less wasteful and less environmentally harmful phenomenon. The accommodative tendency, Hamed Hosseini continues, allows for a 'flexible comingling between *local* apprehensions and *global* concerns.'[10] [italics Hamed Hosseini's] It is of a piece with a better mediated relationship between the local and the global, in a world in which we are witnessing 'the decomposition of national economies into a variety of unequally globalized *local* economies', the world trade system having 'entered into a higher level of asymmetry [...] and a new geography of marginality that cuts across the scales of *globality, nationality* and *locality*'. Hamed Hosseini concludes from this that what is required is 'a transmutation in the conception of the *local-global* continuum towards a more accommodative level by acknowledging the multiscalar nature of globalization processes.'[11]

The new historical subjectivity Hamed Hosseini argues for via the concept of 'accommodative consciousness' is holistic

---

[10]Ibid., 131.
[11]Ibid., 179.

and inclusive because capable of integrating diverse, seemingly disparate tendencies, as opposed to being binaristic. As such it harmonizes closely with the later Glissantian vision which similarly stresses the importance of respecting differences and cultural specificities within a whole or totality which encompasses those particularities. Hamed Hosseini is not advocating any notion of a collective consciousness but a new mindset, a new subjective awareness of self in relation to the whole, with that whole moreover being conceived of as capable of genuinely politically progressive change. A contemporary reformulation of the subject-society/history dialectic of history set out in Sartre's *Critique of Dialectical Reason* is suggested implicitly, and it is a dialectic based on an affirmation of progressive possibilities and potentialities. Once the subject adopts the mindset Hamed Hosseini calls the accommodative consciousness she can act transformatively on a socio-political context which has conditioned her but which cannot imprison her in the thinking which derives from that conditioning. It is not because she has been entirely conditioned to think of globalization as intrinsically capitalistic, wasteful and destructive of cultural specificities and the environment that she must believe that it cannot be otherwise. For Hamed Hosseini, the cry of 'Another World is Possible' clearly begins with individual subjects who begin to understand that economics and politics at a global level can be done differently and that they all have a vital role to play in bringing about such a change.

Glissant's thought is not subject-based but there is nothing to indicate that it cannot harmonize with such a vision which is of a piece with it notably in its political aspects. Indeed, Hamed Hosseini's notion of the accommodative consciousness provides a dimension to Glissant's aspiration to see world politics done differently which is lacking and indeed needed in his later thought. The poststructuralist influence on Glissant's later theory offers advantages but the reticence of poststructuralist theorists when it comes to considering the individual subject as an agent of historical change poses serious problems for any progressive politics. If subjects are conceived of as being so subsumed in existing structures, be they social, institutional, or linguistic that they cease to exist meaningfully as agents, then it is hard to see how any politics of progressive change can be initiated, let alone effectively coordinated and brought to fruition over time.

Moreover, it is precisely the conditioning which technocratic and late capitalist society has foist upon individual subjects which must today be subjected to profound questioning. Poststructuralism and postmodernism have lived and must, like other intellectual tendencies before them, be studied as tendencies which were expressive of, and of great heuristic value to their era – that of advanced Western capitalist, technocratic society – but which have been eclipsed by new social and political realities. This is not to say that they do not continue to offer valuable insights but rather to assert that they are not, or can no longer be, the leading paradigms of our era. In the late 1980s and 1990s, when these theoretical tendencies were in their heyday, the internet and the mass connectivity it affords, but also imposes, were in their infancy; finance capitalism was a new development; the Cold War had just come to an end and it looked as though the Western model of society was poised to become the principal model for the foreseeable future if not, as the US Republican PNAC[12] hoped, for the whole of the twenty-first century; and awareness of the long-term consequences of our industrial, consumerist and lifestyle activities for the environment was much less acute. Today, ever larger numbers of citizens around the globe realize that the world as it is structured at present is unsustainable, a conviction which was not assented to so widely before the turn of the new millennium. Some of the reasons for this unsustainability, and notably exponential demographic growth in many parts of the world, are not easy to act meaningfully upon, but others can be responded to if there is a will to do so. It is precisely these latter areas which the GJM and its descendent social protest movements today wish to impact on. This can only be done if we accept that there are subjects who have it within their power to resolve to act. To say this is not to seek to reinstate some heroically rationalist concept of the subject who, as a rational agent, is beyond all determination exerted on him by factors external to himself. The structuralists and poststructuralists valuably taught us that such a view is misguided and naïve in its triumphant humanism; individual subjects are enmeshed in the structures they inhabit and which condition them entirely, as the even existentialist *early*

---

[12]Project for a New American Century. See the discussion of this American neoconservative group in Chapter 7.

Sartre of the 'Présentation des *Temps Modernes*' (1945) had acknowledged before them. Yet, and this is the value of Hamed Hosseini's notion of the accommodative consciousness, individual subjects they still remain and it is vital that they are recognized as being such. Legal systems recognize it, as do employers, so it would be a little odd if the only socio-professional category of people who do not were contemporary academic theorists.

The subsumption of individual subjects in structures external to themselves does not remove subjective agency but it does have serious implications for any notion of individual responsibility. Such a tendency runs entirely counter to an increasingly pervasive trend in Western societies which seeks to ensure accountability within our institutional systems; individuals at lower levels are constantly required to justify their actions while the elites at the very top continue to act in often seemingly rather arbitrary, but in reality often self-interested, ways which at times pose serious challenges to both legality and democracy. This imbalance needs to be redressed, but it cannot be in any meaningful way if we persist in the view that individuals are not responsible for the choices they make and the actions they engage in. A subject who is conceived of as lacking the capacity for rational self-determination, however compromised that may be by conditioning and circumstances, is an individual who cannot be fairly held to be responsible for his or her actions. It is in this sense that certain strands of poststructuralism and postmodernism have proved to be complicit with neoliberalism. Certainly the fashion for these intellectual trends in the humanities departments of US universities has never given the world-leading financial and business elites of that same nation much cause for worry.

Hence Hamed Hosseini's theory provides a valuable complement to the vision of the later Glissant, offering a dimension that is very largely absent in Glissant's writing. There is no rejection of the idea of the subject in Glissantian theory and his views on politics would seem to rest implicitly on the notion that societies and communities are made up of individuals who are capable of taking courses of action. However diffuse and difficult to pinpoint loci of power in advanced capitalist societies might be, as Foucault argued,[13]

---

[13] See Michel Foucault, *Power/Knowledge. Selected Interviews and Other Writings, 1972–1977* (London: Harvester Wheatsheaf, 1980).

any political agenda pushing for progressive political change, and notably in as inhospitable a context as neo-liberal-led globalization, must repose on the idea of subjects who become resolved to take courses of action in that direction. What Hamed Hosseini has come up with is a valuable insight into what sort of mental outlook or state of mind those individuals might adopt if they are best to see beyond the ideological and political limitations on progressive action imposed on them in their day to day lives, be it that those limitations work at the level of unconscious barriers (conditioning leading them to the conclusion that nothing can really be done, for example) or objective constraints (the political class and legal system protecting the interests of the rich as they have done for so long, for example).

We have observed on numerous occasions in this study, and notably in our discussion of *L'Intraitable beauté du Monde: Adresse à Barack Obama* (2009), that Glissant's politics are characterized by a pronounced utopian tendency. This tendency does not amount to otherworldly idealism because utopianism acts in Glissant's thought as a regulative ideal. Otherworldly aspirations in politics invariably prove to be ineffectual. However, utopian ideals which are meant to serve as an ethical guide for political action do serve a real-world function and are very necessary. Without ideals and principles politics would be nothing but a set of administrative arrangements. No politics seeking either progressive change, or indeed a reactionary embracing of nostalgias for past glory and supposed unitary national identities, has ever been thus limited. Genuine political agendas, whether they be of the laudable or condemnable varieties, have always involved sets of values and objectives some of which are, at the point of being conceived, beyond reach. In fact, it is mainstream politics through official channels today which has for the last few decades been the most lacking in such values, at least in so far as ideals of a socially, economically and culturally progressive nature are concerned. Glissant's utopianism, like that of the contemporary anarchist utopian currents in the alter-globalization movement, is meant in part as a response to this dearth. Utopianism here serves the function of reclaiming a space for progressive political aspirations in an era in which they have become very difficult to uphold. It is not political in a party political or institutional sense, a fact which political realists may perceive as a weakness. But its alternative character is also its strength in that its relative independence from official channels of decision-making is also what allows for a defence of ethical values which otherwise often get pushed to the wayside but which, given the urgency of the problems our globalized world is facing today, we forget at our peril.

Ultimately, debates about the function of utopian ideals in relation to real-world political, economic and cultural agendas link up with broader considerations relating to the status of cultural politics. There has been a growing tendency in humanities discourses over the last two decades or so to assume that political agendas, of the traditional non-identity politics variety, can no longer be constructively furthered through scholarly research. Long gone are the days when it was considered worthwhile to be talking about the class politics or speculating about the continuing validity of historical materialism as a paradigm while ostensibly writing a study devoted to, say, Flaubert. Even as fervent a former believer in the possibilities of cultural politics as Paul Gilroy has in recent years all but given up on the idea that critical discourse can have genuinely positive, politically progressive effects on the wider world around it. His more recent works have very largely lost the militant edge of earlier works like *There Ain't No Black in the Union Jack* and *The Black Atlantic* and Gilroy appears to have lapsed into an emollient fatalistic resignation when it comes to thinking about where we stand in relation to neoliberal-led globalization. In a recent public intervention Gilroy argued that contestatory politics today could meaningfully hope to achieve no more than individual acts of what he termed 'post-humanist humanism'.[14] This theoretical paradigm is most certainly not without interest; indeed it has in my view real potential as a paradigm for approaching progressive politics today. However the way in which Gilroy conceived of its application was largely without value for any collective political project. 'Post-humanist humanist' acts included for Gilroy the example of a brave Greek islander who, upon seeing a significant number of Syrian refugees falling into the sea from a sinking boat, spontaneously swam out to them and brought many to safety. A courageous act of this sort is undoubtedly entirely commendable and exemplary, but it cannot,

---

[14]Gilroy, keynote speech at the UK Postcolonial Studies Association conference, Leicester, 8 September 2015.

in my view, be plausibly considered to be a valid substitute for organized politics, however alternative or anti-hierarchical that form of political organization may be. As a form of constructive action it is not in the same category as political action.

While I am not advocating a view of critical discourse – at once reductive and over-ambitious at the same time – which would have it that the absence of a politically progressive subtext or argumentative framework in critical discourse is detrimental, I nevertheless believe that the evaporation of non-identity based (queer, gender, race) political thinking from humanities research in recent decades is cause for concern. It is true that books like Sartre's politically oriented *What Is Literature?* (1948) or Marxist historian Christopher Hill's *Change and Continuity in Seventeenth-Century England* (1974) never did actually change real-world political arrangements, even in eras that were more sympathetic to left-wing ideas than our own. But to judge them on that criterion is misguided. Of much greater relevance would be an evaluation of their real-world impact in terms of the extent to which they influenced public opinion, and in this regard it is clear that critical discourses, just like all other forms of cultural production, do have a vital role to play. Politics itself, after all, is comprised of discourses and argumentation which are often affected in a myriad of ways by what is going on in the cultural sphere. Any schematic separation of 'real-world' political sphere from some putatively socially and culturally inconsequential cultural sphere should hence be forcefully resisted.

The constructive role which socially oriented cultural production in its various forms and ethico-political utopian agendas can play should therefore not be overlooked, and it is in my view vital that we continue to believe that there is a valid space for such discourses, however ideal-laden they may seem to be. Glissant's oeuvre reconfirms the importance of both of these tendencies, being both eminently and non-reductively cultural (high theory and literary production) *and* socially and politically informed at the same time. Indeed, the later Glissant's utopianism, as we saw in Chapter 6, is integrally connected to his aesthetics. In *L'Intraitablé Beauté du Monde: Adresse à Barack Obama* (2009) and *Philosophie de la Relation* (2009) beauty is not just an aesthetic concept but is presented as having implications for ethics: aesthetics, Glissant argues in the latter text, can provide orientations and directions for ethics. Consider the following statements drawn from *L'Intraitable Beauté du Monde:*

> Exploitation, crime and domination never allow for the feeling of beauty.
> There is no beauty in solitary memories, fundamentalisms, exclusive national histories, ethic cleansing, the negation of the other, expulsions of immigrants and inflexible certitudes.
> Nor in racial or identitarian essence or in capitalist production, in the hysteria of finance, the madness of the markets and in hyperconsumerism.
> This lack of beauty is proof of an attack on the living; it is a call to resistance. It is when there is an awareness of beauty that resistance, our existence and politics draw on the energy of living things.[15]

Beauty is here presented as an ideal and not in just an aesthetic but also in a political sense. A lack of beauty is presented as the basis for resistance and it is in taking beauty as a guide that politics should be conducted. These latter statements, corresponding to the second paragraph above, are of course utopian ideals. Glissant is implying that it is when beauty is lacking that we *should* resist, and that it is resistance, existence and politics which *ought to* take beauty as their guide. Poetics, as we saw in Chapter 6, is for Glissant almost by definition politically progressive: 'The more that Obama's strategies develop in the direction of a *Poetics of Relation* […] the more that virulent racist attacks will continue to be on the rise in the United States.'[16] A movement in a politically progressive direction – and

---

[15]'L'exploitation, le crime, la domination n'ouvrent jamais au sentiment de la beauté. Il n'y a pas de beauté dans les mémoires solitaires, les fondamentalismes, les Histoires nationales sans partage, les épurations ethniques, la négation de l'autre, les expulsions d'émigrés, la certitude close. Pas plus de beauté dans l'essence raciale ou identitaire. Pas de beauté dans le capitalisme de production, dans les hystéries de la finance, les folies du marché et de l'hyperconsommation. Le déficit en beauté est le signe d'une d'atteinte au vivant, un appel à résistance. Auprès de la beauté, la résistance, l'existence, le politique se chargent à fond de l'énergie du vivant (*IBM*, 28–29).
[16]'Plus [l]es stratégies [d'Obama] se développeront dans le sens d'une *Poétique de la Relation* […] plus il y aura une remontée des purulences et des virulences racistes aux Etats-Unis' (*IBM*, 16–17).

poetics is for Glissant progressive almost by definition – will lead to a reactionary counterblast.

Glissant's eulogious homage to the newly elected Obama is the only text in his output in which he expresses real hope – albeit utopian hope – in the possibilities of the official channels of politics possibly allowing for a more progressive agenda than those we have seen in recent decades. This work notwithstanding, the political vision that is expressed in the later Glissant's works otherwise bears similarities to what Curran labels 'post-ideological anarchism', a trend which I discussed in Chapter 7 and which is undoubtedly one of the leading tendencies in the GJM and more recent anti-capitalist social protest movements. There is a powerful utopian dimension to this type of contemporary anarchism which, like Glissant, places emphasis on decentred and non-hierarchical forms of politics. Alter-globalist activists are resistant to authoritarianism in political structures and stress horizontal relationships and international networks of activists, as does Glissant. They increasingly employ on-line connectivity as a means of communicating beyond national boundaries to coordinate activities and aspire to a kind of internationalism involving many nationalities, languages and cultures coming together in a collective political project which challenges neo-liberalism and the cultural and linguistic homogeneity that it encourages. As with Glissant's notion of the opacity of cultures, the basic locus of power for such activists is communities at a local level whose independence should not be compromised by transnational homogenizing forces. Like Glissant, they are profoundly sceptical of universals, being aware that when the idea of universal values and principles are rigidly applied it is because they are connected to the exercise of power; hence supposedly universal values become the expression of the leading ideology of the day and a weapon in the hands of hegemonic majoritarian communities.

Perhaps most importantly, alter-globalists understand that they are engaged in a struggle which is and is likely to remain an uphill one, and yet they persist in making demands for a fairer world than neo-liberalism has to offer. It is in this sense that they exhibit utopian tendencies. They are fully aware that the vision they hold for a world beyond the present unequal state of affairs, a world in which there was a better distribution of wealth and power and in which global warming could be halted, would be difficult to realize in practical terms. And yet they believe that it is not for this reason that the struggle should be abandoned. They are ethical idealists who are resolved to pursue a vision for a fairer world and make that vision into a guide for their actions in the present despite realizing that their objectives may prove unattainable in practice. It is at this level that the alter-globalization mindset is close to and would benefit greatly from Glissant's notion of poetics which involves a projection via the imaginary to envisage the world not as it is but as it would ideally be. Beauty is for Glissant as much a future goal to work towards as it ever exists in the present. Glissant's utopian vision is hence an aesthetico-political ethic of striving to make a better world in adverse circumstances. One strives to reach or attain beauty and this is equated with the socio-politico-economico-cultural ideal of a fairer world devoid of oppression and domination in all their forms. Glissant knows that beauty of this sort is beyond reach in our present-day world and yet he believes firmly that it must remain the guide to our actions regulating and directing them like a sort of moral compass.

The utopian dimension of the alter-globalization movement's thinking and that of Glissant should nevertheless not be overemphasized. In both cases, it is also the case that concrete proposals and demands for progressive policy-making have been made, many of which could be achievable. Utopianism does not in either case amount to an evasion of reality or a refusal to see that the world is as it is. Rather it serves a real-world function: it is a mode of thinking which enables activists to keep their ultimate goals in mind while they are confronting the manifold challenges and difficulties they encounter at a day to day level.

What, though, is to be concluded about the aspiration to defend universal values? Glissant's knowledge of and trenchant opposition to French colonialism and neocolonialism, upheld as they were by the particularly abstract type of universalist thinking that is French republican ideology, led him very largely to reject universal values in the name of a celebration of difference and diversity/multiplicity which sails quite close to that found in the US context, however resistant Glissant may have declared himself to be to identitarian logics. However, in reality, difference is not necessarily entailed by diversity/multiplicity; the latter does not have to imply or involve the former, at least not in the strong form in which difference is advocated in the United States. It is possible for two phenomena not to be the same, and hence for there to be diversity/multiplicity, without it being necessary to go so far as to highlight that they are different from each other. Glissant arguably goes a step too far here. There can for example be commonly shared characteristics between two individuals – be it of a cultural or physical/bodily nature – which are ultimately more significant than those contrasting characteristics between the two which mean that they are not the same. The anglophone, and notably American, lauding of difference involves generating too pronounced a contrast between that which is the same and that which is not (quite) the same. It is not reasonable to assume, for example, that a person who, for example, is black and white mixed race should be considered principally as black and hence 'different'. Barack Obama may have been the first non-white president of the United States, but he was not its first black president as such because Obama is no more biologically 'black' than he is biologically 'white'. To claim this is not to want to assimilate Obama to some stereotypical image of 'white' identity, nor is it to want to dissociate him from 'black' identity; it is rather to associate him with *both* white and black in equal measure, whatever those labels might be assumed to designate in anything more than strictly racial terms.

The types of assumptions I am criticising have far-reaching implications. In particular, they tend to reconfirm the binary oppositions of years gone by while inverting them, such that a phenomenon (here 'blackness') previously treated disparagingly can be celebrated after the fashion of Negritude in years gone by. But the celebration of difference by some is often mirrored by the dislike of that difference in other quarters. The retention of binaries may have advantages but it can also have very serious adverse consequences for members of the very same communities as those who are benefitting from their inversion. Hence the celebration of difference can be liberating, but it can also be a poisoned gift just depending on the position a given person or community finds itself in at a particular place and time. In this regard the example of Frantz Fanon is instructive. Although for some years a supporter of Negritude, ultimately Fanon was to come round to the view expressed by Sartre in his *Black Orpheus* (1948) that Negritude could only be a temporary, even if very necessary, expedient.

At the other end of the spectrum from the celebration of difference, the French universalist tendency to want to iron out differences such that all communities be assimilated to an abstract notion of the collective national identity, is also questionable. Very regrettably, it has contributed to France becoming a key target of the Islamic fundamentalists. If individuals live in a given nation-state it is reasonable to expect that they take their place as citizens of that country, as French republicanism would have it when it seeks to assimilate cultural others to its own value-system. However, to draw the commonly accompanying republican conclusion, in the context of social and cultural policy-making, that the specific characteristics which set one group of citizens apart from those of the majoritarian and putatively more homogeneous community should not be accorded much importance is to fail to respect the particular interests of those communities and to alienate them. The French political class has gone a long way in the direction of acknowledging and actively working to compensate for economic inequalities within French society; at this level, citizens are not instructed to think of themselves as being necessarily the same, or even similar to each other. However, as regards cultural policy, that is at the level of understanding the practical implications of cultural, racial[17] and religious contrasts between communities,

---

[17] In 'Race: from Philosophy to History', in *Race after Sartre*, ed. Jonathan Judaken (SUNY, 2009), Christian Delacampagne reminds us that the French, unlike anglophones, do not endorse the concept of race as such. Whatever the scientific basis of accepting or refusing the concept of race may be – and the question remains a contested one – in practical terms denying the existence of racial difference has manifold implications in particular for members of minority communities. Telling a black person who is a victim of anti-black racist insults that race is of no consequence, for example, is not much use to her as her lived experience would strongly suggest the contrary. In so far as races exist in the mind of the racist, denying their existence amounts to weakening individuals' capacity to defend themselves effectively from prejudicial treatment. It is worth noting that Sartre's position on this issue was a more subtle one than the official French Republican stance. Despite being known for his existentialist defense of subjective freedom and the capacity for self-determination, Sartre argued that each individual had not just a self-defining 'being-for-itself' but also a 'being-for-others'. One's 'being-for-others' is the way that one is perceived by others and the practical limitation which that perception can put on our freedom. If a black person is the victim of racist slurs then to all intents and purposes she is black in that moment, however unconcerned she may otherwise be with the question of her own race. Retorting to the racist that 'there is no such thing as race' will not spare her the insults. Sartre argues, also applying this reasoning to Jews and homosexuals, that however uncomfortable it may be to confront prejudice, the only effective way for individuals to do so is to acknowledge that there is a reality to how they are perceived by others, however misguided that perception may be. To refuse to acknowledge the reality of the situation is a case of *mauvaise foi*.

France still has some way to go if a policy that could aspire to being genuinely inclusive of all its citizens is to be arrived at. Moreover, that the French should be resistant to anglophone cosmopolitan or 'melting pot' models of cultural and racial integration as they often are is understandable for historical and cultural reasons. That they should for so long have demonstrated such a reticence, at least in official channels, to acknowledge fully, let alone embrace the diversity which is today at the heart of French identity, however, is a more open to question. This unwillingness cannot be genuinely shielded from criticism by brandishing the policy of secularism ('laïcité'), however laudable this policy may be in principle; the problem cannot be reduced to religion-related issues alone. Nor can it be justified with reference to self-defensive attitudes in France owing to the encroachments of American-English language and culture, however understandable that anti-imperialist logic may be in and of itself. I would like to stress – and some years ago now such a statement would have seemed otiose because self-evident – that the attitude of cultural inclusiveness and respect for diversity which I am advocating should and must be extended to Muslim communities, the vast majority of whose members exhibit no radical Islamist tendencies. Radical Islamism, and its terrorist sideshow, cannot and will not be defeated by stigmatizing and hence alienating Muslim communities, be it those within Western nations or those in predominantly Muslim countries. Governments around the globe must work *with* Muslim communities to counter the threat posed by Islamism, not against them; failure to do so will only serve to exacerbate the present predicament.

The other, then, is not the same as myself. At the local level of individual subjects no two people are the same. At the level of cultures, religions and communities, there are certainly significant contrasts which have to be taken into account. Such contrasts should also be viewed as valuable in a myriad of ways; cultural diversity is a value in itself, as anyone who has ever spent any length of time in monolinguistic and monocultural environments soon realizes. One particular other, be it an individual, a culture or a community, might be more similar to myself than another other. But to go so far as to place emphasis on the idea that either of those others is different from me while at the same time making that claimed difference into the basis for a social and cultural view of society, and *a fortiori* the basis for policy-making in these areas, is to encourage unwarranted divisions in society and the wider world which are unconstructive and sometimes harmful. The contrasts constituting diversity should hence neither be flattened out as in France nor over-exaggerated as in the US-led anglophone world.

The challenge hence lies in being able to recognize and allow for the fact that we are not all the same while simultaneously continuing to insist that a commonly shared agenda is and must remain possible. It is for this reason that François Jullien's defence of universal values minus universal*ism* offers a valuable perspective on this issue. To dispense with universal values is to jettison the very possibility of an agenda that might be commonly assented to and pursued. Nor can universal values be exclusively founded on the universality of human body, even though this may well be an indispensable prerequisite for them.[18] Although the body is a universal, the matters which diverse communities disagree on are invariably of a cultural nature and any attempt to establish universal values which does not take this fact into account will fall very short. While it is true that it is important to be able to argue that arbitrary arrest and imprisonment without trial ought to be universally condemnable, for instance, the problem remains that it is not the rights of the body of the detainee which are at issue in the first instance. In this case what are first and foremost centre stage are cultural assumptions about the extent of individuals' civil liberties and rights. On what type of universalist grounds, then, are we to argue to the governments of those countries which do practice arbitrary arrest and imprisonment that they should not do it? The hope of identifying values – values involving cultural beliefs and practices – which can be commonly assented to must be retained. It is vital, however, that those values be conceived of as in and of themselves independent of the exercise of power.[19] They are not to

---

[18] In *After Theory* (155–68) Terry Eagleton argues for a universalism which takes the universality of the human body as its basis. Although a valuable contribution to the debate over universalism, in his keenness to counter excessively culturalist tendencies in contemporary theory, Eagleton somewhat underestimates the extent to which any set of universal values which could be hoped to be widely assented to by communities around the globe will nevertheless *also* need to be situated at the level of, and involve, cultural agendas too.

[19] Rada Iveković pointed out in a paper entitled 'Epistemological fractures: the decline of western paradigms', presented at Diasporic Trajectories, University of Edinburgh on 19th February 2016, that one of the principal difficulties thrown up by defenses

be thought of as universal simply because they are being advocated and promoted by a leading world power, a political authority or the sheer coercitive force exerted by big business but because of the integral connection which must pertain between those values on the one hand and truth and fairness on the other.

I indicated in Chapter 4 that Glissant's rejection of universal values is, in my estimation, the principle drawback of his theory because he thereby inadvertently drifts too close to identity-based politics. However understandable this temptation may be for communities which have experienced colonization, and perhaps valuable as a short-term means of self-affirmation, its reconfirming of binaries and potential for inadvertently encouraging sectarian behaviours is a matter for some concern. Consider Glissant's conviction that he 'believes in the future of small countries'.[20] Understandable though it is that he should take this position, it just so happens that today, in an era when the empires of the nineteenth and twentieth centuries have essentially breathed their last, this apparently anti-federalist stance runs the risk of cohering with the nationalism of today's extreme right parties in a manner that is too close for comfort. That said, Glissant's anti-federalism is best understood as deriving from his vehement insistence on the autonomy of postcolonial nations rather than as a rejection of all types of supranational political structures per se.

As I argued in Chapter 4, Jullien's concept of the 'gap' (the 'écart') offers a valuable strategy for negotiating the problem of retaining universal values without letting power-connected universalist agendas back into the equation. As such I believe that it can usefully fill a lacuna in later Glissantian theory. Glissant conceives of the 'Tout-monde' philosophically as a totality, but what of its instantiation in the cultural and social policies of nation-states and indeed at the level of international relations? I am not convinced that a totality conceived of as composed exclusively of differences is the best basis for a political agenda which can bring the different cultures of the world together around at least a limited number of issues that concern them all. The environment is such an issue as it has become clear that it is going to be necessary that there be an

---

of universalism is that historically affirmations of universalism have usually tended to be closely associated with the exercise of political power.

[20] 'croit à l'avenir des petits pays' (*IBM*, 42–3).

international consensus, and one which is binding. The problem of wealth inequality also requires international solutions founded on propositions that are commonly assented to, as does that of illegal arms and drugs proliferation, and that of exponential demographic growth which will inevitably place greatly increased demand on the world's natural resources in the course of the twenty-first century. Jullien's argument that universal values should be retained as a necessary regulatory ideal, but tempered by the 'gap' ('ecart'), would allow Glissantian theory a better modulated instantiation in the sphere of real-world politics than does an insistence on difference. As the 'gap' does not stand in opposition to the Same as the concept of difference does, it is non-binaristic and lends itself much more obviously to the idea of relationality which lies at the heart of Glissant's thought. It involves an implicit acceptance of the multiplicity and diversity of cultures around the globe and leads us to perceive the value of that multiplicity and diversity in its undermining of normative assumptions. When I perceive the areas of conceptual divergence which exist between two or more cultures and languages that I know I become better placed both to question my assumptions and to be respectful of the specificities of (a) culture(s) that is (or are) not my own. I can also better perceive the areas of commonly shared values on the one hand and those areas where we do not see things in quite the same way and have contrasting priorities on the other. In the latter respect, the 'gap' also allows me to understand the necessity of other cultures, like my own, existing in their own contexts and in relation to their own histories while nevertheless *also* existing in an international context in which they must work along with others to arrive at consensus positions on matters of importance for all the nations of the world.

It remains the case that Jullien, like Glissant himself, formulates positions which concern international relations and geopolitics not just in theoretical but also largely *cultural* terms. It is possible to be theoretical and pragmatic in the sense that real-world economics and politics are pragmatic, at the same time. When Glissant advocates greater cooperation between the cultures of the world, and indeed the need to respect the opacity of individual cultures, he situates these issues at the level of language and culture, not at the level of economics. For instance, the threat of Anglo-American imperialism is presented by Glissant as the imposition of a somewhat debased version of the English language on the non-anglophone world.

What he does not discuss are the economic and political conditions that have made it possible for an American private company like Microsoft to take a leading example to extend its influence worldwide through holding a near monopoly on PC desktop software such that computer English and certain underlying American cultural values have enjoyed a global spread. This reservation is not an objection as such. Both Glissant and Jullien are theorists whose disciplinary affiliation is principally philosophy and their choice of focus has more to do with that than to do with a lack of awareness or concern with the more pragmatic dimensions of the issues they discuss.

There are those who are coming to the view that China's future ascendency to the position of leading world economy should be greeted with an attitude of acceptance. Economist Dambisa Moyo is one such voice, indicating in a recent interview how impressed she was with the Chinese vision for future economic policy when it was explained to her during a meeting with Chinese officials.[21] In a public lecture of 2013 Moyo explained that the Western preoccupation with political and civic freedoms is failing to convince many citizens living in the emerging markets. Speaking of a schism between the West and the rest, Moyo argued that 'today, many people who live in the emerging markets, where 90% of the world's population lives, believe that the western obsession with political rights is beside the point, and what is actually important is delivering on food, shelter, education and healthcare [...] if you're living on less than one dollar a day you're far too busy trying to survive and to provide for your family than to spend your time going around trying to proclaim and defend democracy.'[22] Moyo's critique of Western assumptions is of great value to trying to understand how the West should relate to other cultures. The West has long been and remains blind to the priorities of a large proportion of the world's citizens and the real circumstances that they find themselves in. It must make efforts to correct this lack of awareness and demonstrate a genuine humility with respect to cultural others of the sort that it has not shown to date. However, I fear that Moyo's embracing of China as new future world leader is a position which she adopts too hastily. Acceptance

---

[21] Dambisa Moyo, 'The Trouble With Democracy', interview with *Moneyweek*, July 2015: https://www.youtube.com/watch?v=ie-02b0z2w.
[22] Dambisa Moyo, 'Is China the New Model for Emerging Economies?' https://www.youtube.com/watch?v=4Q2aznfmcYU.

of the arrival on the international scene of a new global imperial power in the East is not an antidote to decades of US dominance. Moreover, the argument that many citizens in the world have more urgent matters to worry about than political rights does not mean that those political rights are not worth fighting for and insisting on. This issue should not be conceived of in terms of a binary either/or choice; rather, the challenge is to ensure that inhabitants of emerging nations enjoy *both* an improved standard of living *and* greater political freedoms. As things stand at present, China remains some way off demonstrating a sufficient desire to respect human rights, let alone political liberties,[23] to be accepted as occupying the role of world's leading nation. Its economic pre-eminence in years to come is now looking like an inevitability, but this fact alone does not justify political leadership and, in any case, it is not towards another unipolar but an expansive multipolar configuration that our globalized world would best be directed.

Globalization has spiralled out of control and it has become clear, as many in the political class have come to accept since 2008, that its trajectory will have to be altered if we are not to head into more financial crises as well as a host of other problems, not least of which the bequeathing of an irreversibly disastrous environmental situation to future generations. Finance capitalism and excessive deregulation need to be reigned in, the overproduction associated with free-market consumerist society needs to be curbed, and the tendency of globalization to engender cultural homogenization, including via the imposition of the English language in commercial and political channels, products (e.g. Microsoft computer software, and Google's various monopoly seeking ambitions) and Western (notably) popular cultures, needs better monitoring. Today few doubt the fact that globalization has serious structural problems, but rejecting globalization as a model is not really a viable option. Globalization in some form is here to stay, which is all the more reason that a fairer mode of operation and more equitable practices be adopted. In short, globalization needs *doing differently*: as the GJM slogan goes, 'Another World Is Possible'. It would seem though

---

[23]Take for example a recent article entitled 'Pledge absolute loyalty to party, president tells Chinese media', in *The Guardian*, 20 February 2016, which describes a recent visit of President Xi Jinping to three state-run media outlets. He instructed them to follow the line of the party leadership in 'thought, politics and action'.

that a more precise formulation would be 'Another Globalized World Is Possible'. There can be little doubt that a thorough-going critique, indeed overhaul, of the globalized system is necessary and that this process must first take place within the Western institutions and economic structures which spawned that system. Why? Not simply because the West is to blame for neoliberalism, so should correct its errors, although there is a good case to be made for this argument. But also because those of us in the West need to be clear that if we do fundamentally believe that our system of values, our political heritage, and our institutions have something to offer to the collective future of globalization then we need to adopt a mode of operation which earns us the respect of others; not in order to dictate policy, language or lifestyles to others but to become once again credible as voice in a multipolar global debate about the future of our world.

With colonialism finally coming to an end in the 1960s, and various liberation movements – the American civil rights movement, the women's liberation movement – winning significant victories, the West entered a period in which liberal democratic society was finally beginning to fulfil its promise and live up to its core ideals. Its radical left critics rightly continued to point up its failings, in other words to highlight the ways in which the practice of liberal democracy did not match up to the theory. The fundamental criticism of political liberalism made by Marxism from the mid nineteenth century onwards was not so much that liberal ideals were intrinsically wrong-headed but rather that their flourishing was impeded by capitalist economics; political liberalism was in a sense, for the Marxists, not genuinely liberal enough. Moreover, the manifold errors of neocolonial practices and, most recently, American neo-imperialism leave a bitter taste behind them for those who have questioned the legitimacy of Western hegemony. In spite of these valid criticisms voiced from without and within Western societies, by the late 1960s there were good reasons for believing that the enlightenment inheritance which underlies political liberalism was finally bearing fruit. What has happened since the 1980s is that Western elites, through a combination of ill-judged policy decisions and material greed, have squandered that inheritance and progressively discredited it. Via excessive financial deregulation and deindustrialization the US-led West has adopted an economic logic which has been driving it closer and closer to economic self-destruction while China in the East, following a much better thought out and cannier policy, has enjoyed meteoric growth for the best part of three decades. Russia has also been making an influential return to the world political stage in recent years.

The West, then, has lost its way. This does not mean, however, that it cannot and should not regain some genuine purchase on the situation. But rather that if it is to do so it is going to have to start living up to its liberal ideals in a more sustainable and meaningful way. Liberal freedom cannot be reduced to free speech on the one hand and completely unchecked money and asset accumulation by the wealthy on the other. A conception of society which involves safeguarding the freedoms, but also the rights and opportunities of all, not just of a small minority, is required if liberalism is to work. The West must and can only reassert its place on the world political stage by using 'soft', not 'hard' power. Furthermore, it must earn and win the support of others, not simply foist debased versions of Western thinking on others. I am advocating neither a new form of political or cultural imperialism nor a new brand of universalist thinking of the predominantly conceptual, abstract or inflexible variety. I nevertheless think it essential to continue believing in the possibility and necessity of universal values and a common humanity if citizens of the diverse cultures of the world are to pull together, as is very much needed, rather than in opposing directions. The negotiation which lies ahead of us will be a protracted one and can only be won through persuasive argument, not brute force, be it economic or military.

BIBLIOGRAPHY

Works by Glissant

Caribbean Discourse. Selected Essays, translated by J. Michael Dash (Charlottesville: University Press of Virginia, 1999 [1989]).
Introduction à une politique du divers (Gallimard, 1996).
L'Imaginaire des langues (Gallimard, 2010).
L'Intention poétique (Gallimard, 1997 [1969]).
L'Intraitable Beauté du monde: adresse à Barack Obama (Galaade, 2009).
La Cohée du Lamentin (Gallimard, 2005).
Le Discours antillais (Gallimard, 1997 [1981]).
Le Soleil de la conscience (Seuil, 1956).
Les Entretiens de Baton Rouge (Gallimard, 2008).
Manifeste pour les 'produits' de haute nécessité (Galaade, 2009).
Mémoires des esclavages (Gallimard, 2007).
Philosophie de la relation (Gallimard, 2009).
Poetic Intention, translated by Nathalie Stephens (New York: Nightboat Books, 2010).
Poetics of Relation translated by Betsy Wing (Ann Arbor: University of Michigan Press, 1997).
Poétique de la Relation (Gallimard, 1990).
Quand les murs tombent. L'Identité hors la loi? (Galaade, 2007).*Traité du tout-monde* (Gallimard, 1997).
Une Nouvelle région du monde (Gallimard, 2006).

Other sources

Amoore, Louise. *The Global Resistance Reader* (Oxon: Routledge, 2005).
Assister, Alison. *Revisiting Universalism* (Basingstoke: Palgrave, 2003).
Badiou, Alain. *The Communist Hypothesis* (London: Verso, 2015).
Badiou, Alain. *Deleuze 'La clameur de l'Etre'* (Pluriel, 2013 [1997]).
Badiou, Alain. *The Meaning of Sarkozy* (London: Verso, 2010).
Bancel, Blanchard et Vergès. *La République coloniale* (Paris: Hachette Littératures, 2006).

Bandy, Joe and Smith, Jackie. *Coalitions across Borders. Transnational Protest and the Neoliberal Order* (Maryland: Rowman & Littlefield Publishers, 2005).
Bauman, Zygmunt *Liquid Fear* (Cambridge: Polity Press, 2006).
Bernabé, Jean. Chamoiseau , Patrick and Confiant, Raphael. *Eloge de la créolité. In Praise of Creoleness* (Gallimard, 1993 [1988]).
Bessis, Sophie. *L'Occident et les autres. Histoire d'une suprématie* (Editions La Découverte, 2003 [2001]).
Black, Bob. *Anarchy after Leftism* (Cal Press, 2006).
Blanchard et Bancel. (eds). *Culture post-coloniale 1961–2006: Traces et mémoires coloniales en France* (Editions autrement, 2005).
Bongie, Chris. *Friends and Enemies: The Scribal Politics of Post/Colonial Literature* (Liverpool University Press, 2008).
Bongie, Chris. *Islands and Exiles: The Creole Identities of Postcolonial Literature* (Stanford University Press, 1998).
Bookchin, Murray. *Social Anarchism or Lifestyle Anarchism: An Unbridgeable Chasm* (Spunk Library, spunk.org, 1996).
Britton, Celia. *Édouard Glissant and Postcolonial Theory* (University Press of Virginia, 1999).
Burns, Lorna. *Contemporary Caribbean Writing and Deleuze. Literature Between Postcolonialism and Post-Continental Philosophy* (London: Continuum, 2012).
Burton, Richard. 'Comment peut-on être Martiniquais? The recent work of Édouard Glissant', *The Modern Language Review*, Vol. 79, No. 2, April 1984, pp. 301–312.
Burton, Richard. '"*Ki moun nou ye?*": the idea of difference in contemporary French West Indian thought', *New West Indian Guide*, Vol. 67, Nos. 1–2, 1993.
Burton, Richard 'Modernité et Créolité: Une manière de réponse', *Antilla*, 620 (1995).
Chamoiseau, Patrick. *Solibo Magnificent*, translated by Rose-Myriam Réjouis (London: Granta, 1999).
Chamoiseau, Patrick. *Solibo Magnifique* (Gallimard, 1988).
Chamoiseau, Patrick. *Une Enfance créole I: Antan d'enfance* (Gallimard, 1996).
Chancé, Dominique. *Édouard Glissant. Un 'traite' du déparler' Essai sur l'oeuvre romanesque d'Édouard Glissant* (Karthala, 2002).
Chomsky, Noam. *Occupy* (London: Penguin, 2012).
Coombes, Sam. 'Black postcolonial communities in a globalised world as articulated in the work of Paul Gilroy and Édouard Glissant: a comparative analysis', *Commonwealth Essays and Studies*, Vol. 36, No. 2, May 2014, pp. 11–18.
Coombes, Sam. *The Early Sartre and Marxism* (Bern: Peter Lang, 2008).

Coombes, Sam. 'The genesis, reception, and aftermath of the Creolite Movement in the Francophone Caribbean: creole identity and creolisation re-examined', *Francosphères*, Vol. 1, No. 2, 2012, pp. 106–126.

Coombes, Sam. 'Reaching the public via literary commitment: the development of a revolutionary literature in the writings of Paul Nizan', *The Irish Journal of French Studies*, Vol. 10, Special Issue 'Intellectuals and Public Opinion: A Transhistorical Perspective, 2011, pp. 61–76.

Condé, Maryse. '*Creolité* without Creole language?', in *Caribbean Creolization: Reflections on the Cultural Dynamics of Language, Literature, and Identity*, eds. Kathleen M. Balutansky and Marie-Agnès Sourieau (Florida: University Press of Florida, 1998), pp. 101–109.

Condé, Maryse. *Crossing the Mangrove,* translated by Richard Philcox (New York: First Anchor Books, 1995).

Condé, Maryse. *La Traversée de la Mangrove* (Mercure de France, 1989).

Condé, Maryse and Cottenet-Hage, Madeleine. (eds). 'Chercher nos verites', in *Penser la creolite* (Paris: Karthala, 1995), pp. 305–310.

Cox, Robert W. 'Civil society at the turn of the millenium: prospects for an alternative world order', *Review of International Studies*, Vol. 25, No. 1, 1999, pp. 3–28.

Curran, Giorel. *21st Century Dissent. Anarchism, Anti-Globalisation and Environmentalism* (Basingstoke: Palgrave Macmillan, 2006).

Cusset, François. *French Theory: Foucault, Derrida, Deleuze & Cie et les mutations de la vie intellectuelle aux Etats-Unis* (Editions La Découverte, 2003).

Dash, J. Michael. *Édouard Glissant* (Cambridge University Press, 1995).

Dash, J. Michael. 'Writing the body: Édouard Glissant's poetics of re-membering', *World Literature Today*, Vol. 63, No. 4, 1989, pp. 609–612.

Davis, Laurence and Kinna, Ruth. (eds). *Anarchism and Utopianism* (Manchester University Press, 2009).

Deleuze, Gilles and Guattari, Felix. *Difference and Repetition* (London: Athlone Press, 1994).

Deleuze, Gilles and Guattari, Felix. *A Thousand Plateaus. Capitalism and Schizophrenia* (London: Continuum, 2003).

Descola, Philippe. 'Entretien avec Philippe Descola', *Cahiers philosophiques*, 'Naturalismes d'aujourd'hui', Vol. 127, 2011, pp. 23–40.

Desportes, Georges. *La Paraphilosophie d'Édouard Glissant* (L'Harmattan, 2008).

Due, Reidar. *Deleuze* (Cambridge: Polity, 2007).

Eagleton, Terry. *After Theory* (London: Allen Lane, 2003).

Eagleton, Terry. *Why Marx Was Right* (New Haven: Yale University Press, 2011).
El-Ojeili, Chamsy and Hayden, Patrick. *Critical Theories of Globalization* (Basingstoke: Palgrave Macmillan, 2006).
Falk, Richard. 'Global civil society. Perspectives, intiatives, movements', *Oxford Development Studies*, Vol. 26, No. 1, 2007, pp. 99–110.
Ferguson, Niall. *Colossus. The Rise and Fall of the American Empire* (London: Penguin Books, 2014).
Flesher Fominaya, Cristina. *Social Movements and Globalization* (Basingstoke: Palgrave, 2014).
Fonkoua, Romuald. *Essai sur la mesure du monde au XXe siecle. Édouard Glissant* (Editions Champion, 2002).
Forsdick, Charles and Murphy, David. (eds). *Francophone Postcolonial Studies: A Critical Introduction* (London: Arnold, 2003).
Forsdick, Charles and Murphy, David. *Postcolonial Thought in the French-Speaking World* (Liverpool University Press, 2009).
Fourest, Caroline. *La Dernière Utopie. Menaces sur l'universalisme* (Grasset, 2009).
Francis, C. W. and Viau, R. (eds). *Trajectoires et dérives de la littérature-monde. Poétiques de la relation et du divers dans les espaces francophones* (Amsterdam and New York: Rodopi, 2013).
Friedman, Milton and Schwartz, Anna. *A Monetary History of the United States 1867–1960* (Princeton: Princeton University Press, 1963).
Gallagher, Mary. *Soundings in French Caribbean Writing Since 1950* (Oxford University Press, 2002).
Gilbert, Jeremy. *Anticapitalism and Culture: Radical Theory and Popular Politics* (Oxford: Berg, 2008).
Gilroy, Paul. *After Empire: Melancholia or Convivial Culture?* (London: Routledge, 2004).
Gilroy, Paul. *Between Camps: Race, Identity and Nationalism at the End of the Colour Line* (London: Allen Lane, 2000).
Gilroy, Paul. *The Black Atlantic* (London: Verso, 1993).
Gilroy, Paul. *Small Acts: Thoughts on the Politics of Black Cultures* (London: Serpent's Tail, 1993).
Gilroy, Paul. *There Ain't No Black in the Union Jack: The Cultural Politics of Race and Nation* (London: Hutchinson, 1987).
Hall, Stuart. 'Creolization, diaspora and hybridity', in *Créolité and Creolization*, eds. Enwezor et al. (Osfildern-Ruit: Haatj Cantz Publishers, 2003).
Hallward, Peter. *Absolutely Postcolonial. Writing Between the Singular and the Specific* (Manchester University Press, 2001).
Hallward, Peter. *Out of This World. Deleuze and the Philosophy of Creation* (London: Verso, 2006).

Hamed Hosseini, S. A. *Alternative Globalizations. An Integrative Approach to Studying Dissident Knowledge in the Global Justice Movement* (Oxon: Routledge, 2010).
Hardt, Michael and Negri, Antonio. *Multitude* (London: Penguin, 2006 [2004]).
Hardt, Michael and Negri, Antonio. *Time for Revolution* (London: Continuum, 2003).
Hassab-Charfi, S. and Zlitni-Fitouri, S. *Autour d'Édouard Glissant. Lectures, épreuves, extensions d'une poétique de la Relation* (Bordeaux: Presses Universitaires de Bordeaux and Cathage: Académie Tunisienne des Sciences, des Lettres et des Arts, 2008).
Hoofd, Ingrid. *Ambiguities of Activism: Alter-Globalism and the Imperatives of Speed* (New York: Routledge, 2012).
Joubert, Claire. *Le Postcolonial comparé: anglophonie, francophonie* (Saint-Denis: Presses Universitaires de Vincennes, 2014).
Jullien, François. *De l'universel, de l'uniforme, du commun et du dialogue entre les cultures* (Fayard, 2008).
Klein, Naomi. 'Farewell to the "End of History": organization and vision in anti-corporate movements', *Socialist Register*, vol. 38, 2002, pp. 1–13.
Klein, Naomi. *The Shock Doctrine: The Rise of Disaster Capitalism* (London: Penguin, 2007).
Klein, Naomi. *This Changes Everything: Capitalism Versus the Climate* (London: Routledge, 2016).
Latour, Bruno. *Nous n'avons jamais été modernes. Essai d'anthropologie symétrique* (Editions La Découverte, 1991).
Le Brun, Annie. *Pour Aimé Césaire* (Paris: Jean-Michel Place, 1994).
Loomba, Kaul, Bunzi, Burton and Esty. (eds). *Postcolonial Studies and Beyond* (Durham NC and London: Duke University Press, 2005).
Ly, Mamadou Moustapha. *Édouard Glissant in Theory and Practice: A Diasporic Poetics of Politics*. Doctoral thesis, University of Michigan, 2014.
Maalouf, Amin. *Disordered World* (London: Bloomsbury, 2011).
Maalouf, Amin. *Le dérèglement du monde* (Grasset, 2009).
Majumdar, Margaret A. *Postcoloniality. The French Dimension* (Oxford: Berghahn, 2007).
Mbom, Clement. 'Édouard Glissant, de l'opacité à la relation', in *Poétiques d'Édouard Glissant*, ed. Jean Chevrier (Paris: Presses Universitaires de Paris-Sorbonne, 1999), pp. 75–91.
McCusker, Maeve. '"This Creole Culture, miraculously forged": the contradictions of créolité', in *Francophone Postcolonial Studies: A Critical Introduction*, eds. Forsdick and Murphy (London: Arnold, 2003).

Ménil, René. *Antilles déjà jadis* (J. M. Place, 1999).
Ménil, Alain. *Les voies de la créolisation Essai sur Édouard Glissant* (De L'Incidence Editeur, 2011).
Merleau-Ponty, Maurice. *Les Aventures de la dialectique* (Gallimard, 1955).
Moyo, Dambisa. *How the West Was Lost* (London: Penguin, 2011).
Nail, Thomas. *Returning to Revolution: Deleuze, Guattari and Zapatismo* (Edinburgh University Press, 2012).
Nesbitt, Nick. *Caribbean Critique: Antillean Critical Theory from Toussaint to Glissant* (Liverpool University Press, 2013).
Omerod, Beverley. 'Beyond negritude: some aspects of the work of Édouard Glissant', *Savacou*, Vols. 11–12, 1975, pp. 39–45.
Omerod, Beverley. 'Discourse and dispossession: Édouard Glissant's image of contemporary Martinique', *Caribbean Quarterly*, Vol. 27, No. 4, 1981, pp. 1–12.
Reitan, Ruth. *Global Activism* (Oxon: Routledge, 2007).
Reus-Smit, Christian. *American Power and World Order* (Cambridge: Polity, 2004).
Sansavior, Eva and Scholar, Richard. *Caribbean Globalizations, 1492 to the Present Day* (Liverpool University Press, 2014).
Sartre, Jean-Paul. 'Orphée noir' in *Situations III* (Paris: Gallimard, 1949).
Steger, Manfred B., Goodman, James, and Wilson, Erin K. *Justice Globalism. Ideology, Crises, Policy* (London: Sage Publications Ltd, 2013).
Stiglitz, Joseph. *Freefall* (London: Penguin Books, 2010 [2009]).
Stiglitz, Joseph. *Making Globalization Work* (London: Penguin Books, 2006).
Stiglitz, Joseph. *The Price of Inequality* (London: Penguins books, 2013 [2012]).
Stiglitz, Joseph. *The Roaring Nineties* (London: Penguin, 2003).
Suk, Jeannie. *Postcolonial Paradoxes in French Caribbean Writing* (Oxford University Press, 2001).
Thoburn, Nicholas. *Deleuze, Marx and Politics* (London: Routledge, 2003).
Todd, Emmanuel. *After the Empire: The Breakdown of the American Order* (London: Constable and Robin, 2004 [2002]).
Tormey, Simon. *Anti-Capitalism: A Beginners Guide* (London: Oneworld, 2013).
Walcott, Derek. 'A Letter to Chamoiseau', in *What the Twilight Says* (New York: Farrar, Straus and Giroux, 1998), pp. 213–232.

INDEX

American preeminence 71–2, 120, 130, 186
Anti-Globalization Movement (AGM) 143, 147–54

Badiou, Alain 166
Bongie, Chris
  Friends and Enemies 89–91

Chamoiseau, Bernabé
  Confiant *In Praise of Creoleness* 48, 51–5
Chamoiseau, Patrick
  A Creole Childhood 60
  Solibo The Magnificent 63
  Writing in a Dominated Land 52
Condé, Maryse 60–1, 63
  Crossing the Mangrove 63–5
Creoleness 13, 27, 48, 51, 54, 60, 61, 62, 65, 78
Cultural mixing (métissage) 13, 48

Deleuze, Gilles 92–3, 95–6
  influence on Hardt and Negri, 96
  political radicalism of, 96–7
difference 6, 14, 73, 180

Einstein, Albert
  theory of relativity 8–9

Folklorism 57–8
Fourest, Caroline 80–1

French republican universalism 16, 181–2
Friedman, Milton 133

Gilroy, Paul
  The Black Atlantic 30, 33, 97, 166, 176
  'planetary mentality' 31
Glissant, Édouard
  archipelic thought 39, 40–1
  beauty 178, 180
  Caribbean Discourse 48, 52, 54, 56, 76–7, 100, 107
  Caribbeanness ('antillanité') 48
  'chaos-world' 8–9, 23
  Cohée du Lamentin, La 72, 90–1
  common place, the 42–3
  continental thought 40
  counter-poetics 100
  creolization 13–14, 38, 47, 48–51, 56, 65–6, 99, 169
  detour, the 41, 43
  difference 24, 34
  diverse, the 13, 24
  'echo-world' 8–9, 72
  Entretiens de Baton Rouge, Les 102
  errantry 14, 32, 37–8, 41
  imaginary, the role of the 117
  L'Intraitable beauté du monde Adresse à Barack Obama 90, 118, 120, 122, 175, 178

Introduction à une poétique du divers 13, 32, 38, 56
jazz music 34–5
Malemort 52
Manifeste pour les « produits » de haute nécessité 115–17
Mémoires des esclavages 48, 90, 111, 120
multilingualism 73, 98, 104, 120
nation, the 89
National Centre for the Commemoration of Slavery and Its Abolition 110–12
New Region of the World, A 25, 43, 73
non-system of thought 5, 24, 43
One, the 40, 73
opacity 15, 98–101, 79, 186
Philosophie de la Relation 121–2
poetics 17, 18, 19, 27, 117, 121
Poetic Intention 24, 36, 37, 71, 76, 98, 100
Poetics of Relation 3–20, 56, 87, 98, 107–8
poststructuralist influence on 172
Quand les murs tombent 112–15
Relation 7–9, 11, 14, 19, 22–3, 25–6, 38, 71, 73, 104, 119
Relation identity 6–7, 27
repentance for slavery 114, 120
rhizomatic identity 6–7
standardisation 15, 28, 72
Soleil de la Conscience, Le 71
totality-world 28, 43, 74
trace, the 31–5, 36, 40
Treatise on the Whole-world 36
trembling 35–8, 41
utopian vision of 11, 117, 122, 175, 180
'Whole-world' 11, 18, 20, 23, 25, 26, 29, 36, 43, 74, 120, 185

worldliness 11, 23, 29–30
globalization 62, 65, 125, 161, 188
alternative model of globalization 65, 128, 143, 164
neoliberal-led 79, 131
Global Justice Movement (GJM) 12, 128, 147–54, 161, 110–12, 114, 173

Hallward, Peter
Absolutely Postcolonial 88–9, 107
Hamed Hosseini, S.A. 153, 167–72, 174
Hardt, Michael and Negri, Antonio 151, 165–6

inequality 145

Jullien, François 82–5
the 'gap' ('l'écart') 185–7

Klein, Naomi
The Shock Doctrine 133

Loi Taubira (the 'Taubira' Law) 110

McLuhan, Marshall 134
Maalouf, Amin 81–2
'bridges' ('passerelles') 82, 85
Marx, Karl x, 112, 155–6, 165, 167, 170, 189
early Marxian humanism 116–17
Martinique, 69
'département' status of 70, 74–6
'Melting pot' model of multiculturalism 12, 101, 103
Ménil, Alain 10
Merleau-Ponty, Maurice 109

migration problem *x*
Minoritarian communities *xi*, 3, 16, 34
Monolingualism 73

Negritude 51, 54
neoliberalism 4, 165, 167
New Social Movements (NSMs) 146

oral culture 53, 55, 57

postmodernism 136, 173
poststructuralism 173–4

Sartre, Jean-Paul 109, 181–2
Stiglitz, Joseph 145, 150–1

translation 85, 102–3

universalism 67–85, 180, 184, 185
   Kantian 83

Walcott, Derek 57, 78
World Economic Forum (WEF) 126
World Social Forum (WSF) 12, 147–8, 161, 164
writing and commitment 106, 176

www.ingramcontent.com/pod-product-compliance
Lightning Source LLC
Chambersburg PA
CBHW050139240426
43673CB00043B/1727